P9-CQQ-052

Simply Amazing

Simply Amazing

By

K. C. ARMSTRONG

Sylvester-Aaron Books
A social impact imprint of
Enlightened Financial Press

Enlightened Financial Press
843 N. Rainbow Blvd. , Ste. 3497
Las Vegas, NV 84903
www.enlightenedfp.com

Ordering Information:
Quantity sales. Special discounts are available on quantity purchases by corporations, associations, and others. For details, contact the publisher at the address above.

Printed in the United States of America

First Edition

14 13 12 11 10 / 10 9 8 7 6 5 4 3 2 1

CREDITS

Founder of WMAP Radio and Interviewer
K.C. Armstrong

Copy Editor
Virginia Armstrong

Creative Director
Jessica Sorin Olmeda

Book Cover Designer
Noble A. Drakoln, publisher

Book Cover Photography
Autumn Maglia

Interviewees
Werner Reich
Tom Butts
Jenny Maher
Doug Herald
Virginia Armstrong
Jeanne Beard
Lito Mason
Laurene Hope
Dr. Elizabeth Rodger
Daniella Cippitelli
Shannon Knight

DEDICATION

I wish to dedicate this book to my Mother.
Virginia Armstrong

She has been trying to make me believe I'm amazing
my whole life even when I refused to see it.
I thank God each day for how lucky I am to have such an
amazing, thoughtful best friend and example who showed me how
sacrifices you make for other people are what really matters.
There is no way to put my gratitude in words, but
I thought I would take this time to try.

You're the most amazing person I've ever
known. Thank you for everything.

CONTENTS

FOREWORD

I met K.C. Armstrong through the universe of Howard Stern. We are both renegades, thrill seekers, and like to live life to the fullest. Having such a lust for life often leads to a life of bizarre adventures and an endless search to find the meaning of why we are here on this spinning rock we call Earth.

One thing you can never take away from either of us is our heart. That's what bonded us together and why we are friends to this day. I've called him when I've been down, as he has done the same, to talk each other off the edge. I'm so glad to see him in such a great place and I'll always be here for him, because of his heart.

He has found others with similar hearts and has interviewed them for this book. I hope you enjoy it!

David Arquette

ACKNOWLEDGMENTS

Note from KC:

I would like to thank Matt, the Princess, Ron, Dave and Mary Forgione, and their whole family and staff at Fast File Medical Billing in Port Jefferson, NY (fastfile.com). Thank you, Kellie Koch and my whole staff at WMAP Radio. My idol and friend for life, Coach Dearrion Snead. Dr. Suzie Schuder, Dr. George Fairey and Carol at the Lomax Institute, Bob Wolf and all the wonderful doctors and nurses at St. Charles and Mather Hospitals, all the talent at Long Island Digestive Disease such as handsome Dr. Keschner, Tammy, Dr. Glazer, Dr. Persky, Trish at Pain Management, and so many more. All the hotels in Orange County, Ca. Jack and Terry at the HaHa Cafe Comedy Club, the Irvine Improv, the Melrose Improv, Liam's, and all my KCTV co-horts (Rick, Bruce and Jason).

Patrice O'Neal (RIP), Nick Schwarzen, Jay Woleske, my amazing co-workers at the Howard Stern Show, the sales team at K-Rock, Cathy Tobin, Artie Lange, Dave Attell, Russ Meneve, Jim Norton, Anthony Cumia, Joey "Coco" Diaz, Adam Hunter, Joe Rogan, Coach Jack Harbaugh, his lovely wife Jackie, and their sons John and Jim. All my amazing teammates at WKU Football, too many to list, but I have to especially thank the one and only Buckethead, Moz, Antoine Floyd, Sydney Williams, Latravis Powell, Ron Kelly, Stu McKenzie, Dan and Bryson, Eddie, Willie, Ben, and the Napier Brothers.

I wish to thank all my lead authors, all the guests I've interviewed at

WMAP, my CPA Mike Covati, my business advisor, Mike Gillingham and his wife Carrine. Also Richard Perlin, Mike Newman, Tom Rodger, Ray, everyone over at Max Muscle Orange County, and Tim Sabean.

Thanks also to my business partner publisher Enlightened Financial Press, the whole Kula Community, Johnny Fratto (RIP), Johnny Jr, Ivanka and the entire Fratto family. The Murderers' Row: Scott Demo, Sean Sexton, Jimmy Graham, Jim Florentine, and Bob Levy. The wonderful people at Grumpy Jack's, including everyone in the kitchen: busboys, waitresses, bartenders, including Eric, Dr. Christian Losse, Gavin, Jesse and Dan, Trevor and Anna. The one and only Grumpy Jack and his lovely wife Patty. All the great teachers and staff at Port Jefferson HS and Western Kentucky University: Dr. Lancaster, Ryan, Steve White, Mark White, Maryellen Miller, Dr. Coffee, Dr. Grimm and Judith Grimm, Marissa and the Football Staff including trainers, coaches and players. Till Lindemann, James McMurtry, Johnny Kelly, Josh Silver, Kenny Hickey, Peter Steele (RIP), Jamey Jasta, and Howard Jones. I know I forgot a lot of people, but I'm tired and I just want this thing to be done. When I see you, I'll thank you in person.

From Virginia Armstrong

THANK YOU
John Mtui
Ron Hamilton

My two amazing sons who give meaning to my life: Matthew, who shows integrity, strength, grace, and a father's love in abundance, and KC, who has shown what it means to transform oneself into a loving, successful person who amazes and inspires others, at work and far beyond.

ACKNOWLEDGEMENTS

For your inspiring examples of courage and kindness. You should know why.

1. Kelsey S. Harrington Angel #1
   www.KelseysharringtonFoundation.com
2. Diana Rossi i.e. The Princess
3. Mr. and Mrs. John Parsitau
4. Mr. and Mrs. Joseph Tipanko
5. Joseph Kessy
6. Laura Apol
7. Barb Gregoire
8. Don "Brother" Spence "Who says you can't take it with you?"
9. Dr. P. Paciolla
10. Millie and Aldo Alberici
11. Minerva Clegg
12. Bob Armstrong

I'm sure I've missed some of my top inspirations, possibly YOU, but these were the first to come to mind on a Tuesday evening after 2 glasses of a crisp Chardonnay.

DEDICATION

Dedicated with love to my two grandsons, Jason and Ian.

Please remember, boys, there is no greater achievement or happiness in this world than helping others. You'll see.

From Tom Butts:

It was truly an honor when KC asked if I would be part of this book. I was thinking about how I got here and all the people who have been by my side. I'm one of the lucky ones. My support system is very big and I am very grateful. I think there are a lot of people out there just like me, but who just haven't had the same support system or the right luck. Continue your battle to make it. Keep going! Don't give up. I would like to mention these people that have been with me through the journey so far.

My wife Kaycee, who is my "Yo Adrian" woman who is there for me and keeps me fighting in the ring. My Dad, Jim Butts, forever my Obi Wan Kenobi. My Mom, Connie Torgrimson, for loving and taking care of me as only a mother could. My brother Brad Butts who was my "Mr Spock" through life. My sister Stephanie Z who has supported me and been the glue in our family ever since she was little! My beautiful step parents, Bonnie, Janet, and Carl. My step brothers and sisters, who I wish were together more, Todd, Chris, Maria, Fred, and Anastasia. My kids who I would do anything for, Zackary, Drew, Jade, Quincy, and Drake. I know my grandparents, Grandma and Grandpa Butts along with Grandma and Grandpa Reagan continue to watch over me. My bro in-law Alex, and Sis in-law Jen. Also my in laws who always are there for me, Chrissy, Chris, Jerry, Rene, Big Ed and Lola. The mother of my children Amy. My many close relatives and friends which would be a wonderful book in itself.

There are many friends that have been by my side and there is no way to mention them all. I will do my best here! Ty Palu my best friend since forever. My pal since 1st grade Matt Mitchell. Jay Norris, Darrell Creeks, Scott and Callie Cambridge. Callie was not only a very close friend but was a huge part in saving me personally and professionally with her friendship and legal experience.

My bad-ass wonderful hardworking Nor-Cal Equipment Rentals crew,Peter,Tristan,Tycee,James, Zack(VP)😃, Evan, Bailey

From Laurene Hope:

Thank you to my amazing husband Martin who the angels gave me
Anne Sarah, my little soul sister
My Dad, who I adored
Francis and Steve Gough
Therapeutic Community Aylesbury and Staff – I wouldn't be here without you.

From Lito Mason:

I would like to thank my high school football coach Allan Cox for giving me a chance and not allowing me to give up. I would like to thank my uncle, Lester Mason, and Juan and Barbara Gary for always supporting me when I called on them. I would like to thank my mother, Tarressa Mason, for allowing me to grow without restrictions and my grandmother (RIH) Katherine Simon for always teaching me about life, raw and unfiltered, showing unconditional love. I would also like to thank all that have supported me throughout my journey, especially my high school and college coaches that taught me how to be a leader, not a follower. Last and most important, I would like to thank God for His mercy and grace, giving me the will to keep fighting on my journey!

From Daniella Cippitelli:

Thank you to my two amazing kids, Robert and Ava. You are my 'WHY.' To my mom, Maryann Cippitelli, who always stood behind me even when she didn't understand my decisions at times and was always excited to see where my adventures would lead me.

INTRODUCTION

"KC Armstrong wrote a book? That guy can't spell the word book, much less read one. But write one? OK, it's official- this is the end of times."

I saw that in a chat room, and I thought it might be fun to add on to the thread. I joined the conversation: "Yeah, the book is called Simply Amazing. Really? Let's suggest what the real title should be. I have some ideas to start us off. How about "Simply Amazing to Sell Five Copies?" Or "Simply Amazing I Bought This" or, my favorite, "Simply Shit." Anyway, yes, I did put out this book, and I want to thank each one of you for picking it up. Let me explain.

I have been blessed with an incredible life and unbelievable opportunities. However, I am a complete ingrate who, for some reason, has done my best to destroy everything good in my path- including me. I guess that's where I should start, and I promise to be as brief as I can. I just want you to understand how this book came about and where my idea came from.

First of all, most of you would never know my name if it were not for a genius named Howard Stern. After I played my 5th season with the Western Kentucky Football Hilltoppers, I was offered a job working for the most talented radio visionary of all time. I am so grateful that "The King of All Media" took a shot by hiring me back in 1998. I'll always respect him and, though I'm sure I let him down in the end, I did the best I could and held it all together for as long as possible.

I haven't told many people about this, but after I was fired by Infinity Broadcasting, the years to follow would be spent in some of the darkest places one could imagine.

Several years after I was fired, I was homeless in California, living in a car, that I'll just say did not belong to me. It was then that I was approached by a publisher who offered me a million dollars- that's right, $1,000,000- to think of all the negative and revealing things I might know or have heard about Howard Stern for a tell-all book. The truth is, Howard Stern is human just like any one of us. He isn't perfect, but he gave me a job right out of college and always treated me with respect. In fact, he still remembered my birthday even though I was no longer a cast member and helped me out the best he could.

The point of this story is not to congratulate myself or tell you what a loyal guy I am. My point is to let you know that your mistakes do not define you. In fact they put you where you are supposed to be. As Adam Duritz, front singer, of the Counting Crows said in a song, "Got this little revolver of stupid choices..." I can identify with that. I was fortunate to be able to learn from the best and to meet the funniest and most interesting and loyal fans. I am nothing special, but I never even considered that offer to write a tell all book about Howard Stern. I told the publisher that there was nothing new to tell, and I wasn't interested. Besides, I had just found a nice parking spot to sleep at right next to a Denny's that had a big bathroom, so I was already planning a nice shower in the sink. As you can see, I had much more important stuff on my mind in those days.

There is a lesson here somewhere. My conclusion was that it can always be worse. Yes, I was homeless, but I was homeless in Southern California. As you may know, in Southern California it is just around 70 degrees every day, and it rains maybe three times a year? Nice! Back in New York, when I used to walk to the deli at 5 am to get Howard's breakfast, I would see homeless people sleeping on the subway grates, where the warm air came through, and wondered how anyone could have the mental toughness to live that way.

I remember asking one of the homeless guys a question one morning.

Immediately the gentleman told me that I had to be quiet because the mothership in his navel was about to release a sulfur oxide into his beard, and his appointment with Liberace was cancelled due to the letter his pet lizard wrote to his uncle back when seagulls controlled Parliament. True story.

See, that's how the journey for me for this book began. Obviously, that homeless man was mentally ill and so was I at the time. Yet, we both have a story to tell, I am just fortunate to be able to have a platform to tell mine. In all honesty, I believe everyone has a story to tell, if you are willing to listen. No one can truly say that one story is more valid than the other. We all look at the world through different pairs of eyes. It's funny, but I believe I may have learned this whole concept from Howard. You could be a dwarf, a hooker, a member of the mob, or run through the streets of NY wearing nothing but high heels… and still we all have feelings, experiences, challenges, and a story to share.

I am filibustering and pontificating and probably some other big words too, so let me get to the point, This book is called *Simply Amazing* for a reason. I started WMAP Radio ("World's Most Amazing People") three years ago, and it turns out that the theme of this anthology of my interviews reflects one of the greatest lessons of my life "we are all given talent and opportunities.' Sometimes we use them effectively, but other times we forget our own personal value, and self-doubt and depression can swallow us up whole.

Negativity and destruction can come from the outside, like an accident, act of war, or cruelty from others, or from the inside- like being a coward. That was my poison. I could never understand why victories and successes were empty and unfulfilling, and how it was easier and somehow a compromise to the ones I loved to slowly drink myself to death. The problem with life, and most anything really, if you want something bad enough you're probably going to get it.

My story isn't a story you have never heard before. These are just the simple facts, I have done irreversible damage to my health. Whatever time I have left on this Earth I want to use it to make memories that up lift people, stories that may help someone, who can't, won't or refuses to see the amazing qualities about themselves.

I have been admitted to the hospital over 40 times. It all began with a few mini-bottles of vodka at night, just to loosen up and relax. This "relaxation" slowly transformed into a death sentence. I have always struggled with severe depression. I would find ways to self-medicate. I would use relationships with women to replace the sadness and emptiness I felt inside. I would also use alcohol in the same way.

Again, even though I was fortunate, there was this ungrateful monster that wouldn't go away. My medication didn't help and talking about what was wrong helped even less. The problem was, I couldn't quite tell you what was wrong. All I knew was that there was nothing that made me feel proud of anything, nor did I have any sense of true accomplishment.

When I was young, I really believed that if I was famous all of my problems would be over. I grew up to find out quite the opposite. As soon as I began working for Howard Stern it dawned on me that I *worked* for someone that was famous and had lots of fans, and *he* made me part of his show. It got into my head over time, I was being asked to take pictures with fans, sign autographs, do appearances, etc. It was great, but it began to dawn on me, that although it was great getting this special treatment and attention the attention was because of Howard Stern. It began to make me feel strange. I remember an appearance I did in Chicago and as I was signing 8 x 10 headshots, I looked up and saw a line of people wrapped around the room and thought to myself, "Why the hell would anyone want this picture of me besides my mom?"

From then on celebrity appearances began to make me feel like I was this guy with a huge ego that somehow planned this event and thought I was super special. In truth, Howard Stern, the guy I worked for, he was really someone special, I was just lucky to be around him.

In that environment it's easy to lose track of yourself and believe that you are a celebrity. The real truth is that you *work* for a celebrity and one day that can hit you square in the face. . Finally that happened to me and my lack of self-esteem squashed all illusions I may have had about being a celebrity. I never really believed and and still don't believe I'm any more interesting or better than anyone else.

At some point approximately seven years ago, almost right after my last failed relationship, I just gave up on any long-term goals or even attempting to live the life that I had thought I would. I am not proud of it but I simply began to not care about much of anything. I spent my days and nights drunk. This is really hard for me to share. Essentially

I drank every day to the point where I could not have a conversation or do anything on the rare occasion that I was sober. Anything in moderation is usually OK, but unfortunately for me I had no idea what the concept of moderation was at the time.

While I drank each night, the real problem started when I woke up. It was not the hangover, but the feeling of nothingness. I did not care what the day brought. It was exhausting and torture to fake caring about anything each and every day. I couldn't even make small talk at the grocery store. It simply hurt to smile. So, as soon as I woke up, I made sure I had at least two pints of vodka next to me. I would slam the first one down and drink a glass of water. Now what no one knows about me is that I actually hate the taste of alcohol. So the first pint of Vodka I would slam down would simply burn the back of my throat each time. I would hold it down for a moment, but, like clockwork, the first pint of Vodka would immediately come right back up. This was my morning drill so I learned early on not to take my many morning meds until after I threw up the first pint of Vodka.

Once my body had cleared out the first pint of Vodka, then it was time for the second pint chaser. This one I held down, along with my meds, and I could start my day. It's hard to believe, but for some reason I didn't get drunk or act like an asshole; I just felt normal. I remember sitting in my car one day in a suit about to walk into a job interview at 9 am and, like rapid fire, I sucked down six shot bottles of Vodka, then walked in to the interview and never once was my speech slurred. Drinking like that made me feel like a human. Eventually my drinking progressed to a ridiculous amount. Through out the day I would finish four to six pints of straight vodka with no reservation.

Early on I was deceived by my drinking regimen. I was in such good shape that it took around three years for the daily drinking to start to take it's toll on my body. One morning I wound up with a pain in my stomach that ended up persisting for days. It was so intense I had to be rushed to the ER.

That was the first time I was admitted to a hospital for acute pancreatitis. Acute pancreatitis is when you have drank so much alcohol that your pancreas begins to digest itself. Unfortunately, that's exactly what it feels like. After years of being on the football field and taking blow after blow, this was the most severe pain I had ever felt in my life. They use multiple ways to diagnose acute pancreatitis. In the beginning, they measure your amylase and lipase levels. These enzymes are secreted by the pancreas and liver to break down what you eat and drink. Obviously my numbers were off.

Once diagnosed with acute pancreatitis, it's common knowledge that you are not supposed to ever drink again. Of course I didn't listen. Since that first diagnosis I have gone on to be hospitalized over forty (40) times. You would think that the brutal pain of my pancreas digesting itself would stop me from drinking. It didn't.

After you spend half of your adult life, alone, sitting in hospitals, some soul searching, personal inventory, and introspection occurs. On one of those occasions I calculated how much I drank each day for four or five years. If a shot is 1½ ounces, then I drank 30-40 shots a day. A pint is 16 ounces; that's over 10 shots. A liter is 34 ounces. That's over 2 pints. It took me a week at Mather Hospital to figure those mathematics out, so don't say I never taught you anything. Are you impressed I could figure out that if you add up all the drinks I had? It comes out to about the same amount of liquid as Drakkar Cologne sprayed on a Friday night on the South Shore of Long Island in 1988.

Now, I'll admit what I have to, so you can start reading these special interviews about these amazing people and why I felt compelled to start the "World's Most Amazing People" Radio and compile eleven different interviews into this book, "Simply Amazing".

All the drinking established a pattern for me. It would start with excruciating pain, which after a few days the pain would send me to the ER. Immediately, I'd be admitted to the hospital. Once admitted, I knew the routine. You cannot eat or drink anything for 3-5 days, as they put you on an NPO diet and IV fluids. NPO is IV fluids only, and you are not allowed to eat anything- not even an ice cube.

After the great doctors and nurses at Mather and St. Charles Hospitals repeatedly got me back to health, they told me (after around the 20th hospitalization) that something in my body had severely changed. They told me I was getting so bad that my next drink most likely would kill me, and very soon my luck would run out.

Depression and desperation will make you throw yourself away. I'm sure from the outside it appeared that I had zero respect for life, mine or anyone else's, or that I must really hate myself because I was choosing to torture myself. It's been said that an attack of acute or chronic pancreatitis is one of the most painful conditions to endure. Two mg of dilaudid wears off in 60 minutes, and then you're begging to die for the next hour- dry heaving and feeling like your organs are digesting themselves. Trust me- it is so painful you pray for death. You're helpless.

I have met such amazing doctors and nurses who never judge; they just want you to get better. Their kindness and compassion restores your faith in people, even when the pain is so bad you forget about every dream you ever had, everything you have ever loved. You just want it to stop. You will do anything to make it stop.

This last birthday, I'm ashamed to say, the pain was so severe I no longer prayed for it to stop. I prayed to die. July 17th, 2017 is a day I will never forget. I've had broken ribs, dozens of concussions, been stabbed, tazed, and bear sprayed so I know a bit about pain. This was something different. I pray nobody ever feels pain like that.

I have nobody to blame but me. I beat the shit out of myself mentally, physically, and spiritually to a point where it's hard to ever forgive myself. I never heard a voice inside my head say, "Leave that guy alone... he's not so bad. How much more do you expect him to take?" I only felt disgust, shame, rage, hatred and disappointment every day, every hour, and I just wanted it to stop. That is the best explanation of why I drank, knowing it was killing me.

Something about drinking was the only thing that turned down the dial of spiritual and mental agony I was feeling a bit. I can't say it enough, and if you know an addict and wonder how someone could be so selfish, I assure you they don't do it to hurt or insult you. The addict is no longer having fun or partying. They are most likely doing their best to make it to the next day. I've heard people say things like, "I work a job and have responsibilities. I'd love to get drunk everyday."

No you would not. I promise you.

The nightmare that becomes your life from drugs and alcohol

happens faster than you think, and it's no longer a choice. It will make you think that you are just running out the clock. It will make you start every sentence with "remember." You get to a place where you so badly want that hole in your heart filled with something, someone, anything. You don't care about outcomes. You just want it all to stop.

So I would go right back to drinking. One time I left the hospital and went directly to the liquor store. Other times I remember even bringing bottles into the hospital with me, and as soon as the pain subsided I'd drink again before being discharged.

It's hard to admit all theses things, but I truly want my mistakes and my self destruction to help at least one other person reading this. A lot of people don't think they can be helpe, they feel they deserve a life of agony, but some of them endure it because of the love they have for other people.

I can only tell you how I felt and what I did. I would get so angry and full of rage, living a life void of any interest, ambition or joy whatsoever. Most of the time I would just scream, dig my fingers into my eyes. Every time trying to rip my face off. Other times I would spit at any mirror I saw my reflection in. I was very careful nobody ever saw me go through one of these episodes . I never told anyone. This was the most hatred for any human I ever had in my life and it was all against me.

After around the 30th discharge from the hospital, the doctors were right-my luck had run out. I started bleeding randomly. I started seeing pools of blood immediately after I went to the bathroom. At the time I didn't think much of it, but eventually I got winded and out of breath walking up a small flight of stairs. This ex- college football jock even ran out of breath talking on the air. On top of that, daily, people kept telling me I was so white I looked dead.

One day as I got off the air and began walking toward the exit of the building, thank God, the Princess was there to save my life. I told her I needed to sit down before I could manage the three steps to get to the parking lot. She told me that she was taking me to the hospital because I looked "scary." I said I just wanted to go home to sleep. As soon as she came back from getting the car, she realized I had fallen off a bench and was lying on the floor in the lobby of the office building.

The ambulance rushed me to the nearest hospital. Once there the ER staff realized that my blood pressure was too faint to put in an IV. I was successfully dying. My long-term plan and my hard work of achieving my death wish were about to pay off.

It took two nurses to try and put an IV into my jugular vein, each stopping unsuccessfully after what seemed like an hour before throwing up their hands. As the second nurse gave up, I swear I heard her say, "It's not gonna work." I assumed that this was it. Then a third nurse came over to stick needles and wires into my neck. Now, as I said, I've been stabbed before - and it's quick. Your skin is no match for the blade of the knife. With just a little bit of force the blade goes in with almost a "pop" sound, and then the most pain comes when it gets pulled out, depending how deep it went.

However, the three nurses must have punctured my jugular vein over thirty times. It wasn't just the pain of the needles; it was the mental anguish of seeming to have my jugular vein snaked like getting a clog out of a toilet. After they got the IV into my jugular, I remember being wheeled down to a really bright room. There were several people waiting to take care of me and my pancreas. Yet, for some reason, all I kept hearing in my head was the phrase "dead man bleeding."

Then the news, no one wants to hear on the operating table, came straight from the surgeon himself, I would have to be awake the whole time for the operation. Apparently I was bleeding out, and if they did not stop the bleeding immediately somehow, I would repeat the early deaths of both my uncle (44) and my father (50).

I remember being lifted onto a metal rectangular slab, that was just a few inches deep. To this day I can still feel how cold the metal was against my back, butt, and legs. I can best describe the cold hard metallic container as a bigger version of what you would dissect a frog in.

It freaks me out to think of the spot they cut into first. I was just hoping it was going to be fast. The surgeon made a deep slice into that area below your hip flexor. This is where the inside of your leg meets your groin. There plan was to run a piece of wire, with tiny cameras through my groin to then place a piece of metal around my pancreas duct to stop the bleeding.

For hours during the surgery people were telling me I was "doing great," and to "hang in, there." I remember at one point telling the surgical team I had to go to the bathroom and them telling me there was no time.

Have you ever had to move your bowels so bad that you try not to move because the pressure is so great that one wrong move could be the difference between being uncomfortable and needing to get new pants?

I told them again that I really had to go, and "I'm not kidding." I'm not sure what was stranger, the surgeon telling me to go right there on the table, or feeling what seemed like an endless rush of hot diarrhea pouring out of me. My back, legs and butt started to warm up. That's when I looked around and realized I was lying in what felt like inches of my own warm blood. I could not believe I had so much blood in me.

That day they had to replace the entire blood in my body, 12 bags. After that surgery my pancreas is now essentially held together by a piece of metal in my stomach that I'll have for the rest of my life.

In my near death experience I didn't see any white light or see dead relatives; I just remember pain, wishing it was over, the warm feeling of blood as it surrounded me and turned cold, and then even colder before they could finally clean it off me.

I walked with a cane for a week or two after I was released from the hospital and began to secretly drink again. You would think coming seconds away from death that I would never drink again. That some how I would appreciate my second chance at life, right ? Wrong. T h e years to follow included more hospitals, a fluid-filled cyst being drained from my pancreas and later a liter of fluid taken out of me. The second piece of metal became infected and left me with kidney failure and the loss of 50 pounds.

Regardless, I was a breath away from leaving this place as a selfish, ungrateful coward who was a constant disappointment, a failure, a broken man with memories and unanswered questions.

After forty visits to the hospital for acute pancreatitis needless to say I have done irreversible damage to my pancreas. It looks as if I may have accomplished my original goal of drinking myself to death. "Hey-if I die tomorrow- I at least set a goal in my life and saw it through." More importantly, I made a new and better goal to put this book out, and it's been one of the most positive things I've accomplished in my life to date.

My only wish now is that I am around long enough to see the many ways this book may help people here and around the world

As of March 2018, most of my pancreas is calcified, and I have gone from having acute pancreatitis to having chronic pancreatitis. Simply put, most of my pancreas is dead and it is not coming back. I now have to accept my new life with a piece of metal inside me that keeps me from bleeding out from my pancreas again.

I don't want to risk upsetting my loved ones and my friends by having them act weird around me, so I'm not revealing an expiration date on myself. But I can say honestly, and hopefully can tell anyone who may be where I was, that it's killing me.

But I feel this is getting boring, and so I'll sum it up. I have the beginning signs of pancreatic cancer, and that's one thing I can't fight. If I can avoid that from becoming full blown I could hang on for years to come. Even with that optimism, I have come to accept that the chance of me dying in my sleep of old age is most likely zero percent now though.

If I drink, eat fatty foods and have horrible stress, I most likely will hang on for six months to a year. But I also heard I may have years, so that's what I choose to believe. The problem with this is - if you don't die you kind of look like a liar. I'd rather be anything than a liar, so I'm telling everyone that I am trying to accept some things, but I'm not saying my goodbyes. At the same time, I'm not waiting or putting off anything. My friend Rocky Romanella always tells me we should leave this place better than we found it. So that's why you have this book. Maybe I'm here to help one of you or to introduce you to a person that will change your life in an amazing way.

I have come a hair's breath away from death. Whatever happens, though, I want to prove to you what I know now. I wish I could have learned it a different way, and I wish I could have been nicer to myself because I now realize I'm not such a bad guy, but it's the truth. You are amazing. I don't know you, but you are.

I hope you take from my introduction is not to let the past define you. It's never too late to try again. If you hurt others, if you hurt yourself, spend the time you have left going above and beyond to do the best you can for as long as you can. I have done some horrible things to myself and to other people, but if I get the chance I'd like to be remembered for what I did at the end of my life, not what got me there.

Remember, many of us fall, sometimes to great depths. The difference between a common person and a truly amazing one is in learning, growing, accepting, and changing what we can. I hope you can relate to some of the interviews here. These are all told by people who can encourage us to rise above pain and misfortune. They have all made a lasting impression on me, and I hope they have the same effect on you. I'm just the messenger. But it feels really good to be the messenger of hope as I share the inspiring stories of these truly amazing people.

Maybe this is goodbye, maybe it's not. But I want to encourage everyone to take a minute to listen to other people's stories. You will be surprised at how interesting everyone is. I hope you give people a chance and make a memory with loved ones each day. If you love somebody, or if there is something about them you admire, tell them now. You might be surprised at how far a smile (even if it's fake) or a trivial "I like your shoes" goes.

This book is by and about eleven (11) regular people, and I promise you that reading their stories will be time well spent. I hope the positive messages stay with you. This will be a series of books, and I'll be working on them until I'm called home. Thank you for taking a chance on this one. If tomorrow never comes, I can say this experience of working and creating something that will bring people up for a long long time with my best friend Virginia has been the most meaningful and proudest moments in my life. I'm so blessed and lucky. Maybe it's too late, maybe not, but I'm leaving this place kinder to myself. I hope someone who is where I was, can turn it around and bring someone else up, too.

CHAPTER 1

Werner Reich

Email: info@hmtcli.org
Web Address: http://www.hmtcli.org/
Werner Reich may be contacted through the Holocaust
Memorial and Tolerance Center of Nassau County
100 Crescent Beach Road, Glen Cove, NY 11542

Werner Reich Intro

A few times a year, Mom and Princess travel to local schools around Long Island to pick up clothes that were left in the Lost and Found and bring them to my Mom's house to wash, sort, and fold. Then they bring the clothing to homeless shelters or send them to far off places like Africa. Well, one day they told me they met the most amazing man who was giving a talk to students as they were picking up the clothes.

Werner Reich is one of my favorite interviews I've done in my career. From the moment this man opened his mouth, all I could do was ask question after question with the curiosity of a child and the admiration and respect that comes only from imagining yourself in someone else's shoes. Knowing full well, if put in the same situation, I wouldn't stand a chance, Werner Reich no longer was someone I could relate to. He became more like a hero in a movie.

I tried my best to let him tell his unbelievable story of persecution, capture and torture without interrupting with the thousand questions I had for him. The two hours I spent talking with this morally centered, gentle man absolutely blew my mind and exposed me to horrors I never dreamed existed.

Yes, of course, it's appalling that humans can treat others with such vile disregard for basic decency. Werner Reich was treated with unadulterated, vicious cruelty. He was stripped—or should I say, his captors *tried* to strip him-of his dignity, his faith, and right to live. They mocked him, tortured and humiliated him along with the other prisoners at Auschwitz. He is beyond amazing not only in the story you are about to read, but what I saw during our interview changed my life forever.

I think it was after he finished telling me how they made him wear his prayer shawl as underwear. I am not Jewish, but I could feel a natural repulsion at the attempt to demean anyone in such a disgusting way. I felt many things, but mostly anger at how Werner Reich was treated— simply for being Jewish. I couldn't imagine how anyone could endure anything like this, but I do know how much rage I'd feel.

That's when what I saw changed my life. It was in his eyes. I saw kindness as he related receiving cruelty. I saw compassion and thoughtfulness despite experiencing sociopathy, selfishness and greed. I saw a man looking back on his life and recounting how grateful and lucky he was. I've read the last two pages of his interview over and over. Werner Reich is, without a doubt, one of the World's Most Amazing People.

Interview

K.C. Armstrong: This is the World's Most Amazing People and, guys, I've got to tell you I am so excited right now because I have an amazing guest that I've been waiting to interview for a long time! This individual is a hero and a part of history. Werner Reich is a gentleman who, since 1927, has gone through experiences that we can only begin to fathom or understand. I was saying before that it's so rare that you actually get to speak directly to history, to someone who has been in the places you normally only read about in books. So, without further ado, it is my great honor and privilege to welcome to the program Mr. Werner Reich. Werner, welcome to the program.

Werner Reich: Thank you very much, thank you.

K.C. Armstrong: Werner, I just want to capture every single word that you have to say. Let's start in 1927.

You were born-where?

Werner Reich: I was born in Berlin, Germany. My father was a mechanical and electrical engineer. He worked for Siemens and we lived a very normal, almost perfect life at home in the suburbs of Berlin. My mother was a very fine artist and she was also a very, very proud German. She came from an old family that lived since the Spanish Inquisition in Germany. She had served during World War I in the German military as a nurse and had been awarded the Iron Cross with a citation which said that the gratitude of the fatherland would be with her forever. Not only was she German, but she was also an American because her father fought in the Civil War in the US before returning to Germany. My father was from the Austro-Hungarian Empire. He was from Transylvania, which was the part of Hungary that later became Romania. And he had been an officer in the Cavalry during World War I. So, although my parents were "enemies" during World War I, they somehow shook hands and got married.

K.C. Armstrong: Okay, I'll admit I'm not the best with history—World War II started in what year?

Werner Reich: Well, officially 1939. But actually, in 1933 rules came out which limited various minorities, particularly Jews like us, from existing in Germany. For example, companies were not permitted to hire Jews. So, it wasn't a question just of losing jobs; we weren't even in a position to get a job. So, the vast majority of people who escaped from Germany left in 1933 because otherwise they couldn't make a living.

K.C. Armstrong: Was Hitler gaining power at that time, or was he not even heard of in '33?

Werner Reich: In January 1933 he gained power and he immediately implemented various rules, racial persecutions and so on. He immediately killed his opponents, burnt down the Parliament in Reichstag, and arrested the Communists.

K.C. Armstrong: Were his ideas and methods considered radical at that time by everyday people?

Werner Reich: You know what? Persecution in various European countries was an old thing. You can go back to the Spanish Inquisition where they took Jews and simply burnt and killed them and so on. So, the basic idea as far as Jews were concerned, the basic concept of anti-Semitism, was old hat. You had a set of beliefs that, number one, Jews are Christ killers. Number two, Jews are trying to overtake the world. Then you had stories that Jews are poisoning wells and that they use the blood of Christian children to make matzo, and so on.

K.C. Armstrong: Where on Earth do these anti-Semitic accusations come from?

Werner Reich: Anti-Semitism was really started with the creation by the Jews of the Ten Commandments because the Ten Commandments went against people's basic principles. "You shall not steal, you shall not rape, you shall not murder." These things annoyed people and then, when various religions took over, they wanted to be the only religion in existence; they felt threatened by others. And the Jews were very, very stubborn; they didn't want to convert. And so they became the enemies of various nations. And this has been a tradition forever. Some people say if the Jews hadn't been so stubborn there wouldn't have been any persecution—but then Jews wouldn't exist anymore today! And the other thing was because the Jews were persecuted so much. In other words, they stayed in one place and then they had to move. So, they had to create a portable religion. As a result, most religious services can be held in people's homes.

K.C. Armstrong: Interesting.

Werner Reich: Even today, we don't need a house of worship. And we don't need any priests. Anybody can conduct a service provided that ten people are there.

K.C. Armstrong: I see.

Werner Reich: And since Jews were constantly tossed out of their homelands, they developed portable trades. In other words, jobs which they could take from one place to another. They didn't have flour mills, farms, or anything like that. Instead, they became peddlers, teachers, writers and scientists so they could just pick up and go when necessary. And if you look at the history of Jews, interestingly enough, roughly two tenths of 1% of the world population is Jewish, yet roughly 30% of all Nobel Prize Winners are Jewish.

K.C. Armstrong: The Chosen, God's people . . .

Werner Reich: Well, yes, we believe we have been chosen to spread God's word. When people say we are "the chosen people" I'm reminded of the story of the little Jew who is praying one evening before going to bed. He says, "Dear Lord, for four thousand years we have been the chosen people. Now, please, choose somebody else."

K.C. Armstrong: (Laughs) I've never heard that. That's very good! Now, let me go back, Werner, to your earliest memory. I know you were born in '27, you were in Berlin, and when you were five that's kind of where your big experiences began. But before that do you have other, hopefully happy, memories as a kid?

Werner Reich: I can't remember too much of what happened before I was five. You know, most people's memories don't go much before around 4 years of age. I do remember playing in the garden and going to a local ice cream shop.

K.C. Armstrong: OK, so you're living a normal little boy's life, and everything is okay. But then what happens to change that?

Werner Reich: Well, when I was five my father lost his job, and in December 1933, we left Germany for Yugoslavia.

K.C. Armstrong: Why there? What was happening politically in Berlin at that time?

Werner Reich: Well, in Berlin you had the National Socialist Party (the Nazi Party) taking over, and they tried to solve the German economic problems by simply eliminating certain people that they said were destroying Germany. They were looking to create a racially pure nation, so they went after what they called enemies of the state. They persecuted Jehovah's Witnesses because they didn't want to serve in the military. They persecuted gypsies as being vagrants. They persecuted communists for being enemies of the state. They had basically the same philosophy as the Klan had. The Klan, if I recall correctly, had five groups of enemies: Blacks, communists, Jews, members of the labor unions, and Catholics.

And in Germany it was the same. You know, people always talk about the Holocaust being strictly a Jewish issue. Sure, six million Jews died, but another roughly five to six million people who were NOT Jews died. Roughly 250,000 people were killed willfully under operation T4, which targeted groups of people who supposedly didn't contribute toward the German economy. These groups included the handicapped, mentally ill, and the senile. Huge groups of people.

K.C. Armstrong: Even if you were German.

Werner Reich: Oh yes. I'm talking about pure Germans.

K.C. Armstrong: Well, let's go back to your move to Yugoslavia. Did your father find a job there?

Werner Reich: One problem, aside from a change in language, was that Yugoslavia was strictly an agricultural country. It had a tremendous wealth in agriculture and mining, but that was re-fabricated outside of the country and imported back. So, the country just didn't have any need for engineers like my father. Plus, we had other obstacles. We had left Germany with very little in our pockets. Because it was known that we were leaving the country immediately, we had to sell our house for next to nothing. And also, what little we had was evaluated at the border, and a 25% tax was slapped on it. And then, when I was 13 my father died, and a few months later Germany invaded Yugoslavia.

K.C. Armstrong: Oh, no.

Werner Reich: Now, to have a better understanding, Yugoslavia never existed until 1918. And then it was put together out of different countries including Slovenia, Croatia, Serbia, Macedonia, Bosnia, and Montenegro. These were countries that had fought each other for centuries, that hated each other's guts, but they managed to live under a Serbian king. Anyway, When Hitler invaded Yugoslavia, the country fell apart again. And Serbia became independent and was fighting the Croats, the Germans, and the Bosnians. Croatia aligned itself with Germany and they got virulent anti-Semitic and fascist ideas. There were, I think, five or six concentration camps in Poland. I think five were strictly designed to exterminate people. Interestingly enough, there wasn't one extermination camp in Germany.

K.C. Armstrong: That's surprising. Let's talk about that. What were these concentration camps designed to do? You said some were just designated to kill, but weren't some also work camps?

Werner Reich: There were various camps. There were concentration camps which were built strictly for labor. And then there were camps like Treblinka, Belzec, Auschwitz, and Majdanek which were strictly for extermination. There was even a camp I was in which was strictly for demonstration, in this case demonstrating to the Swiss and Swedish authorities and the Red Cross that the Germans were not mistreating the prisoners.

K.C. Armstrong: How did your life change after your father died and Germany invaded Yugoslavia?

Werner Reich: Well, a couple of days after the Nazis took over my mother was called to school, and I was told that I couldn't attend anymore. I was 13 years old, and that was it—finished as a student. And then people started to disappear. My mother, being an American citizen and having an Iron Cross, felt 100% sure that nothing bad was going to happen to her.

K.C. Armstrong: What did the Iron Cross represent?

Werner Reich: It was a medal given to people for heroic actions in the name of the fatherland, whatever that may be.

K.C. Armstrong: Okay. So, you are no longer allowed to go to school. Was that because you are Jewish?

Werner Reich: Yes, because I am Jewish. I was told I had to stay at home and then, after a couple of months, my mother introduced me to a couple, husband and wife, and I was told to move to their apartment. I never knew what their names were, but I moved in with them though I couldn't wear shoes because the people in the apartment below would hear me. And I couldn't go near the window because people from the street would see me.

K.C. Armstrong: Were these people that were hiding you Jewish?

Werner Reich: No, they definitely were Christians.

K.C. Armstrong: And what happened to your mother and sister?

Werner Reich: My mother stayed at home, still believing she was protected. She tried to get to the US, but that wasn't possible without huge bribe money, which she didn't have. So, she then placed my sister in hiding with one couple, and me with the other couple.

K.C. Armstrong: That must've been hard being separated from both your mother and sister. So, you're with a Christian couple, and they're raising you?

Werner Reich: No, they didn't raise me; they hid me.

K.C. Armstrong: Why did they take you in?

Werner Reich: Well, one of the couple was going out during the day and coming back later with film. I then learned how to develop these films and make enlargements of the pictures and so on. I did that for two years until I was discovered. There was a knock at the door at about 6 o'clock one morning, and half a dozen Gestapo men rushed in. They wore black coats, boots and black leather coats. They turned the place upside down. Everything in the cupboards and drawers was thrown on the floor, and then the couple was dragged away while a guy with a gun watched over me. I told him I had to go to the bathroom, which he allowed, but he told me to keep the door open. After I relieved myself he told me to get dressed and he took me down to the Gestapo headquarters, which was lucky.

K.C. Armstrong: Why do you say that?

Werner Reich: Because if the Croats had taken me they would have cut my throat. That's how they killed people. They had competitions to see who could cut the most throats in one day. Well, anyway, I was locked up in a little cell in the headquarters basement, which had been a coal cellar before. It was just me—no bed or anything. Just concrete floor and a bucket.

K.C. Armstrong: Did you understand the weight of what was going on?

Werner Reich: No. I didn't have the slightest idea. Apparently, I didn't show the proper respect, because the Gestapo agent came over to me smiling, hit me, and I absolutely flew across the room.

K.C. Armstrong: Oh my God.

Werner Reich: And then he told me to get up, hit me again harder, and I slammed into the desk and cut my head. I was bleeding and crying all over his carpet, but that didn't bother him.

He enjoyed hitting me. He questioned me for quite a while about where the films in the house I was staying in came from and who the films were given to. I didn't have the slightest idea; I mean, I wasn't involved in that. I hadn't been told anything. The Gestapo must have suspected that I didn't know much anyway because why would those people tell me where the stuff came from? Who knows what the Gestapo had already done to the couple? They'd probably killed them by then.

K.C. Armstrong: How long did they keep you?

Werner Reich: Three days in the dark basement, tossing me a liverwurst sandwich every so often. After the three days

I was put into a car and driven to Slovenia. Now, I was in German territory. Up to that time I was in Croat territory, but now I was in German territory. And they locked me up in a border town in a little jail cell, like a wooden hut.

K.C. Armstrong: Was this just yourself?

Werner Reich: By myself, yes. And it must have once been a drunk tank. There were millions and millions of fleas in there and they got into my nose, my ears, my hair. I mean, they drove me absolutely bonkers.

K.C. Armstrong: Itchy, right?

Werner Reich: I was itchy and also swollen all over. I was wearing a short-sleeved shirt and short pants. But after a few more days I was transferred by car to Graz, Austria.

K.C. Armstrong: What happened in Graz?

Werner Reich: I was locked up in the police station there, and that's where I had my only revenge on the German government because I infected my cell, and all the adjacent cells, with fleas!

K.C. Armstrong: Good job, Werner!

Werner Reich: I was locked up with three other kids. Two had been arrested for burglary, and the third kid had murdered his mother. I was the fourth criminal there.

K.C. Armstrong: Were the other kids Jewish?

Werner Reich: No, no. They were Austrian.

K.C. Armstrong: Now, throughout this whole time while you're being brought to jail, put in a car, brought to the next jail, were you more concerned with what was going to happen to you next, or were you thinking about your family? You must have been thinking of a million things. Can you go back to that time and remember what was . . .

Werner Reich: I found myself in a state of basic apathy because there was nothing I could figure out. The total atmosphere—I'd never been in jail before; I didn't even know where I was. I found out about these things later on.

K.C. Armstrong: But did you ask them "What did I do wrong?" or "Why am I here?"

Werner Reich: No. My basic attitude was that within the next day or two they'd find out they made a mistake and let me go. I was naive. I mean, I had been highly protected because of the Victorian background of my parents. They never discussed unpleasant issues in front of my sister and me. And so, I found myself in Graz locked up for six weeks. And then we were taken down to the police station yard and were allowed to walk around. One day, from my cell window, I saw my mother walking around that prison yard with a bunch of other women. She wore a grey dress. And that's the last time I ever saw her.

K.C. Armstrong: That's the last time you saw your mother. How very sad.

Werner Reich: She had been arrested. They obviously had laughed at her Iron Cross and American citizenship. You know, the beauty of the Germans was that they really did not get involved in minutia, you know. So anyway, I was next transported to Vienna where I was deposited in a synagogue which was destroyed during the Night of the Broken Glass.

K.C. Armstrong: What is that?

Werner Reich: Kristallnacht happened in November 1938, I think it was the 8th. In one night something like 7,000 Jewish businesses were destroyed, 1,600 houses of worship were demolished or vandalized, and 30,000 people were arrested. Within a month, I think 1,000 were murdered. This mad display of violence took place throughout Germany, Austria and Czechoslovakia.

K.C. Armstrong: I heard about that in school, but it never sounded real.

Werner Reich: It was. To me it's a sign of the obscenity that happened in Germany because in one town, the day after the Night of the Broken Glass, all the schools were closed so that the big boys could take the little children around town to show them how to break Jewish windows.

K.C. Armstrong: That's pretty unbelievable.

Werner Reich: Yes, I know. I find some of these things very, very—I don't know-incomprehensible even now.

K.C. Armstrong: Right, right. To even get the children involved in that way. So, you stayed in one of these destroyed synagogues?

Werner Reich: Yes, with a couple of hundred other people. They all had luggage with them and I had nothing. I didn't even have fleas with me.

K.C. Armstrong: You generously gave them all to the Germans at the Graz police station! So, these other people with you in the demolished synagogue were from all over?

Werner Reich: From Vienna. And the next morning we get loaded into a railroad car and go on a two or three-day trip to a place called Terezin in Czechoslovakia. Terezin was an old Austrian fortress. There were about 2,900 civilians living in that town and working the fields around the town. When Hitler occupied Czechoslovakia in 1939, all the civilians were tossed out and he opened a concentration camp, a demo camp.

K.C. Armstrong: Demo Camp?

Werner Reich: That's right. It was established to prove to the Red Cross and the Swedish authorities that the Nazis adhered to the Geneva Convention, which demands civilized treatment of prisoners of war.

K.C. Armstrong: Okay, I see. So, Jews were now considered prisoners of war?

Werner Reich: Yes. Prisoners of war. And so, what they did was take all the intelligentsia of Germany,Czechoslovakia and Austria and later on, I think, a few from Denmark, and they dumped them into Terezin. They gave them musical instruments and they gave the kids pencils and crayons and so on.

K.C. Armstrong: On the outside that probably didn't seem so bad.

Werner Reich: Theoretically things did not seem bad, but there are a couple of facts which I think may be worthwhile mentioning. One of them is that before, 2,900 people lived in Terezin. When the Nazis took over, they dumped 60,000 people there. So, the overcrowding was a huge problem. When the inspections came, a couple of things had to be done for appearance. Number one, the food improved dramatically.

K.C. Armstrong: From what to what?

Werner Reich: From garbage to little cakes and decent soup. No meat, but, you know.

K.C. Armstrong: So, they were putting on a show.

Werner Reich: They were putting on a show. People were even given postcards and told to write anything that was nice and good, and they did. This was part of the whole fraud. And, besides having to change the food for the inspectors' visits, they also had far too many people there. So, before the inspections, they packed people into trains and shipped out maybe ten, twenty, thirty thousand to reduce the population. They shipped them to Auschwitz where they gassed them. Let me put it to you this way: 141,000 people had been shipped to Terezin and about 17,000 survived.

K.C. Armstrong: Incredible.

Werner Reich: By putting on this show, the Germans were protecting themselves from international investigation. So anyway, I was working in Terezin on all different projects. I was laying railroad tracks. I was exterminating bugs in buildings. I was making brooms; I was making baskets. I even helped hold the lights for a concert performance of the opera *Carmen*.

K.C. Armstrong: So, while you were doing all these things, the days at Terezin weren't horrible?

Werner Reich: No, no, it was bearable. I knew nobody there. Most people spoke Czech. I still saw myself leaving there, perhaps the very next day, so I was a naïve kid.

K.C. Armstrong: I know you said you were there in Terezin for ten months. Was the next stop Auschwitz?

Werner Reich: That's right, KC. One day they called up a whole bunch of us and they took us down to the railroad tracks to a bunch of cattle cars. And in each car, they put one bucket and loaded about a hundred people per car.

K.C. Armstrong: How much room could you possibly have had?

Werner Reich: We were sitting on the floor and that was it, finished. They closed the door and loaded the next car. After loading the entire train, we started moving, and we travelled like that for the next three days. And the bucket they had given us for a toilet was filled very fast.

K.C. Armstrong: You said ONE bucket?

Werner Reich: For a hundred people. And so now we were lying in our feces and urine. Some people, the very old and the very young especially, died right there in the cars. After three days the doors were opened. We were all scrunched up in pitch black on the floor when suddenly the bright daylight hit us, blinding us. People screamed at us to get out of the cars. There were SS men walking around and also . . .

K.C. Armstrong: Did they have guns?

Werner Reich: No. They didn't have guns; they had walking sticks. They were prisoners with striped uniforms and sticks.

They went inside the cars and hit people over the head and wherever they could. Eventually we managed to get out of the cars. Some people had suitcases which they were told to leave on the railroad track. They separated the men from the women, and we were taken into the camp.

We saw the electrically charged barbed wire to hold us in, and there were buildings with huge chimneys where smoke poured out. We didn't know where we were, so we asked. We were told we were in Auschwitz II, which was the extermination camp. There were actually three Auschwitz camps in the immediate vicinity. There was Auschwitz II, strictly for extermination. There was Auschwitz I, which was a bunch of brick buildings for German criminals, as an overflow of the German penitentiary system. And these were German murderers, thieves, crooks, child molesters—you name it. Plus, they also imprisoned gay people there. And then there was a third camp, Auschwitz III, which was strictly a manufacturing plant that made artificial rubber, but that was a couple of miles away.

K.C. Armstrong: My question is why would they send you to an extermination camp? You were a strapping, healthy kid in your teens, right?

Werner Reich: I was 16 at the time.

K.C. Armstrong: 16. You could work. Why would they send you there?

Werner Reich: Who knows? From what I've heard from people who were in some of these working camps, I'm glad I wasn't in one of them.

K.C. Armstrong: Did you know at the time that Auschwitz II was an extermination camp? Did you know what those chimneys were for?

Werner Reich: We learned a little at a time. Once we were in the camp, we had to strip naked and walk to a table where a guy grabbed us by the arm and tattooed a number there. Then we had to go a little bit further to sit on a chair where they cut off all our hair. We had to stand, and they used one of these cut throat razors to shave off our pubic hair and then painted the area with something that just burned like hell. We were given some underwear, a striped uniform, shoes and socks, and that was it. They changed the underwear every couple of weeks or so and on a couple of occasions I was given the biggest insult they could think of. They gave me underwear made out of prayer shawls.

K.C. Armstrong: Oh no. That really happened? How sick. Why the shaving?

Werner Reich: The Germans were terrified of lice, and they wouldn't mind burning thousands of people just to avoid getting lice.

K.C. Armstrong: I see. Were the men and women still separated?

Werner Reich: At that time in Auschwitz, that was a very unusual camp. It was temporarily what's known as a family camp. For a couple of months married men and women were together in some barracks, but after that the only groups where the genders were put together were Gypsies and Jehovah's Witnesses. There was one area for each of those groups, but they were all killed.

When we first arrived at the camp, the prisoners who had been there a while told us that within six months we would be leaving the camp through the chimney. We thought it was a stupid joke because there was no way in hell that we could imagine anything like that happening.

K.C. Armstrong: I'm sure you just couldn't believe something so horrid was actually true.

Werner Reich: This, by the way, is a normal reaction to any really bad news. People would first assume they were hearing a bad joke. You know, if somebody came and told you your brother was run over by a truck, even if it happened, your first reaction is . . .

K.C. Armstrong: "No, it didn't happen." You don't believe it because it's so shocking and you certainly don't want it to be true.

Werner Reich: Right. So that's what happened to us, and we were within a few hundred yards of these four buildings, these four crematoria. We saw the people being led to the buildings and then the huge flames that shot out of the crematoria and smelled the burning hair and burning flesh all through the camp. A few months ago, I was in my kitchen cooking, wearing a short sleeve shirt and got my arm too close to the gas burner. It must have singed a couple of hairs, and it brought back those memories of Auschwitz, yes.

K.C. Armstrong: Really? How awful! It's still such a part of you.

Werner Reich: Yes. It was as if I was back there. So anyway, it took me about three weeks in Auschwitz to believe that what was happening was real.

K.C. Armstrong: Who were the people chosen for the crematoria?

Werner Reich: When people arrived at the railroad tracks, they had to stand in a long line and wait for SS men and SS women to do the separation. Anybody under the age of 12 was rejected. Anybody over the age of about 40 was rejected. Pregnant women, handicapped people, people who were unable to work, they were all rejected and sent in one direction. The remaining people were sent in the other direction. Later, when the Hungarian Jews came, they didn't even go through the selection; they were all just sent directly to the gas chambers.

K.C. Armstrong: They didn't even do the separation with them.

Werner Reich: Right. The same thing applied to Jehovah's Witnesses and to Gypsies. They were all sent to death.

K.C. Armstrong: If you will, Werner, take us through a day. I'm sure it was unbelievable.

Werner Reich: A typical day in Auschwitz would first consist of lining up and getting some brown water, made out of burnt acorns and two ounces of bread made from flour and sawdust. That was breakfast. Then sometimes you had to work. I left the camp a couple of times digging beets outside the camp, but most work was inside the camp, leveling out the ground, for instance. One day an SS man didn't like the way I was leveling the ground and he hit me with a shovel in the kidneys. I thought I was going to die.

K.C. Armstrong: Oh, man.

Werner Reich: In the morning we stood in line in lots of ten and were counted-sometimes twice or three times. If one person was missing we had to stand there in snow, sleet, rain ice, whatever, until that person was found. For lunch we got a cup of "soup." I've never been able to find a real term for it. Just salt water with little pieces of unwashed dirty potato pieces or beets. In the evening we got another one of these soups and another piece of bread.

K.C. Armstrong: Made out of sawdust?

Werner Reich: Yes—flour and sawdust. There are some estimates that we got about 400 calories a day.

K.C. Armstrong: What about water? Did you have enough to drink?

Werner Reich: Yes, there was water to drink. And that's it. And in the evening, we went back to the barracks and frequently had joke sessions because it was the only thing that took our minds away from the camp—the only thing not connected to our reality. Most people talked about food or their home life.

K.C. Armstrong: Do you remember talking—or fantasizing—about one particular meal?

Werner Reich: No, I just remember being hungry. I was worried about my life, and I didn't like to think about that. It was very, very difficult. In the daytime you spoke to people, but when you were lying next to each other in the bunk touching each other, at that point you were very, very lonely. The closer you were to these people, you know, the lonelier you got.

K.C. Armstrong: Really?

Werner Reich: Yes. Well there were people from all over the world, really, in Auschwitz. At night I often acted as translator because we had people from Russia, Poland, Germany, Hungary, Italy, Denmark, you name it.

K.C. Armstrong: So, there were language barriers. Did you translate their joke sessions?

Werner Reich: Oh yes. I didn't tell them, but I translated them. People would tell old jokes from home the way today you would send email jokes.

K.C. Armstrong: Like sitting around a bar trading funny stories?

Werner Reich: Yes. It helped take our minds from reality. But then July 6th was a defining date in my life.

K.C. Armstrong: Why is that?

Werner Reich: On July 6th, all the young boys in the camp between the ages of 12 and 18, and there were several hundred of us, had to take all our clothes off and run past Dr. Mengele and his SS men. Dr. Mengele was a German doctor.

K.C. Armstrong: The "Angel of Death."

Werner Reich: Yes. The "Angel of Death" who experimented on people. And so, we ran past him, and occasionally he nodded his head and the person he indicated was sent to the other side of the field. And we were running for our lives; we were trying to look taller and stronger and happier and healthier . . . When we were finished there were roughly 300 of us on one side. Then we had to run again and there were 200. After a third time there were 89 of us.

K.C. Armstrong: What was he looking for?

Werner Reich: I haven't the slightest idea. And of the final 89 boys, ten months later, when the war was over, only 46 were still alive. After the 89 of us were selected, virtually all the other 4900 people in the camp were sent to the gas chambers. So approximately 46 of 5000 people at that camp survived the war. That's a 1% survival rate. I alone, for some reason, was sent to Auschwitz I.

K.C. Armstrong: That's incredible. Absolutely insane. Did you have any personal experience with Mengele?

Werner Reich: I heard him speak, but I had no direct contact other than the running. The only thing we didn't know was, when he split people, which group went to death. We felt we should look strong and healthy, but there was no way of forecasting. Also, even if he kept you alive, he also may have then used you for experiments.

K.C. Armstrong: I read about what he did with twins.

Werner Reich: Yes, with twins and dwarves, and you don't want to read that stuff. No, don't; it will spoil your evening.

K.C. Armstrong: I love the way you can keep your sense of humor even when talking about this atrocity.

Now as you spent more time at Auschwitz II, were people still lined up going into the chambers?

Werner Reich: Yes. 1944 was the height of gassing. After one gas chamber was destroyed by sabotage, though, the war pretty well came to an end. The camp was liberated on January 27, 1945. So, I was there in May 1944; Mengele's selection was in July, and in September I was transferred to Auschwitz I.

K.C. Armstrong: Was that mostly work?

Werner Reich: I was sent there because they needed some people. I was assigned to work with horses.

The SS men had military horses which needed to be brushed, cleaned and fed. I didn't mind; it was my first *stable job.*

K.C. Armstrong: I get it. And throughout all this, was there any word about your sister?

Werner Reich: I didn't know anything about my sister or anyone else I had known before. So, I was at Auschwitz I, and at the end of the year we kept hearing gunfire. Russian prisoners of war were brought into Auschwitz, lots of them. And then, after hearing news from them, we were speculating that everything was, you know, over.

K.C. Armstrong: You were waiting for the . . .

Werner Reich: I was waiting to be released.

K.C. Armstrong: Right.

Werner Reich: Now remember, Auschwitz I was strictly for criminals. They had movie hours for the criminals, they had a brothel for the criminals, and they also had better food for the criminals. Above everything else, these were Germans. I mean, they screwed up, but you know, they were still valued as German citizens.

K.C. Armstrong: Yeah, I guess. When you were in Auschwitz II did you ever come across a guard or one of the SS that you could tell wasn't really okay with what was going on? What would happen if a guard didn't obey 100% and showed some kind of compassion?

Werner Reich: To begin with, the SS men who worked in Auschwitz were all what's known as "Sonder Kommando." They were special commanders, volunteers who had been tested. They were told when they applied for the job to go over and kill a particular prisoner, and they would do it. If they didn't, then they were rejected, you know, if they couldn't do it. So, the closest niceness, if there is such a word, I ever experienced was from an SS man when I was in the camp just a short while. I walked close to the electric wire and this SS who was standing on the other side told me, "Go away or I'll have to shoot you." And that was the closest . . .

K.C. Armstrong: That was the closest thing to someone being human to you?

Werner Reich: Yes, K.C. When December came, all the criminals in the camp were being put into German uniforms, and they were being shipped to the Russian front.

K.C. Armstrong: So, the army obviously needed more fighting men. How did things change in the camp for you with these criminals being recruited and leaving?

Werner Reich: There were fewer of us prisoners, and one day we were given a piece of bread, told to take some extra uniforms and start walking. This was the beginning of the "Death March."

K.C. Armstrong: Explain that, please.

Werner Reich: Over 60,000 of us were being evacuated from the camp. We walked for a couple of hours in subzero temperature. There was snow and ice on the road and we were very weak. We trudged along the road for a few hours and then we stopped. Those who couldn't get back up were shot.

K.C. Armstrong: Unbelievable.

Werner Reich: And we continued like that throughout the day, and the only water we had was the snow and ice. The first night we slept in some stables and in the morning when we started off many people were stumbling on their feet. That night we slept in a silo. On the third day we were loaded into railroad cars, but already about 15,000 of us were dead.

K.C. Armstrong: You mention ice and snow. What were you wearing? Did you at least have shoes?

Werner Reich: We had our work clothes and worn shoes, but remember we were dealing with subzero temperatures. It was the coldest winter in the 20th century.

K.C. Armstrong: You can remember how cold you were?

Werner Reich: It was numbing cold. And then we were loaded into open railroad cars, travelling four days.

I remember the first day, but after that my mind goes blank. Once we arrived at Mauthausen in Austria, over half the people were dead. At first, we tossed bodies out of the cars, but then we didn't have the strength to do that anymore. Once out of the train, those of us still alive were herded into a shower where we collapsed from the heat and pain—excruciating pain because all of us were frostbitten.

K.C. Armstrong: What a nightmare.

Werner Reich: Many people died on the spot. After about three days my feet started to rot, and a Serbian prisoner of war got some tools from somewhere and cut off my toes on one foot and parts of the toes on the other foot. He saved my life.

K.C. Armstrong: By cutting off your toes? And without anesthesia?

Werner Reich: Right. He had some paper bandages, and that was that. I was completely awake; there was no anesthesia. Anyway, my feet were so numb that I couldn't feel it. They're still numb.

And then things got really bad because there was no food. We were squeezed in between the Russians and the American forces. There were huge piles of bodies all over. There were diseases in the camp, and I slept next to a dead man for three days just to get his ration of a spoon full of moldy bread.

K.C. Armstrong: Oh my God.

Werner Reich: And on the 5th of May we were liberated by American forces who certainly didn't know what to expect when they entered the camp. All they had with them was the standard issue rations.

K.C. Armstrong: What's that?

Werner Reich: These little boxes that held a can of high-caloric food and a couple of cookies, three Chesterfield cigarettes and a piece of chewing gum. I ate a can of chewing tobacco without knowing what it was because I didn't speak English.

K.C. Armstrong: Let me go back a minute. Before the Americans came and liberated you, did you know that was going to happen? I don't know how you didn't give up by that time. And you were sleeping next to a dead man. I mean, there is only so much a human can take.

Werner Reich: But no, I didn't give up. No. I was a teenager. I just knew I was going to survive. The trouble is that millions of others thought the same thing.

K.C. Armstrong: Why were you different?

Werner Reich: I wasn't different from the rest. Only they didn't survive, and I did. You can't ask those who died what they believed.

K.C. Armstrong: Was there something that you held on to? Did you think of your family, your faith, anything to get you through all this insanity?

Werner Reich: You see, your problem is you're an adult; you don't think like a teenager. Teenagers think they are invincible. That's why they do stupid things like driving 90 miles an hour, you know, jumping off cliffs and doing other nonsense.

K.C. Armstrong: Werner, when you were finally freed from the camp in Austria, do you remember that moment clearly? What were you doing?

Werner Reich: I was lying in my bunk beside that corpse, and we were all told that the Americans had entered the camp. They shared the rations they had with us. Approximately 20,000 people died eating that food.

K.C. Armstrong: I don't understand.

Werner Reich: Well, you give somebody a can of food with 800 or more calories-somebody who hasn't eaten in a long time—and it's like me giving you a bottle of olive oil to drink.

K.C. Armstrong: So, it was too much for their systems that were actually starving. I assume everyone must have been just skin and bones.

Werner Reich: When I was liberated I was 17 years old and I weighed 64 pounds.

K.C. Armstrong: Oh my God! That's incredible.

Werner Reich: And I was lucky. I was lucky.

K.C. Armstrong: You said the Americans weren't prepared for what they found there at the camp. What did they do for you?

Werner Reich: Well, only a very small number of Americans were charged with straightening things out.

They went down to the village and picked up local town inhabitants and forced them to bury the dead in mass graves. And their basic job was to make sure that the prisoners didn't run out of the camp. A couple of them did escape and went right into town and killed and ate somebody's cow. Others robbed the townspeople and spread all sorts of diseases. So, the Americans had to make sure the freed prisoners didn't run away, looting and spreading disease all around the countryside.

K.C. Armstrong: That's something I never thought about. It must've been so hard, not only for the freed prisoners who just wanted to get out of there, but also for their liberators who had to keep some sort of order.

Werner Reich: Those men (the liberators) worked very, very hard. They fought through Europe, the Battle of the Bulge. I later got to know a beautiful human being, a man who fought his way through Europe to become my liberator at Auschwitz. He died a few years ago—we became very good friends here in the US.

K.C. Armstrong: Werner, I've heard you speak publicly a few times, and one thing you always come back to is the question, "Where were the good people?" What are your thoughts on that?

Werner Reich: Well, some people are bystanders. They often don't want to get involved because they think some situations are not their concern, or they feel that if they open their mouths they're going to get hurt. Why should I get hurt for somebody else? If only one person gets up, obviously that person will get hurt. But if many others get up, then nobody is going to get hurt. In any government or group, you have what is needed for someone to succeed the way Hitler did. All you need is a ruthless leader, a small group of people who are willing to implement that person's rules, and a large population that doesn't give a damn. And you had that in Europe. You had exactly that situation.

K.C. Armstrong: Why did the large population do nothing?

Werner Reich: Because it was safer for them. They didn't want to get involved. They didn't want to get hurt, and they wanted to live in peace. But we have to stand up for each other. We cannot be quiet. The United States got up and fought for the people of Europe and the world, and in the process, during World War II, 407,000 Americans lost their lives. 407,000! Do you know how much land we gained from that? Not one square inch. That's really fighting for each other's rights, not for personal gain. This is so important, because if you don't stand up for the others today, who is going to stand up for you tomorrow?

K.C. Armstrong: Most of us can't even imagine living through a single day of what you have been through.

We might think we would feel absolute rage. But is there anything that you can tell us about faith or hope or acceptance? About believing in people even when no one was there for you—to help you throughout all this horror?

Werner Reich: Well, the Americans came.

K.C. Armstrong: True. I understand. That's huge. How do you think your experiences have shaped your life?

Werner Reich: Number one, I enjoy life very, very much. Number two, I am not terribly interested in material goods. I'm very much interested in people, in human beings. I am very much interested in seeing people enjoying life. Life is very limited. I didn't realize it was that short when I was young, but as I'm getting older it's shorter and shorter, and to me life has been very, very good. I have no complaints about life. I could have been killed in the camps, but I was spared. I have been married to an absolutely fabulous, wonderful lady for 61 years. She died a couple of month ago.

K.C. Armstrong: Oh, I've heard that. I'm sorry.

Werner Reich: Yes. But life has been good to me, and when life is good, it's absolutely fabulous. And whatever you do, enjoy it. Don't think that the world owes you anything. I went to college for ten years at night to get my degree, and nobody paid for it except me. I worked very hard all my life, but I had a ball, and I hope everybody else enjoys their life too.

K.C. Armstrong: How important do you believe family is for people in the whole experience we have here on this planet?

Werner Reich: To me, family is very important. It's not just a question of family, but of responsibility. If we bring to life other human beings, then we should also have a certain responsibility to make them human beings that can live and enjoy life. It's not a question of creating some monster or creating somebody who feels in any way limited. I have two sons who are not only my sons, but they are very, very good friends. And they married two girls who are also very good friends to me. And I have grandchildren who are fabulous.

I think it's just a question of how you look at life and how you shape what's around you. Mind your own business when it's necessary, but don't sit by when you see other people suffer. We can't afford it and we can't do it, because tomorrow you may be the one who will suffer.

K.C. Armstrong: You met my little nephew who was here in the studio earlier. If you could sit him down and tell him, "I have lived an amazing life and I have so many experiences. There are so many things I can teach you." What would be the top three things you would tell my nephew about this world and what you know?

Werner Reich: That's difficult! I never thought about that. I would say be nice to everybody. Not because they are nice, but because you are. Ignore lots of minor things; they aren't important. It's totally unimportant whether the person next to you puts sugar on his French fries or ketchup on his apple pie. That's unimportant, so mind your own business. But when it comes to another person's safety or wellbeing, jump up, be the first to help. People have helped me, and I've helped others. It's a beautiful way of living.

K.C. Armstrong: That's great advice: Be Nice, ignore the unimportant, be the first to help others. I'll play this for him later. I do have something else to ask, if you don't mind. How do we stop something that happened so many years ago-something so horrible, so evil—from happening again? You, me, normal, regular people. Our listeners, our readers. What can we do to prevent the rise of such evil in today's society?

Werner Reich: I think one problem in the United States is that fewer and fewer people are attending religious institutions. These were the places where ethics were taught directly. Many parents today feel that the schools should teach ethics, and the schools feel that the home should teach ethics. As a result, it's very difficult to add ethical teachings in the school systems where sometimes people will complain that you are including religion, when you aren't, really. And people at home say you're not doing your job in school. I don't know, somehow, we have to determine how to do that.

But I think ethical behavior is very basic. You know, if I teach you to be honest, then you'll be honest when you do your shopping, you won't cheat on your income tax, and you won't jump over a turnstile in the subway. But instead, you see, people are being too specific: don't jump over the turnstile and forget about the others waiting, for example. It's the basic principles, like honesty that create decency. Very basic principles like don't steal, honor your parents. You know, 50,000 smaller rules come from those basic concepts.

K.C. Armstrong: I couldn't agree with you more. Like treat people the way you'd like to be treated. It doesn't have to be complicated.

Werner Reich: That's right. I'd like to say to your listeners and readers to just be nice to each other. Life is beautiful, and it doesn't take a lot to be nice. It takes a lot of pain and a lot of anger to be nasty. Much easier to be nice. And 99% of the things that you worry about are really not important.

K.C. Armstrong: Great advice, Werner. And finally, years from now when you are no longer here and people who knew you share stories and memories about you, what would you hope they say? How would you like to be remembered?

Werner Reich: Just if they could say, "He was a nice guy," I would achieve everything I ever wanted.

CHAPTER 2

Tom Butts

Phone: 916-388-9850 **Fax:** 916-381-6048 **Email:**
tom@nor-calequipmentrentals.com
Address: 9400 Jackson Rd Sacramento, CA 95826
Web Address: https://www.nor-calequipmentrentals.com

Phone: 916-388-9850 **Fax:** 916-381-6048 **Email:**
tom@nor-calequipmentrentals.com
Address: 9400 Jackson Rd Sacramento, CA 95826
Web Address: https://www.nor-calequipmentrentals.com

Tom Butts Intro

I was introduced to this man in the first two months of operating
WMAP. I'm not sure I remember where I found him, but as soon as we
got on the air he was like a friend I had known for years. During the
first interview, I was inspired by his integrity and attitude about running
a business. I had always worked for someone else, so as he spoke I was
mentally taking notes. I immediately had a mentor.

Tom was a tough guy who lived hard, and I felt a connection right
away. What I took away from his interview was that to be successful
like him the most important thing is to have integrity and treat people

with respect and fairness. During that first interview he told me that a business owner needs to "say what you do and do what you say." I never told Tom this, but this was a pivotal moment for me.

To make a long story short, at that time I had one of the best salesmen in the country in charge of sales and advertising. Tom made an appointment to talk to him about buying some commercials and some possible advertising options. Something came up, and Tom was not called at the assigned time. This is when I made a decision that defined how I was going to run my business. Tom had already shown me how in his interview.

I told the salesman I was taking over the account. I had no experience in sales, but I was going to implement what I learned from Tom, and it was then and there that my business standards were set. I told Tom that I owed him an apology, and my company made a mistake by not respecting his time and for not saying what we'd do and doing what we had said. I offered him half price and a promise to earn his trust. Tom signed that day, and our business relationship and friendship began. Tom's integrity is a direct model of how to treat people with respect and how being accountable and responsible can rub off.

I hope you are inspired by his story as much as I was. It's amazing how one person can affect so many others just by doing the right thing. Thanks, Tom.

Interview

K.C. Armstrong: Guys, I am excited today because there is a gentleman that I am about to speak with that you guys know pretty well. This is a guy who has been here from the start, and he is pretty much what this station is about. I'm talking about Tom Butts, of course, over at Nor-Cal Equipment Rentals in Sacramento, California. Tom Butts—perseverance, determination, thoughtfulness, honesty, integrity. Those things are what we built this station on.

Tom Butts is the owner, the CEO, the brains and the brawn behind Nor-Cal Equipment Rental. This is a guy with a story that is just perfect for this station and I'm going to stop here and, with no further ado, it's my honor and privilege to welcome back to the program, Mr. Tom Butts. Tom, thank you for being here. How are you today?

Tom Butts: I'm doing great, KC. Really appreciate you having me back on man, it's been a while.

K.C. Armstrong: Yeah, I know. Tom, you've become a fan favorite and favorite in my book. I love how you do things, and I'm really excited to talk to you today because we're going to go through your story in this interview. We're going to find out from start to finish how Nor-Cal Equipment Rentals came to fruition and you personally became a successful businessman. So, are you ready for this ride?

Tom Butts: I'm ready my friend. I'm looking forward to it. I always enjoy your show and I think you're doing a great job. Anyways, the respect is mutual.

K.C. Armstrong: Now, Tom, when you were growing up I know your old man and your mom were both very supportive of all of you guys. You had a big family. I know you had a brother and, did you have sisters too?

Tom Butts: Yes, I have one sister.

K.C. Armstrong: And how many brothers?

Tom Butts: I had a brother, and as life went along I ended up with three more step-brothers and two stepsisters, kind of the modern family.

K.C. Armstrong: Right, exactly. The modern family. Tom was telling me the story about when he was going into school, and how his younger brother, and he were so different . . . Tom you know the story I'm talking about, right?

Tom Butts: Yeah, yeah, yeah. We all have different skills and my parents were very good early on at recognizing and helping us in whatever our skills were. We were very, very young. My brother, I should say, was way more skilled in school than me and I always walked around with a can of cars. You know, hot wheels, matchbox—and my brother would be reading books even though he's a year younger than me. I think even before kindergarten he was able to read these kid books, not only normally but upside down, and I'm over here making car sounds. The point of the story is there's nothing wrong with that; we all have different skills and, you know, my brother has gone on to good things including college and I did not. But again there's nothing wrong with that and here we are today. I'm proud of what I've done, but yeah, I've had a lot of support.

K.C. Armstrong: That story is awesome because you're right. but the reason I'm laughing so hard is because it paints a funny picture! I've gotten to know Tom and he's a huge, intimidating-looking guy. I can picture him playing with the cars while his younger brother is reading upside-down children's books—and, right, to each his own!

Tom Butts: Yeah.

K.C. Armstrong: It's a cool story. It's a good memory. So, alright Tom, you're in high school, you have a great voice for doing voice overs. I don't know who told you that entertainment would be your future, but I know you were interested in it. Tell me about wanting to get into films.

Tom Butts: It's just weird with me. I guess somebody could say I have a big ego or whatever. It's my personality to always envision myself being in movies and TV. I can't explain it, but as I walk through life I'm always envisioning myself in front of a camera. I grew up with the monster movies, Star Trek, Star Wars and all, and my imagination just soars with it. As I got a little bit older I started getting into a sport called BMX. It's a lot of visual, dirt bike stuff, but I always envisioned being behind a camera. When I was in junior college, for my brief career of about a year and a half, my favorite class was film.

K.C. Armstrong: Wait, Tom, is that because the professor told you beforehand if you guys show up you're going to get an A?

Tom Butts: Yes it is, I started my project and thought, "Oh my God, now I know why I'm at school.

It's for this class!" And I'm dedicated; I'm just buying pencils and paper and here we go—this is my calling. Then when I asked the instructor how our film was going to be graded, he said, "You're all getting A's because it's not about the result; it's a process." And I said, "No problem. I'll be here every day early." Unfortunately, when he gave me that green light, as a young kid in college drinking beer, he never saw me again!

K.C. Armstrong: I appreciate the honesty, Tom. You mentioned before you think it was an ego thing. I don't see it as that. I see it as something where you knew even at a young age that you were going to be successful at whatever you chose to do. Whether it was doing something in the media or whatever because you knew yourself you had that work ethic, which I guess was passed down from your father and your mother. I know your dad was an engineer and must have instilled some great qualities in you guys.

Tom Butts: Oh, yeah. I've been fortunate, I keep saying it over and over, but having a good family around you, especially as you get older, makes you realize how lucky you are. My parents are divorced but we still can all get together, go to one of the parent's house, and the other parent is invited. It's unique, and they've just always supported us. To me, the strong work ethic helped me literally look at everything as half full rather than half empty. You can watch the sand running out or you can say, "Nah, I got half a tube still here." And that attitude, boy, you've got to have it in business.

We were in California, which is a really tough environment for business in general, and there's a new rule or a new law or a new fee to pay every other day, it seems. You have to be able to roll with the punches, and I find myself at times not being able to. It gets very frustrating. I've got to take a knee, take a time out, or just walk away. Sometimes it sucks, but we're fortunate to be where we are, and the key is looking at the glass as half full.

K.C. Armstrong: And you're touching on something here. I want to talk about the business, and how it all came about. You're talking about seeing the glass as half full. I can't picture you, Tom, when things were really tough in the middle of starting this big successful business that you have now. When things were so tough with all the challenges that you had to overcome, did you always see the glass as half full or were there times where you wanted to break the glass or say there's nothing in the glass?

Tom Butts: Overall, there have been a few moments when I couldn't take it. I actually remember one; I think it was about 2006. I called my dad when we were being looked at to be purchased by another company. My business partner at the time did not agree with the way I thought of things, and I just told my dad, "You know, don't be disappointed, but w.e may have to sell. I've just had enough." Those times are rare.

I went through a divorce in 2009, and I've always been a family guy. I had to move away from my young kids, but I was lucky enough to have my mother take me in. My dad was financially supporting the situation, but going through a divorce and going through a business divorce at the same time was very, very rough. I have to say, against all odds, I still always believed in the brand, the Nor-Cal Equipment Rentals brand, my company. I mean, I can bore you for days with stories.

K.C. Armstrong: It's not boring.

Tom Butts: Well, it may not be, but I always have had all of my money tied up in the business and also had job offers to shut down and walk away.

K.C. Armstrong: To sell it off. People would buy this from you and all the headaches would be gone.

Tom Butts: Well, we could have shut it down. I had real job offers to go to work for somebody else. The attorneys that were handling things for me, my family, my friends, business associates, everybody said, "Hey, no shame. You did everything you could. It's just time to shut it down, and you need to take care of your family." I heard them, but I stuck to my guns. I kept going and I felt, boy, if this backfires I'm going to be alone in an alley.

K.C. Armstrong: You're all in at this point. You're putting all your cards in.

Tom Butts: Yeah, all in. Your soul is in, your blood is in, and your reputation is in. Everything.

K.C. Armstrong: You believed in it, though.

Tom Butts: One hundred percent. I always had, even during the difficult times. I'd be like a cheerleader to myself, literally. I'd be walking around saying, "Oh yeah, we owe all this money, but you know what? We just made ten grand!" Really, just not looking at the whole picture as maybe a numbers person would, but I knew maybe we got a new customer or we did this, or we did that, or we were bringing in another piece of equipment. You know, baby steps. I always knew the business could be something special. It's hard to explain until you walk that walk. I was going to say like Sylvester Stallone with the Rocky script. I mean, the guy had to sell his *dog* to stick to it. Stallone said, "I'll sell you the script, but I'm going to be in the movie." Everybody said no, but he held out and—there he was.

K.C. Armstrong: So, what gave you that determination and belief in yourself and in your product? You pretty much put everything on a table and said, "I know this is going to work and I'll be damned if it's not."

Tom Butts: Well, I started in the industry in 1989, and I know what you are supposed to do. You do A, B, C, D, E and F, and it *should* work, even though it *wasn't* working. And I knew that my dad had always joked about me. For example, there was a time when I was working for somebody else. I probably should have left and done something else when I got passed over for a promotion. I was irate to the point where I was pulled aside and given some days off to calm down, but I stuck with the job. My dad always says, "You know, I would have quit in two seconds!" But that was a joke, and he always pointed out that for whatever reason you stick to your work, and that really came through when I started this Nor-Cal Equipment Rentals.

I've always envisioned the future, envisioned something bigger than where I was at. Believing in your dream or your vision is a tough thing to do, except I'm real visual-oriented, so I've envisioned since 2004 owning a Peterbilt delivery truck. And at the end of this year it finally happened, 12 and a half years later. Somebody driving by the shop might look over and say, "Cool, Nor-Cal's got a delivery truck." For me, it's a real point in time; it's a real mark in Nor-Cal equipment history, or history for myself. And you just have to write your goal out, put it on your computer, or put it in concrete in your brain. You've got to have those dreams which are what keeps you going.

Tom, how did the idea to rent huge equipment to small businesses and people taking out a pool in the back yard or something like that first come about?

Tom Butts: Well, the rental industry has been around for a long time, and I graduated with a friend whose dad had started that sort of business. We all went to work for the rental equipment industry. And I had a grandfather who had his own Peterbilt and worked on caterpillar equipment. For me it was natural. Like I said earlier, I always played with cars and trucks and I even drew them. I was into drawing and the arts so I already knew I liked this stuff, this was cool to me. And then fast forward on up the road; I started as a yardman. I got promoted to a 1 ton driver, then to a low bed driver, then senior low bed driver, then a dispatcher. Next, I became manager of what became, 15 years later, a hub store for a national chain in northern California.

K.C. Armstrong: But you thought you were going to work there for the rest of your life, right?

Tom Butts: Oh, yeah. I have an uncle who worked for Wonder Bread, and he worked his whole career in one place. I remember having a chat with him that I'd be the second guy that starts and finished at the same place. But when I heard we were getting bought out by a national chain I was really, really disappointed. I understood it, but I was disappointed. I thought we had this home forever. And so I started looking around. I think it was about 2000 or 2001 that I got the urge to go out on my own. You learn how to do this first by making other people money. You buy an asset for $20,000, it makes $30,000 a year, and then you buy a second one. You start doing the math that, hmm, this is pretty lucrative.

And so, with my dreamy type of ideas and celebrity type of goals, I started saying, "I'm going to have my own business." I went out, made contacts, and actually got way over my head as a young man. I only had my two sons; my daughter wasn't even born, but I had struck a 3 million dollar deal with no money down. Equipment was coming in. I guess I was really good at selling it to all the people involved because they were all backing me. And then in September, the Towers were hit in 2001.

K.C. Armstrong: And you wouldn't think that something like that would affect a gentleman on the West Coast that's renting out equipment for people, but apparently it did.

Tom Butts: Oh, yeah. I remember the day it happened. We had to start moving stuff to Travis Air Force base. I remember feeling, "Is this the right time to not only start a business but go massively in debt really quick?" I mean, you're owing some big money in that world. I'm this young man with cojones that you wouldn't believe, but was the reality that after selling myself and striking all these deals, maybe this wasn't the right deal and the right time? I settled back down, but I still had that dream.

K.C. Armstrong: Wait, you didn't take that 3 million dollar deal, Tom?

Tom Butts: No, no, no. Basically I had property lined up, and because the value of the property was $200,000 more than that I was buying it for, I was using the 200,000 down on a million-dollar building loan. I had all these equipment vendors ready to bring in millions of dollars of equipment. You're talking about *if it works* you're instantly doing well. But *if one brick in the wall goes bad*, it's all bad. I believed in myself, believed in the company that I was creating. I had some people lined up to go with me. I think it was part of being young, but I believed in my dream, 100%, and obviously other people did too because 3 million dollars lined up is hard to do. Looking back, I had a young family, and working toward my dream could have been great, or it could have been disastrous. It just wasn't the time. Then another opportunity came up in 2004, and that's the one we struck on and moved forward on.

K.C. Armstrong: And that's when Nor-Cal Equipment Rentals was pretty much born.

Tom Butts: Yeah, May of 2004. We were actually going to buy an existing 20-year business in a completely different location. I went through the complete process of buying, where you line up banks, money, equipment. Again, going through the whole process, we even went and counted the guy's equipment, sat in the store watching the operation, and went through his employees to see who we were going to keep, who was going to move on. All these things, and when we got down to signing paperwork the guy says, "I forgot to tell you. I have a first right of refusal with another company." So, it completely shot us in the foot. We couldn't move forward on it, but the people that had backed us said, "You want to start your own business?—we will absolutely back you. So, that is how it happened.

K.C. Armstrong: Were they just pretty much believing in you, Tom, to back you?

Tom Butts: Yeah. Believing in us and our reputation in the industry. Never met the people that put the money up, besides talking on the phone. You have to verify everything, but I don't know if you can do it today. You know, just, "Hey, I've been in the business for this long. I've got a good idea, what do you think? Can you give me a couple hundred thousand?"

K.C. Armstrong: Yeah, you've got to think twice about that one! But the one thing that I want to convey to the audience here is, Tom, you were not a person that had a load of money that was given to you to frivolously try a bunch of different things. There were times when you were building this business that you couldn't even afford a cheeseburger.

Tom Butts: Yeah. I think I've mentioned that to you. I don't know if it was on or off the air but there was that point. My mom doesn't really care for this story because I was living at her home during the divorce and she feels guilty, which she should not. I felt like Will Ferrell in *Wedding Crashers*, you know? I'm the guy who is coming up the road yelling, "Mom, meatballs!" Actually, I didn't, but my mom just catered to me because she was really worried about me. And so, when I tell this story she is like, "Oh my God, you were hungry! It's my fault!" I hope she's not listening right now.

K.C. Armstrong: Sometimes Moms needs to turn the radio off! "Ma, turn it off for a minute."

Tom Butts: (laughs) So, the story is, I'm down there, at the shop. The ex-business partner is there and I start feeling that hunger that's just like "I got to eat now!" And I had not one dollar on me. I remember I called people in the area, "Hey, Jim, are you there? Hey, can you grab me a hamburger?" Anybody that was available, and I remember just going, "Oh my God, I'm going to start throwing up here. I'm starving!" I remembered there was an aluminum recycling bin on the side of the building. So, here I am, big business owner with a successful business, throwing aluminum cans in the back of the truck to recycle so I can get food.

K.C. Armstrong: That's awesome.

Tom Butts: I'm telling you, maybe God had that in the works for me because I've never forgotten it. To really be hungry, and, what am I going to do here? Call my mom and dad from an hour away to come down here and bring me food? I had to get creative and, you know, it was a true wake-up call to value a dollar, I'll tell you that. And, I think anybody that owns a business at some point is going to face that struggle.

K.C. Armstrong: Right. I think it's remarkable that you remember that, probably because you can see how far you've come. And you don't forget about those days because you remember what it took to get you where you are. So, I still want to hover around that time. You find the cans and you're returning them to get lunch, and at the time you were doing every job there was.

Tom Butts: Oh, yeah.

K.C. Armstrong: Right. Tell me about what you were doing. This was just in the start, right?

Tom Butts: No, we started out really strong and then the economy crashed, and so things got very thin. So, this is about midway through. When businesses take off like that you're expecting life to be good from there on out.

K.C. Armstrong: Like, hey, this is easy. I can do this—there's no problem.

Tom Butts: Oh, yeah. What's the big deal? Anyway, this is happening in about 2009 or 2010. I was going through a divorce and my head was not into anything. If you're in a breakup or divorce you know what I'm talking about. And you still have to go down and meet customers and shake their hands.

I remember this one time like a comic book; you know when they do the quotes over the head? I'm sitting in there nodding and smiling to customers, answering questions about a backhoe and doing the company thing, but in my mind, I'm worried about my three kids. I remember the agony of acting, literally, putting on that smiling face. I knew we had no money in the account, people were coming at us left and right for payments, and there was no way that was going to happen.

And yet I'm out shaking hands and telling people how great we're doing because what are you going to do? Say, "Oh my God, we're in trouble"?

K.C. Armstrong: Right, you've got to put up the front. You've got to roll with it.

Tom Butts: I'm doing sales calls and, say I get a deal and the guy says, "Yeah, deliver that over to that drop site." I would jump into my truck, go flying to the yard, get a trailer on the back, throw the thing on, and deliver it to the site. Then the guy is calling in the office saying, "Wow, man, you guys move fast. Tell your driver thanks!" We did that for years.

K.C. Armstrong: Wait, Tom, let me stop you for a second. So, you were doing not only the day-to-day operations of a business, but you were doing the sales, you were doing deliveries, and then for the guy that called you back, you must have been doing reception. Is that true?

Tom Butts: Oh, yeah. I'd be answering all the phones too. Yep.

K.C. Armstrong: Incredible. And how many hours would you say you worked a day?

Tom Butts: Oh, in that time, minimum 12-14 hours a day. Had a family, everybody's playing sports, or everybody's got events. I answered the phones for about 11 years, Monday through Sunday, 24/7. You know, a lot of equipment business is emergency stuff at night: light towers and a lot of rain happening out here. People need chippers or whatever, and I have some really good people that work with me now. I'm able to hand that ball off, and be completely confident that things are going well. Tristan is the one who answers the phones for us on the counter and he's getting a taste. Actually, he's getting a real good dose because we had our best year by a huge margin last year.

So, we're growing, but yeah, in the archives of Nor-Cal Equipment there are some funny stories! And, you know, we were competing against companies that had literally 20 times the inventory and 20 times the people. And through relationships I would get an order. I'll give you an example – light towers. You can tow one light tower behind your truck, or you can load them all in a big rig and do it all in one sweep. So, if I had six light towers that needed to go all the way across town, 45 minutes away, guess what? We're doing them behind pickup trucks. A big company can just throw them on a truck. I would say yes to the order, and we'd be running until 9 o'clock that night getting them out. I can laugh about them now because I'm not doing it anymore, but man at the time it was grueling.

K.C. Armstrong: So, Tom, we're basically talking about the ins and outs and the struggles and the successes of building a business. So, let's see, you took ownership in 2004 and were still doing pretty much everything with limited staff until about when?

Tom Butts: Well, we had a limited staff, you will laugh at this, but basically until the end of 2012. And you've met a friend of mine, Ed, with ECO Foundation.

K.C. Armstrong: Great guy.

Tom Butts: Ed is not just a customer, he's a friend. But originally, he was a customer. He had his product in my yard. I'm having Ed watch the store while I do a delivery. So imagine, you've got your own Radio Shack or you've got your own Let's Go to a VCR thing. You're having your buddy who rents the movies from you cover the counter while you go deliver some movies and pizza to a couple of houses down the road.

K.C. Armstrong: Incredible.

Tom Butts: That is the level that we were doing. I had another company that also had some space with us. They were great guys, Dennis and Allen. They would cover the counter when necessary for a very long time. It goes right along with acting like you have a staff of 20 when you have two. Then in 2012, again, Ed came to me and said, "Look, you're killing yourself. You've got to start bringing some people in," and that was a very tough thing for me.

K.C. Armstrong: Was it that or was it that you felt that you couldn't afford to pay them?

Tom Butts: Well, I felt I couldn't afford to, but I could. That is a big part of it, KC. I had money finally starting to build up and I didn't want to spend it.

You know, it was one of those "I'm not going to waste it on that," and then I found out the better people you have around you, the better you're going to do. This was a very tough lesson for me. Not only just finding people that want to work, but people that are going to work within your system and your beliefs and your style. We're an equipment rental place; there are thousands of them across the United States. But we try to have our own little niche to it, kind of all the West Coast Chopper slash Gas Monkey style to it. You know, we try to be a little bit of characters here and there. When people come in they look at our walls of stuff and, you know, it's almost entertainment when they come in. They're not just getting a tractor so, that's part of it.

K.C. Armstrong: Tom, if you look back, can you pinpoint a time when you were able to say, okay, here's our turning point? This is when I was able to remove myself and not do every single job and to trust other people that I'm hiring, and this is where we really turned the corner?

Tom Butts: I would say midway through 2013 I was feeling that. Basically, I took things over in 2012, and it's kind of like taking over a body on life support. You know, what do we have to do here? You gather some professionals, you gather some help. I had great support from my bank. American River Bank stood by me through thick and thin. So for me I think I can comfortably say about midway through 2013 I started to feel, you know what? I think we're going to do this thing. And I was doing little things, like buying a small piece of equipment. It might only be a $2,000 piece of equipment, but I was able to write a check for it, and we didn't miss a rental. In my business you've got to have the toys lined up, or you're dead.

K.C. Armstrong: Right.

Tom Butts: I tell you these stories of wearing all these hats or acting like we have three delivery trucks. Well, we didn't have a lot of equipment. So, our equipment had to be really maintained because that equipment could literally be bouncing on three jobs in a day. You know, from this guy to the next guy. He's done, go pick it up.

And that's all fine and dandy, but to really be competitive you've got to have a lot of soldiers lined up. I was able to start slowly building inventory so that today I feel very confident.

K.C. Armstrong: Tom, what about the wear and tear on these machines? I know you keep your equipment pristine, and you're offering the public the best that's out there, but don't these machines have a life, an expectancy of when they're not going to be useful anymore or are outdated.

Tom Butts: Well, out here in California not only do we deal with what you just said, the life of the equipment, but also dealing with an air resource issue, horsepower ratings, and things that the environment is regulating. So, yeah, you have to keep updating equipment, which means you are always cycling equipment. You're cycling it for depreciation reasons, and you're cycling it just to keep up with the Joneses. And that's where I can finally say we're able to compete with some other companies. I am not the biggest guy, but we provide a very good product and we have good customers and really good loyalty.

We also rely on dealerships for these brands to really support us and help us, which they do. Caterpillar, Ditch Witch, Kubota, Chicago Pneumatic—these guys have done a really good job of giving me programs that are affordable, gear that's perfect. Everything's going to break; you've got to realize that. Everything is. I don't care if it's brand new or five years old, it's going to go down. Who do you have to help you replace it or who has got the parts? So with the help of our salesman and manufacturers we've been able to create a pretty good system of maintenance.

K.C. Armstrong: How do you have such a great relationship with Caterpillar, Ditch Witch, and Kubota? You've even had some John Deere and some Magnum too, didn't you?

Tom Butts: Oh, yeah. But the reality is I started in this industry in 1989, and a lot of the guys that are still in our industry have known me through the years. So, I am able to keep these relationships through longevity and doing what I say. You know, everything is who you know, how you negotiate, and how you come through and prove yourself. For instance, if you take on a $100,000 tractor and the payment is whatever it is a month, you better make the payments. And so, those are things that we've been able to do a good job at. Likewise, we've had some really good support in this area. They've just been more than a support system. They've been friends and it's really made a difference.

K.C. Armstrong: So, are you saying, Tom, that a big part of the success of your business is your word and your integrity?

Tom Butts: I think so. I've not only had really good fortunate relationships on the equipment side, but a lot of the customers I have are very loyal, as well. There are a lot of people to thank. You know, there's Rick at Procida Landscaping, Corey at CPM, I can go on down the list.

K.C. Armstrong: Well, go ahead. It's going to be written, so please get it out!

Tom Butts: These are guys that gave me a shot with their company.

For whatever reason, they gave us a shot. They saw something, and they've been loyal to us ever since. You know, as time rolls on and you have good relationships with these guys, it really counts. It takes time but, yeah, your word and your reputation are critical. If you're going to survive, you have to do what you say you're going to do.

If you get a call to do something that's not in your means, say you can't do it. "Call this company here; they can do it." When I've done that, I found people continue to come back. Everybody is afraid they're going to lose their customer. What a customer doesn't want is you jerking them around and saying, maybe I can do it, maybe I can't—and then you leave them hanging. Just take care of them even if it's not through your company, and that's been successful for us.

K.C. Armstrong: You know, you make it sound simple. From what you've been through and from what you've endured, all these challenges that you've hurdled, from what I'm getting here from this very honest and frank conversation is that basically it comes down to your word, your integrity and your willingness to work and for people to trust you. Is that right?

Tom Butts: That's exactly right. When somebody comes into your business to spend money with you, you better treat them the way you want to be treated if you go to a restaurant or you go into your local hardware store. I get real worn out on bad service, and it's a great lesson for anybody that wants to come into our business. Don't be like that. If we're on the phones and people walk in acknowledge them, give them a thumbs-up, be right with you bud. I know when I go into a store and somebody does that to me, I feel good.

I think our customers also feel they've helped us survive and they're helping us grow the business. I truly believe that they feel they have a stake in it. Their money is just not going to some corporation back where ever, and the dollars mean nothing. They know when they spend money with me our business is expanding, we're all growing. I'm going to have more toys to help them on their jobs. They get a new free Nor-Cal hat and jacket, everybody's happy!

K.C. Armstrong: Tom, your story is so honest and revealing. But my next question to you is if the Tom Butts that I'm speaking to right now in 2017 could talk to the Tom Butts of 2004, what type of advice would you give that gentleman, or would you just want to shake his hand and say, "Look, I know what you've been through"?

Tom Butts: Well, that's a good question. I actually have not thought of that. I would pat him on the back and say, "You better pad up my friend."

K.C. Armstrong: Well said!

Tom Butts: Once in a while I'll hear somebody wants to open a business and I'm all for that, but I'll also challenge them real quick because I basically lost everything and have had to regain it. I'll ask these people, "Do you have six months of money built up to survive? Not only personally, but to run your business."

My advice to some guys is, "If you're really not into it, you better have this much money set aside." They'll kind of scratch their head and I'll say, "If this is your ultimate dream and desire, you should go for it because if you don't do it now you will always regret it. Having said that, man if you're going to put everything in jeopardy, and you're not committed to it, I don't recommend it."

K.C. Armstrong: Right.

Tom Butts: It is a tough, grueling battle. It's worth it to be talking to you and telling stories with a laugh and be upbeat about the future—but it doesn't happen for everybody. Part of my success could be luck or however the stars aligned. I don't know, but I always believed in it. If I could tell Mr. Tom Butts his future I'd tell him he'd have long hair and look like a Sons of Anarchy guy! I do have to point out also that when I met my wife I was living at my mom's. I was in one of her rooms, and we called that "Apartment 1A." You know, that was the joke. It's very embarrassing, but when I met Kaycee I could not take her to the movies or go get a drink. My mom would give me $20 like a 16-year-old so I could date Kaycee, but she didn't care.

K.C. Armstrong: That's a good woman right there. She must have seen something in you.

Tom Butts: It was never about money with her. It was never about it. I had all this family Support, and, you know, having a woman like Kaycee on your side is just the best. You can't explain having that kind of unconditional support.

K.C. Armstrong: You could be President with Kaycee behind you.

Tom Butts: Yeah, it was such a big deal. You know, when you have a little bit of money in your pocket you can meet some people, and not know if you're getting their true feelings. When I met Kaycee, I literally had nothing, I mean it was pathetic, but it was cleansing. I'll tell you that because whatever happens in the future, I tell you I will always remember starving and not having enough money to take her to the movies.

K.C. Armstrong: Dude, that is the coolest story! And it really is something special the way you can talk about it now and you can talk about Kaycee, and how she saw something that a lot of people wouldn't. You said it was cleansing and I think that's the best way to describe something like that because you really weed out a lot of the people that are in a relationship for different reasons. You found somebody that saw Tom and believed in Tom. Without her I don't think we'd be talking right now.

Tom Butts: Well, I think you're right. You've got to have some light in the tunnel, and whether it's candlelight or a light tower, you've got to have something that you look forward to. Let's be honest, going through a divorce and being separated from your kids is about as low as it gets for a man.

K.C. Armstrong: And add on that your business is dissolving too.

Tom Butts: Oh, yeah. You know, there's no money to do anything. And you have job offers to change it all, but you say no to them. That was the key.

K.C. Armstrong: Tom did your faith play a part at this time?

Tom Butts: Yeah. I grew up a Catholic, although, if you were to judge me with the Catholic rulebook I think I'm heading the wrong way.

K.C. Armstrong: I think everybody is, Tom.

Tom Butts: But deep down I feel I have a real good relationship there and I'm trying to explain that to my kids now—that you need to have an inner relationship or faith. I'm not going to sit here and define it for you, but I'm telling you when you're in the dark and you can't sleep, you've got to find peace. I was able to find that through my relationship with God. So, you need to find your faith, whatever that is, for the times you need to call upon it.

K.C. Armstrong: What a great story this is. Guys, this is Tom Butts from Nor-Cal Equipment Rentals and you can get more information, at *nor-calequipmentrents.com*. Also check out their Facebook or Instagram page. Tom is just an amazing guy, his wife, Kaycee, and his offspring—Zack, Drew, Jade, Quincy and Drake.

K.C. Armstrong: I know a bunch of them are part of the business.

One calls himself the VP, and you have him working down there, right?

Tom Butts: Oh, yeah. Mr. Zack is quite the character.

K.C. Armstrong: Tom, I really appreciate spending the time with you. I think this story is remarkable. It's so honest, and I can't thank you enough.

Tom Butts: Oh, no problem. I always like being part of your show KC. It's an honor, and I appreciate it. Someday I want to visit the studio and check it out, my friend.

K.C. Armstrong: I would love that. Actually, I need you and maybe one of those Ditch Witch or Caterpillar backhoes. I just took down the wall here, and I'd like to take down this whole other side because it's giving me a lot of problems. At any rate, Tom Butts, thank you so much for being a part of WMAP from the start. I'm so happy to share your story so people can read about your drive and the sacrifices that led to your successful business today. Thank you so much, buddy.

Tom Butts: Alright, pal. Thank you. Have a great one.

K.C. Armstrong: Tom Butts. What a great guest, man. And that's what it's about, being true to your word—honesty, integrity and rolling with it. That guy has been through the mill. And when he was in the middle of that people said, "Here, here's a job. Just forget your dream. Here's a job. Safe." And he said, "No, I still believe in this." And that's a pair of stones if you ask me. Nice.

CHAPTER 3

Jenny Maher

http://sbpra.com/jennymaher/

Jenny Maher Intro

Jenny Maher can be contacted through her email jmaher0415@gmail.com or her website www.themindbodyandspirit.net that shows her array of publicity interviews, art work, and excerpt of her most recent book, *Finding Faith in Darkness*, as well as her personal contact information for any questions.

If someone told me this woman's story, I would absolutely not believe it. We've been on the air for close to three years now, and Jenny is one of the people I find myself telling people about. I'll let this interview speak for itself, as it has to be told by Jenny herself. When I asked what she would change if she were to face her ordeal all over again, she absolutely shocked me by replying, "KC, not a thing."

Jenny lives to help other people, and I often think about her and this interview when I get in a mood where I think the world is cold and harsh. Jenny brings light despite going through the very depths of darkness.

Interview

K.C. Armstrong: Alright guys, back here, WMAP, the World's Most Amazing People. The theme of this station could not be more fitting than what you'll hear from my next guest. I feel terrific that I can bring her to you.

Let me start off with a quote from Jenny Maher who is going to be our guest here in a minute. "I wrote this book not just to tell people my story but to show people who have given up, lost hope, or don't think that they can make it another day to not give up. Life is full of obstacles, that's what makes it interesting. I've found that as long as I keep moving forward, even if it was baby steps, I was doing well. Even when sometimes I took a few steps back or feel down, I learned with God's help to get back up and keep moving. I hope the people who read this will find the determination in themselves and not give up."

That's from Jenny Maher, and her first book is called *Never Give Up: How Determination And God Gave Me A Better Look at Life.*

Her story is so incredible and I'm happy to have her on the program. Guys, with no further ado, it's my honor and privilege to welcome to the program Ms. Jenny Maher. Jenny, how are you today?

Jenny Maher: Great. How are you doing, K.C.?

K.C. Armstrong: I'm doing great. I'm so excited to have you on, and this is exactly what our station is about!

It couldn't be a better fit, so the listeners are in for a treat since we have you here.

Jenny Maher: Well, thank you for having me.

K.C. Armstrong: There's so much we're going to cover. Let's take you back to your first memory of your childhood. Can you tell me that?

Jenny Maher: Well, it was probably when I was about seven years old. I woke up and my mom was on the couch blurting out all these numbers and letters and just weird things. She wasn't really coherent. We got my mom to drive us to an ATM and when we tried to get her to go back home, she wouldn't go back home. And she kept driving with the signal and the different lights on and everything. And I was able to direct her on the freeway to her psychiatrist. When we got there I was screaming and crying, and I ran up to the psychiatrist and told him to come see my mom because she's not right. And he just said, "It's okay just go home." But they ended up taking her to the hospital and they put me and my brother in foster care. That was the first time I remember the real crazy experience—where I went to foster care.

K.C. Armstrong: Wow, so, Jenny, where was your father during all this?

Jenny Maher: My father died when I was three in a hit-and-run.

K.C. Armstrong: Oh, man. Okay, so you grew up without a male dominant figure, and would you say that your mother was mentally ill?

Jenny Maher: Yeah, she had bipolar disorder with psychotic episodes. So, you never knew what was going to happen. Like one time she dropped my brother off for a football practice in the middle of the street, and she was actually stopped by the police because she was walking down the middle of the street naked. And so it seemed spur of the moment when the police would show up and place us into foster homes.

K.C. Armstrong: So, you would go into a foster home, and then would you go back to your mom?

Jenny Maher: Yeah, every time she got stabilized we'd go back.

K.C. Armstrong: She was medicated? Did she just not take her medicine sometimes?

Jenny Maher: No, she took her medicine, but I'm not sure exactly because I was young. But because of her mental illness the medicine didn't always stabilize her. So, we were wards of the courts. They had social workers come out and make sure everything was fine. It usually happened like once a year that we were placed in a foster home or something like that.

K.C. Armstrong: And what was it like in the foster home? Was it as tough as they say?

Jenny Maher: The foster homes I was in were not nice. They usually housed the kids that were in the system longer.

The older ones pretty much took control of everyone else. This was in Los Angeles, so it's a whole different kind of system from many other places. And so, the parents really didn't take control of anything or do anything. I was abused in some of them.

K.C. Armstrong: What type of abuse are you talking about?

Jenny Maher: I was sexually abused in the foster homes by the other foster kids, but I'm really not comfortable talking about that.

K.C. Armstrong: That's completely alright. I want you to be comfortable here because you're so brave to tell this story. Okay, you're in and out of these places, which are horrible, and you're walking around on eggshells at home wondering when your mom is going to have an episode again. Now, I know you were younger than your brother, but did you take a kind of motherly role in the house?

Jenny Maher: Yeah, I was the more responsible one. My brother, he mostly got angry at her when she wasn't acting right. He also got into drugs, and he'd take his anger out on me. I usually was the one that took care of my Mom when things weren't going right or, you know, she got upset and threw things around the house. I'd clean it up and . . . So, I mostly, I held in a lot of my emotions because I had nobody to talk to. And my Mom actually grew up in an abusive childhood too, and so she didn't really know how to care for us or give affection. I was never tucked in at night or given hugs or comfort or anything like that. So, it was mostly, you know, take care of ourselves and so I had held a lot of my emotions in. As a young child I had migraines and stomach issues and nightmares and all kinds of stuff just from holding all my stress in.

K.C. Armstrong: Right. Jenny, it's so sad that you were forced to become an adult at such an early age and still you must have been yearning for some companionship and some sort of protection from somebody. So, later in life did that affect your relationships?

Jenny Maher: Oh, definitely. Because I didn't know how to reach out to talk to people about how I felt or what was going on. And I didn't have the teaching, like, I didn't have close friends. I played sports after school, but I didn't really talk about what was going on at home. A lot of the teachers tried sitting me down and talking, but I always was afraid that something bad would happen if I was honest with them.

As I got older I didn't really know how to approach people and start a conversation. And I had a lot of problems with post-traumatic stress disorder where any sudden noise would make me jump out of my skin. Or, you know, I didn't like people being close around me because I'd feel trapped. I never really had a true relationship, especially with a male figure since I didn't have any male role models. I didn't have a grandparent or a father. So, pretty much male figures were out. It's really hard to be brought up and learn about different things or how to be around boyfriends when you don't have anyone in your life to teach you about it.

K.C. Armstrong: Right. Or even see it because you weren't brought up around it. Now, tell me when you did finally have a relationship with somebody, was it hard to accept love?

Jenny Maher: Yeah. Because it just felt awkward. I wasn't sure, like if I was kissing a boy I wasn't sure if that was the way you kissed a boy. It felt weird even holding hands or just being close to someone. It just didn't feel right, I wasn't sure. I had more boys that were closer as friends than as boyfriends. And I didn't know, I still didn't know, how to hold a conversation with anyone. I mean, I can talk about sports and football or anything like that.

K.C. Armstrong: Because you were a tomboy.

Jenny Maher: Yeah, I was definitely a tomboy. I played sports, everything. So, it was easy to hold a conversation about that. But to talk about being treated wrong or something that was bothering me, or the hurt inside because of something my Mom had done, I couldn't talk to anyone about that.

K.C. Armstrong: Right, but you said something before (and I know this stuff from going through 10 to 15 different psychiatrists because I've had my share of mental illness too), but you said something about being very angry. Now, throughout your junior high and your high school years, you told me that you didn't really have anybody to talk to or to share your feelings with. So, the natural thing that would happen is all that anger that you had gets turned within, and therefore it gets viewed as depression. Did you have a lot of depression in high school?

Jenny Maher: Well, I didn't really show it. I kept busy and that was my main thing. I played after-school sports, I did school; I even worked and stuff. So I stayed really busy and nobody really saw it, but I tended to hurt myself. Like I started cutting to get rid of the emotional pain that I was dealing with, and that was my release.

K.C. Armstrong: How old were you when you started cutting?

Jenny Maher: I was eight or nine and stopped at 36.

K.C. Armstrong: So it was something that was always there.

Jenny Maher: Yeah, it was an addiction. It was just automatic. My pain was in my chest, so my heart was hurting. I had to release it by feeling physical pain. It wouldn't even always be cutting. I'd punch a wall or punch something to hurt my hand or do something to hurt myself. Any way to get the physical pain to take away the emotional pain.

K.C. Armstrong: And if you think of it, what's really happening there is someone suffering so much that the only thing they know that's real is this physical pain, and that's so sad. I'm sure you would rather have that physical pain than the emotional pain. And to start cutting at eight or nine just shows how lonely and how dissatisfied you were with things that were going on. With the anger, and then doing this.

Jenny Maher: It was odd the way I started; I was actually playing with my mom's razor and accidentally cut myself. I realized that was when my Mom gave me attention. It got to be that if I hurt myself, then I would get the attention I needed from my Mom. So it started out as just a way of getting the attention I needed, and it came to a realization that I was actually feeling my emotional pain.

K.C. Armstrong: Right. So, through high school you kept busy and learned to be a good actor and put on this face that nothing was really bothering you. You masked it and kind of buried it away. So what made you join the AirForce? And was that right after high school?

Jenny Maher: Pretty close. It was because on my 18th birthday my Mom kicked me out of the house and made me live with one of my high school friends that I played sports with. I didn't really have a choice. She just set it up and so I had to live there. It was just like the spur of the moment; I never knew why she did it. I assumed because I was no longer a ward of the state because I turned 18, but she's never given me an explanation. So I lived with my friend and basically after high school had no place to go. I didn't have the money for college, and I didn't have any place to live. So I ran into recruiters at school one day, and I decided to join the AirForce.

K.C. Armstrong: And it wasn't like you had a real interest in it. This was just a place to go. Is that accurate?

Jenny Maher: Yeah, at first it was, and then I thought about it and I looked into it a little bit more. Then it seemed like the perfect thing for me to do because I had always loved the medical field, and I loved children. I had wanted to be a pediatrician and I wanted to do something in the medical field. And it so happened that I got a good enough score on the entrance test that I was able to become a medical lab technician. It kind of dropped into my lap and worked out really good for the time.

K.C. Armstrong: Okay, so there, finally you get a bone thrown your way, something good happens. But if I'm not mistaken, the Air Force didn't work out. Do you want to expand on that?

Jenny Maher: Yeah, even though I was away from my Mom, because I hadn't really talked about what I'd been going through in my childhood it never really went away. The pain stayed there, and there was nothing I was able to do to feel better about myself. That's when I started really getting depressed because I was living in the dorm by myself. I didn't really know how to reach out to people. So, I was getting more and more depressed, and it got to the point where I had to be admitted into the mental health unit.

After a while I didn't talk to anyone and I just went through a lot of different places that tried therapy. It ended up that they finally released me with a medical discharge for bipolar and post-traumatic stress disorder and depression.

K.C. Armstrong: How did that feel since, as you stated before, your mother had these things too?

Jenny Maher: I was scared at first because I knew what she had gone through, but then I realized that I wasn't having psychotic episodes like her. It was more the highs and lows, depression, the drops in depression. But it was aggravating because it's really hard to treat, and I didn't have any support system. I was basically just going through life one day at a time, and it wasn't really productive or anything.

K.C. Armstrong: It wasn't what you thought life should be.

Jenny Maher: No.

K.C. Armstrong: And you were probably disillusioned and disappointed. But when you get out of the Air Force and you're classified as having these mental illnesses, where do your travels take you next?

Jenny Maher: I moved to Colorado with a friend that I had met when I was stationed at the Air Force Academy. I was stationed at Andrews Air Force Base in Maryland, and that was when they kicked me out. So, I was able to move in with a friend and her family who lived in Colorado. She had two kids, and that actually was really good because I was around people. And, you know, the kids were around.

K.C. Armstrong: You were taking care of the kids, right?

Jenny Maher: Right. I was helping out. And people were around me, around my life and it was actually getting really good. But then her husband actually tried to sexually assault me, and it was back all over again. I just felt like I had a target on my back.

K.C. Armstrong: Did you think people would believe you if you reported what happened?

Jenny Maher: I actually called somebody, a crisis line or something. I was about ready to jump off a bridge, but I was talked down. That's when I was first hospitalized in the VA hospital. But when I got out, my friend was mad at me because of her husband; she thought I was lying. So now I had nobody again and I was all alone again. It was like starting from scratch.

K.C. Armstrong: Right. So Jenny, where do you go now after you're out of the hospital?

Jenny Maher: Well, thankfully I was able to buy a house, and I moved into my house. I started with nothing, no furniture, no nothing, and I became close with my neighbor. But you can't get away from those inner demons without letting lose somehow. And my Mom came back into my life. I needed her for some support, but she was still the same. She wasn't having the psychotic episodes, but she was still pretty unstable. She wasn't taking her meds, so she would scream at me for any little thing. It was hard living. Even though it was my house, I just put up with her because I needed somebody.

K.C. Armstrong: Yes, you were lonely. But in a way it seems like you always find someone to take care of, like the kids with your friend and your mom. It seems like that's probably where your comfort level was. Being there for someone else when you yourself needed care. Maybe something subconscious made you do this, made you keep seeking out people that needed you to take care of them. Is there any accuracy to that?

Jenny Maher: Yeah, it was easier for me to take care of others than letting somebody help me because I felt that I was being a burden on people, that I was taking up their time. If they wanted to talk to me or they wanted to help me with something, I thought that I was bothering them, or they could be doing something else and I didn't want to upset them. So I didn't feel comfortable with people helping me, and it was a lot easier to be there for others. I loved helping people, no matter what it was. And even if I ended up being taken advantage of, that was the kind of person I was used to being—the caregiver.

K.C. Armstrong: One could think that you had really no self-esteem, but yet you still had this thing inside you that made you fight and still be determined. You were able to take such abuse, and such horrible events happened to you, and you had to carry this for so long. When did the depression get so bad that you started to think about suicide?

Jenny Maher: It was off and on through from like 32 to 34, a lot of times that I wished I was dead. But I was afraid that if I tried something I'd end up comatose or a burden on somebody. I was trying to find ways to hurt myself so I'd end up in the hospital and be around people. But then they discharged me, and I was alone. So, it was kind of in and out of hospitals for a few years, and that wasn't working.

But it became really serious when I was 34 and my Mom again disowned me because she got mad at me at a movie theatre. I'm not sure what exactly she got mad about, but she started sending me really hateful emails, and I finally thought that there's no hope left, there is nothing left. You're taught your coping skills, you know, different ways to cope when you feel that you're at your end point.

I was seeing a psychiatrist or psychologist, and I didn't want to tell her I was suicidal because I didn't want to go to the hospital. So I tried just using the coping skills, finding some comfort food, finding distractions, calling somebody and talking to them. I was going to school to work as a CSI, and I was hoping that would be a diversion for me. But by the end of the night nothing had changed, and I made the decision to end my life.

K.C. Armstrong: How were you going to do it?

Jenny Maher: I had just gotten a prescription for my medications that I took for sleep, nightmares, and depression. I was on six different medications and they were real potent.

K.C. Armstrong: Probably narcotics too.

Jenny Maher: Yeah, some were narcotics. And it was enough that if you take two or three it'll knock you out. I wrote the note and took a lot of pills, and it ended up that my dog woke me up. I was mad because I was alive. And I had hallucinated or something; I thought there were police at my door. So I took more pills, and I hid in the closet, and that's the last thing I remember until I woke up in the emergency room three days later.

K.C. Armstrong: Oh my God. There are so many questions I have! First, what did your note say?

Jenny Maher: I don't remember exactly, but it was to my Mom. She had torn it out when I got back to the notebook I used, so I don't know exactly what I wrote—but it was specifically to her.

K.C. Armstrong: It was to your mom, okay. So you wake up in the hospital. As soon as you open your eyes, tell me what you're seeing, what your experience is.

Jenny Maher: Well, I'm lying there, and the doctors sit me up, and my Mom is sitting there in the corner of the room looking at me. The doctors are asking me if they can intubate me because I guess I'm having trouble breathing. I told them no because I know that when you intubate it's hard to get off of it. When I sat up, I couldn't move anything.

K.C. Armstrong: Jenny, I'm sorry I don't mean to interrupt you, but just to clear something up, what does *intubate* mean?

Jenny Maher: It's to put a tube down your throat to breathe for you.

K.C. Armstrong: Alright, thank you. They want to do this procedure to you, so you could breathe better, and you say no.

Jenny Maher: Right. Because I was still breathing, but I guess my oxygen level was low. But when I sat up I realized that I couldn't move my arms. I couldn't move anything. I could barely even keep my head up.

K.C. Armstrong: Oh my God.

Jenny Maher: And they didn't know exactly what was causing it, and so they laid me back down, put me on oxygen, and ran a bunch of tests. I had sores on my back and feet from sitting in the closet for whatever time that I sat there. And apparently from the MRI they found my spinal cord was swollen with lesions. They hoped that by giving me treatments which decrease swelling I would eventually get sensation back in my arms and legs.

K.C. Armstrong: Did that work out?

Jenny Maher: Well, after two weeks they had gotten all the test results back and nothing had changed.

The doctors would come in and want me to squeeze their fingers, and nothing was changing. After the two weeks they got all the test results back and they told me that the paralysis was going to be permanent. I was going to be a quadriplegic. At the time the only thing I could move was my head back and forth on the pillow.

K.C. Armstrong: Oh my God.

Jenny Maher: My Mom had been visiting me off and on, but I was still caring for her more than she being there for me. When the doctors finally told me it was permanent, I called my Mom. I was crying as I told her that I was going to be a quadriplegic. She told me that I could cry for one day and that was it. And then we hung up the phone.

K.C. Armstrong: How horrible. I know when sometimes my foot has been in the wrong spot it falls asleep, and it feels strange. But when it's your whole body? What was that like?

Jenny Maher: It was definitely weird. The nurses would try to get me in a position on my side or whatever to get me comfortable. I felt like I needed to lie in a different direction, even though I couldn't feel it; it was just weird. They kept telling me it was because I was in ICU for a long time, because of my oxygen level and everything. They told me to just try to go to sleep. For the first week, I didn't get much sleep; I just couldn't. I couldn't do anything for myself. I mean, I could barely even push the nurses' button. They had a big button taped to the pillow and sometimes it would come off, and I was too afraid to have them close the door to my room in case I couldn't push the button. And so, they had to do everything for me, feeding me, sitting me up, you know—everything. I was just going through life being so dependent on everyone for everything. It's still hard to get used to, but I'm more able to cope. But that helplessness was the biggest problem I ever had.

K.C. Armstrong: And isn't it strange, Jenny, that you probably prayed your whole to just have someone pay attention to you, someone to take care of you instead of taking care of everyone else? Isn't it ironic that God chose this for you, because now you're helping so many people while having someone take care of you? Where was your faith in all of this?

Jenny Maher: Well, at the beginning I didn't have religious beliefs or anything. I believed there was a God, but I didn't understand religions. I hadn't read the Bible, so I wasn't really following a religion. But after I woke up knowing that I survived, and I lived through the pills I took, I knew at that moment that God saved me for a reason. I didn't know why, but I also realized that making me a quadriplegic meant that I couldn't hurt myself anymore. And basically, I had to have some-body with me and I couldn't be alone. And it was like His way of taking care of me because I couldn't do it myself.

K.C. Armstrong: Because that's all you wanted your whole life, isn't it?

Jenny Maher: Right. I mean, I didn't want to be taken care of totally like I am.

K.C. Armstrong: Right, of course. Jenny, how long were you in the hospital before they let you go?

Jenny Maher: I was in the hospital for three years before I actually got out, and they told me I'd be in a power chair my whole life. They told me I'd be dependent on others for everything and that I'd never be able to live in-dependently. I decided I was not going to listen to them. Instead I was going to fight as hard as I could to, you know, push myself in a manual wheelchair. I was going to do what I could to live independently. There were just so many fights and so many obstacles that I ran into. The treatment that I was given at the VA from the caregivers was just not helping me when I needed help. And you know, my Mom basically was not an advocate for me, anyway. I was being abused in that VA from some of the aids. The nurses didn't really take care of us, so I had pressure sores that got infected and ended up having amputations. It's been a constant battle from all the different places I've been.

K.C. Armstrong: After your suicide attempt, did you feel that you regretted doing that, or did you ever feel like giving up again after this happened to you?

Jenny Maher: Yes. When I was living in the nursing home in Colorado, under the Denver VA again. At that point I didn't have anyone. The staff or the supervisors are supposed to be there for you and weren't, and I wanted at times to bring my chair in front of a bus and kill myself. But I was afraid that I would just be worse somehow. I had thoughts about that because I still felt so alone, and nobody cared about me. I was at the dropping point where I couldn't do anything for myself and I couldn't get away. I mean, I counted on people to get me up, to put me to bed, to do lots of things for me, even though I was able to do a lot more on my own now. But I still depended on them for daily routines.

K.C. Armstrong: You must have felt so helpless.

Jenny Maher: If I just wanted a cup of water that was sitting right there on the table, inches from me, I couldn't get it. I'd push the call button and could hear the nurses talking out in the hallway. But they don't care about you; it just makes it that much harder when your caregivers just don't care.

K.C. Armstrong: It's such a bittersweet story because here you are, someone who always had to take care of themselves and you want some help. You wanted companionship but you always just did things for yourself because that's the only person you ever could depend on. And now you need other people's help to get a glass of water. How did that make you feel? Did it make you angry at God, angry at yourself?

Jenny Maher: I was never angry at God. I never got mad about my situation because I had done it. And I never blamed God because I didn't have faith in God at the time.

It's not like He let me down or anything. So, I mostly just felt helpless, where there is nothing I could do or say, and I had no control over what I was given. For instance, they could stop my physical therapy even though they weren't supposed to. I could go to a supervisor, but it didn't matter. It's not like you can call the police when you're at the VA hospital and tell them they're not treating you right. You have no control over what's not being taken care of or what is, and so that's the helplessness of that. It made it that much harder.

K.C. Armstrong: And if you were some kind of being that could stand above and put your whole life into fast forward looking at all the things that you went through—just watching your life panned out from when you were born until now—what would that being say about Jenny Maher? What do you think the initial response would be if you ask this being to comment after watching your whole life?

Jenny Maher: Well, first, I wouldn't have been strong enough, when this happened to me, if I hadn't had to take care of myself or go through the abuse that I went through. If I was pampered and taken care of, I don't think I would have been as strong as I was. But because of all that's happened, I grew close to God, and because of that my faith has grown, and I've become stronger and more confident. My faith and trust in God has shown a way in my life that makes me happy because I now do know that someone is watching out for me and that He is there for me. And as long as I have that faith and trust, I don't have to worry.

K.C. Armstrong: Are you saying that your faith took away the loneliness?

Jenny Maher: Yes. I mean, now I live. When I was in the nursing home I was invited to church and that was when I first found that people were nice to me, accepting me. It took years to grow in prayer and it wasn't just like a quick turn of events, but I've conquered things that no one thought I would have been able to. I live independently and I have caregivers that care about me and I enjoy life. I still try helping people.

K.C. Armstrong: And you have the two cats.

Jenny Maher: I've got my cats. Yeah, and they take care of me. And I go to church and the people in my church love each other. I wouldn't have had any of that if I had continued the life I was living.

K.C. Armstrong: How did you get to find a way to look forward to each day, to find the beauty in each day, and why was it so hard for you to go through all of this to have something that you're supposed to have when you're a kid? You look forward to the days now, you see beauty in life, you connect with people, and you help people. Why did you have to go through something so hard to do what you're doing now?

Jenny Maher: Because, I think, if you have an easy life and then you suffer something drastic, you really can't be out there to help others to do what we're supposed to do. We're supposed to be there for each other and help each other out. Because of all the trials and tribulations that I went through and experiences I had, I can talk to someone else and say, you know, I've been there. I've been where you are, and I know how it feels and I know what you're going through. And your life doesn't have to continue this way, this doesn't have to be the end.

I still have off days. I'm not going to say that every day is a glory day, but I always realized that there is a reason for whatever is happening. I don't understand it at the moment, but there's always a reason for it. I just have to trust God that it's for the best. And when you have that mindset, that the world is not against you, but that everything is not going to be a bed of roses either, then you know that it's going to be okay.

K.C. Armstrong: Jenny, what could someone listening to this interview on WMAP or reading your chapter in this book learn through your experiences?

Jenny Maher: That if I was able to make it after going through everything that I've gone through, they can make it too.

K.C. Armstrong: What do you think they'd be most impressed with? What might they think is your best attribute after hearing your story?

Jenny Maher: My perseverance. I fight, I fight a lot. I continue to fight, and I don't give up. If I have to be on the phone calling in all different directions to get something taken care of or something done, I'll keep on fighting even if it hurts. I'll fight to get whatever I need to get done and that's what a lot of people tell me, that I persevere.

K.C. Armstrong: What a great lesson that people can learn from you. And is that why you named your book, *Never Give Up?*

Jenny Maher: Yes. And the easiest way to get it is just going to my website sbpra.com/jennymaher. I've also just published a new book, *Finding Faith in Darkness*, also available through my website.

K.C. Armstrong: I think it's admirable for you to tell your story to help others. That's what makes you one of the world's most amazing people. I have to ask you though, what if somebody is going through what you were going through in any way? Maybe as a kid, or as not knowing what to do, not knowing where to go—thinking about suicide, thinking about ending it all. What kind of advice could you offer these people who might be where you were?

Jenny Maher: Well, I think the most important thing that I learned is you have to find a release. Find an outlet, especially if you don't have anyone you can talk to. It might be writing, music or painting or drawing or anything. You need a way to get that out that's safe. That's what I found that's most helpful. Like right now I paint, and my painting is my escape. So, just find some safe avenue of expressing yourself, don't keep your emotions in.

K.C. Armstrong: Got you. Advice is to be taken very seriously coming from you, since you have lived through this experience. Now, Jenny, this is a tough question, but if you were to look back on your life would you have changed anything?

Jenny Maher: No. I wouldn't.

K.C. Armstrong: That tells me so much. The wisdom you have now has been worth the journey. Is there anything else you'd like tell our listeners and readers?

Jenny Maher: Having a belief that someone is there watching out for you is important. For me, having a church with a group of people that love me and take care of me is key. It's not something that cures everything, I mean, I still have meltdowns when I'm stressed, but I don't let that control my life. I think that's the hardest thing that people have to realize. You can't let that anger and despair or depression control your life.

K.C. Armstrong: Incredible. Jenny, you are definitely one of the world's most amazing people. Thank you so much for sharing your hard-won insights with me. I really appreciate it, and I know the listeners and readers do, too. I'm sure your honesty and candor will help people to a better understand of others, and perhaps of themselves.

Jenny Maher: No problem.

K.C. Armstrong: So, I will talk to you soon and, wow, just thanks again for really doing such a great job. What a story! Jenny Maher, guys. We can all learn from her.

CHAPTER 4

Doug Herald

Phone: 1-877-478-9471 **Email:** info@timeandeternity.net
Web Address: *www.timeandeternity.net*

Doug Herald Intro

As soon as we moved into our own building, I interviewed a man from Kentucky who had been using his faith and generosity to bring food and support to those in need from Cincinnati to Africa. Doug became a friend right away. He told me, when we decided to work together, that he was looking for a long-term relationship with anyone who wants to make a positive difference in people's lives.

Doug has been on the air with me many times, and each time he tops himself. What makes him so amazing as a person and as a guest is his courage to present his vulnerability openly to others in an attempt to help them with their own struggles.

As a man who appears to have it all, Doug honestly shares with us the emptiness he felt for years. It took a very long time for Doug to replace this void with acts of charity, friendship and gratitude. Most importantly, his faith has shown the way for Doug to realize how blessed he truly is and encourages him to share his good fortune and understanding with others.

Introduction

K.C. Armstrong: Alright, guys, next up is Doug Herald, who has a story which I've been telling you about for the past year. His journey is absolutely what this station is based on: determination perseverance, hard work, and faith.

Doug is a successful author, entrepreneur, speaker, and all-around incredible gentleman. He was born and raised on a family-owned farm in Grant's Lick, Kentucky, not far from my old stomping grounds of Bowling Green. When he decided to leave the farm, he did his best at every job he took to get promoted to the next. Great work ethic. Got to the top. Promoted. Next job. He grew up not having all the luxuries that a lot of people did, but he climbed the ladder through hard work and his strong faith. He was influenced by his mom and grandparents who helped create the amazing person he is today. I wish I could interview them too because of what Doug has become. So, guys, with no further ado, it's my honor and my privilege to welcome to the program Mr. Doug Herald. Hey, Doug, what's going on, buddy?

Doug Herald: Hey, KC! As Elvis would say, it's a rainy day in Kentucky, but it's okay. Everything is good.

K.C. Armstrong: I mentioned that you were born on a farm. I've known some Kentucky farmers; how long was it before you were thrown into doing all those necessary chores? I know there's always heavy work to do on a farm.

Doug Herald: When you're on a small family farm, what you grow and what you butcher are what you live on. So, I don't know. I like to tell folks I thought my name was "Milk the cow!" until I was 13. When you're old enough to sit on a tractor and steer, you do that while everybody else throws hay or tobacco on the wagon. By five or seven you're helping and watching, and by 12 or 13 you're actually very productive.

I always swore that when I got off the farm I'd never go back. But now, looking back through my last 50 years, the principles that work taught me and the character lessons were invaluable. You know, my dad left when I was an infant. My mom, my brother, sister and I went to live with our grandparents and my uncle in a four-room house of about 700 square feet. I was probably nine or ten years old before we had indoor plumbing. Financially we were poor, but we were never hungry. And really, with work ethic and family, we were wealthy in a small little town called Grant's Lick, Kentucky, that I hope to make famous one day.

As a young boy, I started working to add value to the family because we were sort of all in it together. So certainly by 12 or 13 years old, I was doing almost everything around the farm that a grown man does. Unfortunately, now we let adolescence draw out until about ages 25 or 30, and that's beyond me. I'm really thankful for the opportunity to have learned how to work. I may not be the smartest guy in the world, but I figure I can outwork anybody, and that's really paid off over the course of my life time.

K.C. Armstrong: I know that about you, Doug. I always wondered what it's like on a farm when it gets really cold. Are you still out there working when it's really, really cold? I'm a city guy, so I don't know.

Doug Herald: Well, one thing about farming is that your livestock always have to eat and drink.

The cows still have to be milked, and the pigs still have to be sloped. That's just the reality of what it is. And while there are no crops growing in the wintertime, we had to make sure we cut ice from the pond, so the animals could drink. It's not a lot of fun, but it's the nature of farming. It never ends—seven days a week, and sometimes 24 hours a day. I have a friend now that has a cattle farm, and he's watching the cows all through the night. When they're getting ready to birth, he's down there helping them. It's constant.

K.C. Armstrong: Doug, do you think you missed out on anything since you were working so much at such an early age?

Doug Herald: We worked a lot and grew up fast, but my mom and my grandparents tried hard to make sure we had extracurricular activities, too. Sports were certainly a big deal in Kentucky, especially basketball and baseball. I played football in high school, and I don't even know where that money came from, KC, but my family always made sure we were at practice and the games. Honestly, before this very minute I never even thought about that. But I do appreciate it. We were always given that privilege, maybe because my grandfather loved sports so much. And my uncle, who is only three years older than me, was really a superstar athlete.

It was really a special life growing up, but the financial poverty was very real. I remember as a young kid asking my mom to bring me home a bag of Fritos, which at that time cost 30 cents. When my mom got home, and I went out to her car, she was sitting out there with tears in her eyes. I asked her where my Fritos were, and she said, "Honey, I didn't have the money to get them." So, you know, financially things were really, really tight, but we were never without love, we were never hungry or without responsibilities and duties. We always had good food, especially pinto beans, cornbread, and biscuits and gravy. And now those are my favorite foods! My little girl tells me, "Dad, you grew up lucky because you got to eat your favorite food every single day."

K.C. Armstrong: That's cool. And you know how I love my biscuits and gravy, too! You can't spend time in Kentucky without forming that attachment! I was just thinking as you were talking though, about what a lady your mom must have been, how proud she must have been of her family, and how much you took from her strength.

Doug Herald: Yes, that's accurate. My mom was only 20 years old when she had me, and I was her second child. She literally dedicated her life to us three kids. Even today at 70, she is still very beautiful. I grew up with a country song, "If you happen to see the most beautiful girl in the world . . ." I thought that song was written about my mom. To this day she has never remarried. She went through a lot of abuse inside her marriage in lots of ways, but she did her absolute best for all of us kids. And what do you say about that? It's very humbling, and I'm very thankful because nowadays a lot of people won't even take responsibility for their kids, while I have a mom that would devote her entire life to the three of us.

K.C. Armstrong: That's something special, and your mom is definitely one of the world's most amazing people! Doug, I have to ask, during this period in your life, did you stash away a notebook or something like that? Because later on, of course, you became a very popular and effective writer.

Doug Herald: Actually, I didn't start back then. I sort of bluffed my way through high school. I was always the teacher's pet. But to be honest with you, I was a functioning illiterate; I couldn't read at the age of 25, literally.

K.C. Armstrong: Wow. That must've been a real problem.

Doug Herald: Yes! And then I was called into the ministry where I learned to read and put myself back through school. See, in Kentucky your education was just not important back then, certainly not in my family where life was just about work and then just getting a job. I could probably only read on a first or second grade level at the age of 25. So, I've probably read or listened to seven or eight hundred books in the last four or five years. I'm very proud that I've got three daughters that have been through college, and one is in law school.

K.C. Armstrong: So, you really grew beyond the expectations of your family and people around you in your youth, it seems.

Doug Herald: Yes, KC. By the age of 40 I had outdone most folks in my family monetarily and through position in life, and yet I was sort of empty. By that time, I had been through college and learned how to read and write. I had just gotten promoted to director of maintenance and engineering and began to make more money than I ever thought I'd make. And, honestly, now that I've looked at it and worked through some things, I realize I always worked really, really hard to prove that I wasn't a "piece of garbage," to keep it a G-rated program. But I never believed that in my heart, and that caused me a lot of pain. I tried to give folks to the outside of me what I thought they wanted. But the inside of me was just broken, and I was terrified others would see what was on the inside. After that last promotion, I recognized that if there's not something more to life, then I don't want to continue. For five or six years I went to a child psychologist to understand why I could be so full and rich on the outside and yet so empty and broken on the inside. I started thinking if I can't fix this thing, then I don't want to be here.

K.C. Armstrong: Oh, my God. That's when you know it's tough. I understand that attitude, too. I mean, you probably grew up old school. Like, what would your grandfather think about you going to see somebody for help? Do you think he would understand that?

Doug Herald: No, I don't. The reality is that there's a stigma, certainly in Kentucky and the Midwest, about seeing a psychologist. You know, "What's wrong with you?" I mean, we were told that in the Christian world, all you need is Jesus. But for me, I just knew that something had to be better.

K.C. Armstrong: Something was missing.

Doug Herald: Right. I began to work emotionally on some stuff with a psychiatric professional.

It's literally been ten years since then, and there's been nine and a half years of pretty consistent counseling. What really happened I guess, KC, is that I never thought much about my being lovable. Honestly, there are folks all over the world right now that really do love me, but I never saw myself as lovable. And what we do emotionally until we learn that we really are something special, we put people in a situation where they can never please us. If my wife and daughters bought me a Corvette or a tie for Christmas, my reaction would have been the same. If they bought me a tie, that's what I thought I deserved because I'm a piece of junk anyway. If they bought me a Corvette, well, what'd they do that for? Because I'm a piece of junk and I don't deserve it. That's the sort of thoughts I had my whole life.

You know, if somebody is an alcoholic and stays sober for ten years, as soon as they take a drink or stumble everybody says, "Well, I knew they couldn't make it," instead of celebrating the fact of making it for ten years. And for me there are still peaks and valleys where I struggle; the only difference between me and the alcoholic is that my struggles are not seen. The problem is not the alcoholic taking the drink; the real problem is how he deals with the pressure that caused him to want to take a drink. And how I deal with my ideas of who I am at a base level is the cause of my personal suffering.

K.C. Armstrong: Right.

Doug Herald: That's what I have to deal with. When I have low points, I don't stay there as long as I once did because now I have some tools. In the big picture of life, I've made tremendous progress. When I look back beyond ten years, unfortunately most of the time my measuring stick was perfection, and that's—death. But if we can look back and just say, "I'm making progress," then when we slip and fall down, we can get back up and keep going. That's the continuous improvement part of life, and that's what I've learned.

By no means do I have all the answers, but I promise you I've got more answers than most people. I realize now that sometimes our deepest struggles are actually gifts that God gives us to affect the world. Everybody has an opportunity, and I believe as long as you're still breathing, there's hope. I believe that with all my heart.

K.C. Armstrong: I couldn't agree with you more. You know, Doug, you're somebody who is so successful, who's risen to the top in pretty much every professional endeavor you've tried. I'm sure you must have met people along the way that didn't do right by you. Do you forgive them and give them another chance, or do you not do business with them? Maybe you can talk a little about that.

Doug Herald: Well, I'm not going to tell you that I've always done this perfectly. But I believe that even in business we need to look from a collaborative standpoint rather than a competitive one. And I realize that folks, including me for a long time, generally look at business as a competition. But several years ago I realized that there's plenty of success to go around, and we serve a God of abundance. We can be collaborative and not have to be in competition about everything. At the end of the day, maybe some people have done me wrong based on the best they knew how to do. But, honestly, I have such a huge appreciation and gratitude for what's been given to me and done for me. So, humbled by the gifts and opportunities and by what's taken place in my life, I don't hold grudges. I can say with all of my heart that there's nobody in the world that could call me, and I wouldn't go to them. And there's nothing like having that kind of peace—and opportunity.

What I've come to realize is that people may hurt you, KC, but most of the time, it's hurting people who hurt people. Most of the time people hurt you out of the darkness of their hearts and out of the darkness of their lives. But I think it's important that we do forgive. I believe that you reap what you sow. I want to reap love and friendship, so that's what I try to sow. The older and more mature I get, the more I recognize how amazing is the life I've been given. So, it's pretty hard to harbor any hard feelings toward anybody when God's been as good to me as He has.

K.C. Armstrong: Well, that's quite admirable. You met all these challenges, becoming operations manager, project manager of the Gerber line and director of maintenance and engineering and then getting involved as VP of Wornick foods. You certainly worked hard for all these accomplishments. But once you rose to the top, you had the honesty and bravery to admit that you weren't really fulfilled. Do you think that God loved you so much that He wanted to test you extra, like Job of the Old Testament?

Doug Herald: You know, I don't think God wanted to test me extra. But being raised without a dad in the middle of Kentucky back in 1966 to 1976 wasn't like it is today. We were definitely odd. We were called out as being little bastard children. And that wasn't a condemnation; that's just how people looked at it. Certainly, being raised by grandparents having a different last name was unusual and confusing. I remember as a boy telling folks who I was, and they'd say, "Well, whom do you belong to?" Somewhere deep inside that affected me to a point where I never felt like I had a home. I never felt like I belonged. And it was probably nothing more than what I put on myself because I was never mistreated. I was never without love. I mean, I had uncles that took us places and helped raise us. And my grandmother and grandfather. But, it really irked me that we were looked at differently because we didn't have a dad. It's hard, even right now, to think about it without getting emotional. The only thing that I ever wanted in life was that wholeness of a family.

I remember when we were young, my mom, my brother, my sister and I would go down by the pond at night and have a picnic on a blanket, gazing up at the stars. And we would hope for a falling star, so we could wish that we could just have our own little trailer house, a little mobile home, you know. I remember things like that and how deeply they affected me. Only four or five years ago I recognized that I really don't like holidays, especially Christmas and New Year. My wife always had a family to go to, as she was raised in a traditional home, but I never felt I had a real home in my life. I always felt welcomed, but I never felt that I had a place. It bothered me so much, and so I would work really, really hard to prove that I was something. And I worked to protect what was going on inside me, but I realized I was carrying around too much pain.

K.C. Armstrong: So that must've been the point when you knew you had to get help in finding and appreciating your own self-worth.

Doug Herald: Yes, it was definitely my low point. You know, my dad died on a Tuesday, after eight years of Alzheimer's, and everyone was worried about me. I had a lot of questions to ask him that he was not able to answer because of his illness, and that bothered me for a while. I hadn't seen him in so long, and then the opportunity to get information passed. When he died, I didn't feel much; I didn't know what to feel. And that Thursday, as I got into the shower getting ready to go to the funeral home, it all hit me. The dream that I'd held for 47 years, to have a relationship that every son and daughter wants to have with their dad, was truly gone. The hope for a relationship with him was gone even though there hadn't been a lot even before that. But it was final, and I stood in the shower that day and wept bitterly.

K.C. Armstrong: You just broke down.

Doug Herald: Oh yeah. I remember looking at my wife and other folks who had a great relationship with their dads, and I would covet that. But with that being said, I know now that I'm the person that I am because of my history, and I now can affect millions of people positively. I know I would rather be here with the opportunity to affect the world and give people hope than I would having had a regular, normal childhood.

K.C. Armstrong: Doug, that's so selfless. Now here enters your creation of *Time and Eternity*; everything has led up to this. Tell us about that and your book *In Hope for Time and Eternity* and the whole movement surrounding both.

Doug Herald: Originally, I wrote the book because I knew that I had something that could help other people, and I just wasn't going to hide it.

K.C. Armstrong: That's awesome. I would think, Doug, that writing that book was probably one of the hardest things that you ever had to do. To admit all these things and come clean about your problems was very brave. You were almost like a sacrificial lamb because you were looking out for other people more than yourself.

Doug Herald: Well, yes. But honestly, we live in the greatest country in the world, yet folks can have everything they could ever imagine in life and still be broken on the inside. We don't have to live that way, KC, and I just learned that.

K.C. Armstrong: Please tell us more about that thought and the project.

Doug Herald: Well, *Time and Eternity* is a company that I founded about 3 years ago with my partner, Dr. Bobby Sparks. One day a few years back a woman named Theresa Black told me I needed to tell my story, but I didn't even know I had a story! The reality is that I started working on my emotional development when I was 40 years old. And by age 45 I had gotten a huge amount of help through therapy and scripture. There's a passage in the book of Romans that says, "*tribulation worketh patience; And patience, experience; and experience, hope: And hope maketh not ashamed.*" I literally live that passage. I saw so many people of my generation in the northern Kentucky/Cincinnati area that go to bed broken every night. They have everything the world says they should have to be happy, and yet they're not. That had been me and my story. For so long I thought there was something wrong with me, but the more I worked and studied, the more I realized that I was more normal than I thought. And I wanted to tell my story so folks could understand there is hope, and that the things they struggle with are normal, too. It's okay to raise your hand and say, "Hey, I'm struggling. I need help. Would somebody help me? I'm hurting." And I really had gotten so much help myself that I wanted to pass it along to other folks.

K.C. Armstrong: You spoke about the stigma of seeking help for emotional problems. Was that still an issue?

Doug Herald: To an extent, yes. Actually, when I wrote my book and literally told all, I lost some Christian friends. I lost preacher friends that backed off from me. You know, everybody has a box for you, and as soon as you begin to get out of that box they begin to get uncomfortable. I was telling my story one day when a lovely lady out of Columbus, Ohio named Theresa Black came up to me and said, "I want to write your story." And I didn't even know that I had a story! But that was the seed. I finished my book along with Theresa and Dr. Bobby Sparks. My goal is for folks to understand that what they struggled with in their 40's and 50's is absolutely normal. We spend so much time showing everybody the outside because we're terrified that they'll see the struggles going on inside. And yet, the inside is where all that's precious comes from. To learn to be real and vulnerable is where all power and strength comes from, and that's how we affect other people's lives.

K.C. Armstrong: What is the main platform of *Time and Eternity?*

Doug Herald: Viewing *Time and Eternity* as a business ministry, I write about how people develop in both business and in personal development. I believe that in life we should be continually improving, so we have those two platforms inside the business world. First, how do we lead people, how do we engage them to perform better for the mutual prosperity of the employee and company? That's the leadership piece inside the business of manufacturing or any other business. Secondly, we say the greatest investment that a person can ever make is in themselves. This is the personal development side.

There's a myth that when formal education is done we stop growing, and unfortunately that is sometimes a sad reality. When people stop growing, they stop living, so we stress personal development. We have a couple of books out now and a third coming out this summer. So, lots of really good things are going on to allow us to help people to get the most out of life. I believe that all of us have a certain potential which a lot of folks never reach because of their mindset, fear, or whatever else they may be struggling with. I've lived that in my own personal life and still fight every day to press through barriers my mind tries to impose.

K.C. Armstrong: When you were coming up with *Time and Eternity,* Doug, and you went full force with it, tell me about some of the challenges that you had. Something like this can't be easy.

Doug Herald: Well, I'll tell you, KC, in September three and a half years ago, God showed me a vision of what my life should look like, and that's when I began to write the book and develop the *Time and Eternity* business plan. But honestly, I desperately wanted to be a pencil in the hand of God. My whole life had been forced by me, and I had gotten to the place where *Time and Eternity* was God's; it belonged to Him. I wanted to be that vessel in His hand that affects the world.

And the reality is, I've been *walking by faith,* meaning going as far as I can see and relying that when I get there, I will see how to go farther. I really wasn't crystal clear about what I was doing, KC, up until our first interview in January. That's when God put all the pieces together in my eyes; that's when the business plan truly was birthed. Up until then I was walking by faith, knowing a direction but only seeing pieces of the final product. I could never explain my idea in the practical business way I felt in my heart. And when we had the opportunity to do that first interview on a rainy night here in Kentucky, I was able to manifest what's been in my heart and what's been my vision the whole time. When I got through with the interview with you that night, when I was sitting in my car in the Outback Steakhouse parking lot with my wife and friends inside eating, I had complete clarity of the whole vision for the project to become *Time and Eternity*.

K.C. Armstrong: Oh wow!

Doug Herald: Until then I frustrated a lot of people because they would only see pieces of my idea. It was a really big vision, but I couldn't, I really couldn't, give a clear picture because I didn't have it myself. But now I do, and my goal is to go into poverty-stricken areas, whether it be in downtown Cincinnati, West Africa, China . . . no matter where. I want to be able to reduce hunger and poverty in Third World Countries, to build manufacturing and food production so we can give those folks an opportunity, maybe even affect them for eternity. That's my goal.

K.C. Armstrong: That would be so amazing!

Doug Herald: That's what I want to do. I have the skill set and the people to do it. I will soon have the backing to do it.

And it's not about making a lot of money. There is so much money already available, that we can literally change the world with a really good plan. We just need a sustainable business plan at the grassroots level where folks living in poverty can be taught how to work to make businesses thrive and grow.

K.C. Armstrong: Doug, I knew from our first conversation when you really exposed your soul to us that you had been through challenging times. But I also thought to myself, "Whatever has to be done, this guy is strong, and he's going to make something important happen. And his story needs to be in our first book." And my prayers were answered!

You mentioned that making a ton of money is not part of your goal; however, we know that bills have to be paid. How will you manage that? Is this a non-profit organization?

Doug Herald: *Time and Eternity* is for profit, and we've now registered a non-profit, the *Time and Eternity to Eradicate Poverty.* Ultimately, I believe that we can run a not-for-profit-organization that can get at least 90% (90 cents from every dollar) to exactly where it needs to go, and that's to help wipe out poverty. Obviously, there have to be some administration fees in order to talk to governments and such. But my goal is to never let those fees go above 10% of all the funds that I have been given. A full 90%, at least, would actually go into sustainable work. I'm not talking about giving people a fish. I'm talking about teaching people to fish. I'm not talking about dropping off tractor trailer loads of rice and killing fragile economies. I'm talking about helping folks work smart in order to revive their economies.

It's been proven that just giving food and money to Third World Countries does two things: make the rich richer and destroy the local economies. So, our goal is to take monetary donations to places like West Africa, say, build a mango plant, teaching the native population how to dehydrate mangoes. So, 90% of the mangoes that grow naturally won't continue to rot on the ground. We'll put people to work and make a sustainable business. *Time and Eternity* would own part of the asset, but over the course of three to five years there would be an exit plan. At that time, the ownership would transfer completely to the national partners in whatever country we're in.

My goal is not to own stuff and to run stuff. I do that now. Instead, my goal is to set up businesses that treat people the right way and then let them run and grow businesses themselves. For example, right now there's an opportunity for a food manufacturing plant in Senegal. I was also asked this week to present a plan to the government of St. Lucia to potentially establish a factory to dehydrate naturally-growing bananas. Our goal in all areas is to create jobs, not to just give things away.

K.C. Armstrong: Awesome! I've seen those documentaries you mentioned that show how well-meaning give-away programs actually harm rather than help these developing countries. Your plan is to employ people to build communities and economies, which is a huge difference. What an incredible, humanitarian project, Doug!

Doug Herald: I told you I was going to take you all over the world, KC!

K.C. Armstrong: Every time I talk to you, Doug, it rejuvenates me to see how another human being can do so much for others. The result of your hard work, personal struggles, therapy, and all your experiences have led you here, to this point of humanity, which makes you stand out as one of the World's Most Amazing People! And people like you are a blessing to all of us and the reason for our radio station and publications. So, thank you, Brother.

Doug Herald: I appreciate that, KC, and I appreciate all you have done to help us spread the word. There are really a lot of great opportunities for the many people that want to get involved and just simply don't know how. People can join us in creating something really special, but it really doesn't belong to us. It belongs to all people that want to make a difference in the world. And the vision belongs to God that gave it to me; it's really His.

K.C. Armstrong: Anything else you'd like to tell us?

Doug Herald: You know, an undertaking like this brings a lot of fear. But, again, I believe you only get one bite at the apple, one chance at this life. I think the biggest regret you can have is getting to the end of your life and finding that your dreams are unfulfilled. All the things you wanted to do and could have done are left unfinished. All you could have accomplished, your hopes, your writings, and your projects—all undone because you were afraid to unleash them. That's tragic. I believe that every individual has a God-given potential, and I think we should not be afraid to try to reach it. It's sometimes hard and even discouraging. Sometimes you skin your knees, but

I believe, at the end of the day, it's going to be well, well worth it.

K.C. Armstrong: I agree 100%. Doug. I can't thank you enough for what you're doing and for sharing your story with us. I hope everyone will visit Doug's site *timeandeternity. net* to see more about what he's doing or even to help. And Doug, I'll be in touch soon for your biscuit and gravy recipe—Kentucky style!

Doug Herald: You got it! Thanks so much, KC!

CHAPTER 5

Virginia Armstrong

Email: info@leavingfootprints.org
Web Address: https://www.leavingfootprints.org

Virginia Armstrong Intro

This chapter was definitely the hardest to do. My mom, as you know, is my favorite and most important person in my life. To interview her about the time she almost left me alone in this terrifying and wonderful place was, let's just say, more unpleasant than if Edward Scissorhands was your proctologist or if somehow you were getting a massage and all of a sudden the table turned into a taut rope of barbed wire and the place you rest your face in turned into High Pitch Eric's sweaty naked ass after I chased him around with rotting bluefish for an hour in a sauna. How's that for an image? So if my description confused you—I'll just say hearing about my mother's near-death experience on Mt. Kilimanjaro when her fingers swelled to the size of balloons made me have *immense discomfort.*

So I distracted myself by cracking jokes, being inappropriate, and trying my best to dance around the details. Although tough for me, I did have to "man-up" and get her real story so I'll just tell you: this is a story about my Mom in Africa. (FYI-during her trip I was in jail at OCCJ—next book!)

Interview

K.C. Armstrong: So why don't you tell us exactly how and why this adventure came about?

Virginia Armstrong: Well, as a retirement gift to myself, after 30 years in the classroom, I set my sights on the top of the "Roof of Africa," the great Mount Kilimanjaro. At 19,300 feet, The mountain is the highest on the continent of Africa and tallest freestanding mountain in the world—the source of many legends, dreams and heartaches. This was my goal; but I died 762 feet from the summit at Gillman's Point on the Uhuru Crater rim.

K.C. Armstrong: Don't remind me! But let's start this story with some background which led up to that. You know I love teachers, and you've been teaching forever, in and out of the classroom. How does it feel to be an integral part of the lives and successes of countless young people?

Virginia Armstrong: Thank you for asking! And thank you for the opportunity to lecture you. I don't get that opportunity much anymore! *Success*, in my opinion, is creating and then achieving a goal of personal importance, and I want that success for my students. Depending on our tolerance for true self-knowledge and for dedication, that goal can be as small as a vow to stop biting our nails, or as large as being elected the President of the United States. Self-knowledge drives the recognition of where our passions lie and what we would most like to achieve. Do I want to be a smart entrepreneur? A civil rights activist? A teacher, explorer, athlete, health professional? I've tried to explore these options with my students and empower them with the skills and confidence needed to follow their dreams, once they determine what they are. A teacher's greatest gift is seeing former students happy and successful.

K.C. Armstrong: Let's go back to what made an amazing person and an amazing teacher—what was growing up like? I always am fascinated where greatness and great values come from.

Virginia Armstrong: As a child I was groomed to be a helper: dusting the milk bottles on the back porch, changing my doll's diaper, walking with my mother to collect funds for various charities, and delivering fresh eggs to the Convent each Sunday morning. In school, I brought the popcorn maker for the class party and decorated the gym at homecoming. I was taught to stop at Church when I walked past, even if "just for a minute." (*Jesus might be lonely* . . .) The emphasis was always on others, so that became very normal to me.

K.C. Armstrong: Big Family?

Virginia Armstrong: I'm the oldest girl in a family of seven children. I was expected to care for the younger ones regularly, and I learned to make dinner for a large extended family at a very early age. This was simply what we did; the family pitched in to take care of everyday routines. No one complained, balked or nagged.

K.C. Armstrong: So, this is where a life of altruism starts?

Virginia Armstrong: You're too kind, KC!

K.C. Armstrong: And handsome.

Virginia Armstrong: (Laughing) Yeah, of course! So the "altruism" you speak of brings some unforeseen problems, such as bouts of enabling and being manipulated, but that is part of the process of learning to give of oneself within boundaries. Something I realized along the way is the imperative of learning. I was not a great student, but rather an independent one. When a teacher mentioned something that sparked my interest, I would research and discover—with joy. When my 12th grade English teacher, who was more interested in analyzing the football team's playbook than TS Eliot, assigned *The Return of the Native* by Thomas Hardy, I spent the rest of the term reading all Hardy's other novels—and poems—in class while x's and o's were making their way onto the chalkboard. Stubborn but rewarding—creating self-awareness!

K.C. Armstrong: Stubborn but rewarding, that's the name of the sequel to this book

Virginia Armstrong: (Laughs) Literature became a tremendous part of my life, never failing to provide education, entertainment and inspiration to this day.

I also participated in lots of physical activities, though I just thought of them as fun, most notably dance and horseback riding. And walking in the woods with my dog, Misty, which I later discovered was called *hiking*. A loving relationship with nature was followed, with snowboarding, skiing, ice-climbing, cattle driving, horse herding, backpacking, swimming, biking, and even competitive boxing the eventual results. Achieving goals and dreams often requires operating outside one's comfort zone.

K.C. Armstrong: So, by your own definition, what were your early successes that led to becoming who you are now?

Virginia Armstrong: Well, I guess my childhood "successes" were meeting my responsibilities willingly and proudly, developing my mind and imagination, performing kind deeds, and pushing to my personal limits in fitness and sports. The process was learning what made me happy and then upping the ante for each new endeavor, by setting progressively greater goals of attainment in each of my interests.

K.C. Armstrong: What do you think prevents others from becoming successful? What are some of the things that you did differently?

Virginia Armstrong: I would guess the biggest distraction in finding one's own success would be lack of self- knowledge and self-confidence. It all starts within us. If we were offered a business design and financial backing, could we create a success? That will only work if we find within ourselves the enjoyment or passion for what that particular business entails. You need to believe in the vision, and then you need to believe in your capacity to construct it. Only then will you have the motivation to research all you need to do to get the enterprise working, and you will have the necessary confidence to follow through on your plans. Without either the passion or the belief in yourself, the business will not prosper. The same can be said of all our self-imposed challenges. Self-awareness, passion, and confidence are needed for effective goal setting.

K.C. Armstrong: How does one find these qualities? If they have not grown within us from childhood, are they still attainable?

Virginia Armstrong: I would hope and believe so. The human mind is capable of almost anything. But you have to recognize what it is you are looking for.

K.C. Armstrong: I'm going to repeat some things I thought I heard you say one way or another. Did you say something about self-knowledge?

Virginia Armstrong: Yes, Self-knowledge. What makes you happy? What gives you a feeling of satisfaction?

Do you like working and playing closely with others or prefer a more solitary setting? Meditate. This is not a realization that strikes when you are navigating city traffic.

K.C. Armstrong: Believe in yourself?

Virginia Armstrong: Believe in yourself. Absolutely. First, start with realistic goals. Research funding and the learning curve, you will have to master for your goal. How will you educate/train yourself? Who can you talk to who has done this sort of thing already?

Once you know your plan is achievable, don't look back. You've already assessed the possibility; now move forward replacing doubt with certainty and a problem-solving attitude. In my case, I was fortunate to find out early that I could always find happiness and fulfillment in reading, learning, spending time with family, helping others, enjoying the outdoors, and being active and healthy. My teaching career built upon and expanded this self-knowledge and I shared these interests with my students as possible sources of their own pleasure and growth.

K.C. Armstrong: I get it. Self-awareness, passion, and confidence may be the winning combination for successful goal setting, but how does all this relate to your story of "dying on the mountain"? First of all, why Kilimanjaro?

Virginia Armstrong: It's kind of a long story, got time? I had always told myself that I would retire from teaching on the day I stopped seeing my own two sons in the back of each of my classrooms.

K.C. Armstrong: At 41 years old I did graduate.

Virginia Armstrong: Well, that never completely happened (the part about not seeing you in the back row), but your faces did dim a little as my contemporaries were drawing their teaching years to an end. I was able and wanted to leave the profession while I still loved it and also while I was still well enough to enjoy an active retirement. Once the decision was made to announce my retirement date, I wondered what to do to mark the occasion.

K.C. Armstrong: So, I assume the common thing to do when a teacher retires is to have a keg party, take ecstasy and go to a monster truck rally wearing nothing but neon bead lights, right? That's normal right?

Virginia Armstrong: Maybe it's best you didn't go for a teaching degree. Anyway, when deciding on an appropriate celebration for my retirement, I knew a special dinner, or perhaps a luxury cruise (as you and your brother suggested), just wouldn't do it. I wanted something monumental and challenging! I consulted my love of exploration, nature, and adventure . . . The decision didn't take long to envision. This was undoubtedly what teachers of children's literature call the "Aha! Moment."

K.C. Armstrong: I believe this is what I call, as a son, my Aha NO-ment!

Virginia Armstrong: Kilimanjaro! The highest peak on the continent of Africa and highest free-standing mountain in the world! Come on! Mystery and legend surround the Great Mountain named by the ancient Maasai. Yes! Even better, this was a mountain selected by Ernest Hemingway to write about mortality and reflection, two topics I was now considering as I left a major emphasis of my life for an unknown future.

I loved climbing the White Mountains in New Hampshire, the Adirondacks in New York and the Presidential Range in Colorado, particularly Mount Elbert, the highest peak of the Sawatch Range and the entire Rocky Mountains. It was there on my 55th birthday that I first experienced a 10,000' altitude headache. I remember leaving

our campfire early that night on Elbert headed to my tent with two aspirins and great plans for an early summit the following morning. I woke with a headache unlike the post-birthday headaches I'd experienced in the past! All of these previous climbs were difficult but rewarding, even exhilarating! But let's take it up a notch to provide a truly incredible adventure and put body, mind and spirit to an ultimate test!

K.C. Armstrong: What were you thinking? Oh wait, I know, "My kids have made me worry about the stupid crap they do for years, I'd like to give it back to them." That's what you were thinking right? I'm just kidding . . . how did you begin?

Virginia Armstrong: Payback time! All those years of white-knuckling my stadium seat on the bleachers and wrestling stands! Actually, my attitude was more like "I can do anything I put my mind to" coupled with "my most meaningful competitor is myself." You know exactly what I'm talking about. My experience included lots of physical training, including hiking, mountain climbing, weight lifting, and a biathlon here and there. In my years of teaching, while I strove to be the best I could be, I designed and taught many courses and proudly touched many lives. I was an independent self-starter, but my focus had always been on others—"the helper"—more than on myself. Raising a family also fosters self-sacrifice, as any parent knows, and my children were always the top priority and greatest joy in my life. Honestly. But now, as a retirement gift to myself, this was about ME!

K.C. Armstrong: I can say that's 100% true!

141

Virginia Armstrong: I researched tour groups. Unlike most mountains, Kilimanjaro cannot be attempted by individuals. You must be part of a licensed and registered expedition. There are many guides available, and I immediately knew that my main criteria would not be price or comfort, but safety. After much searching I found a reliable company in New Hampshire. The trip leader had been to the summit of Kili previously, as well as Everest and other challenging climbs. He and his wife were both experienced mountain guides and had run many successful expeditions. Food would be plentiful which I needed to check, since my blood sugar levels can drop quickly with physical strain.

I learned that Mt. Kilimanjaro is composed of three distinct volcanic cones: Kibo 19,340 feet (5,895 meters); Mawenzi 16,896 feet (5,149 meters); and Shira 13,000 feet (3,962 meters). Uhuru Peak is the highest summit on Kibo's crater rim and the fourth highest of the "7 summits" (highest mountains of each of the seven continents).

K.C. Armstrong: So, safety was first. Good. But how did you make that judgement?

Virginia Armstrong: I did my homework. When I interviewed the operator from New Hampshire, I was confident that I had made a good choice. Not only would we be cared for by two to three porters per climber, we would be carrying emergency oxygen, and also a "Gamow bag" which is a pressurized bag large enough to fully enclose a person and decrease effective altitude for use in extreme cases of high-altitude cerebral and/or pulmonary edema. OK, fine. Now I could tell my children of my plans with confidence.

K.C. Armstrong: How did your family feel about this "celebration"?

Virginia Armstrong: Although not overjoyed with my choice of celebration, the "boys" – you and Matt—supported my decision. I could tell you would have much preferred my selecting a lounge chair on a Caribbean beach, but shortly after closing my classroom door for the last time, less than a month after my retirement from nearly 30 years of teaching . . . . I was on a plane to Kilimanjaro, Tanzania, East Africa! I believed in my vision and I believed in my capacity to construct it.

K.C. Armstrong: Tell us how the trip began.

Virginia Armstrong: After landing outside of Arusha, before the expedition was to begin, our group met at a hotel in the town of Moshi under the looming grandeur and mystery of The Great Mountain. Here we were to recover from jet lag, repack our personal gear which we would carry ourselves each day, and organize the 35 lb. packs that our porters would transport for us from camp to camp during our eight-day trek. The next two days were spent sightseeing as typical tourists to recover from any residual jet lag and explore the amazing African landscape. However, in our explorations around town, I became intrigued by the uniformed children walking to and from their schools.

After asking some questions of a shopkeeper, I was told he would gladly walk me to the nearby primary school and introduce me to the principal.

The woman in charge of the Kibo School, Ms. Elly Sunguya, couldn't have been more welcoming, and I was invited to meet the children and then to return the next day as a guest teacher!

A new excitement overtook me. This was as exciting as preparing for the trek! Teaching children—in Africa!

K.C. Armstrong: Have you ever taught abroad before, and what was your first impression of the African school?

Virginia Armstrong: No, this was all new to me and in Tanzania, children learn both Swahili and English in the classroom. So, when invited to address the class I decided to conduct an "immersion lesson," meaning I would evaluate the students' English structure, vocabulary, and fluency while they had the chance to hear and interact with a native speaker. My topic was my traveling experience. These kids had most likely never left their own rural village, much less their country. I would tell them a bit about the US and the world they could explore one day.

But the poverty in Tanzania was overwhelming! The school was structurally unsafe for the children. The eaves and roofing had gaping, rotting holes and looked ready to collapse. Six grade levels were assigned to the school, but since there were only four schoolrooms, only four grades could attend each year. A system of rotation was developed. Children walked long distances and attended only if their parents could afford to let them leave their homes each day; many children had to work or help around the house. And there was the matter of the cost. Even in public schools, children must buy uniforms and school supplies and pay various fees, prohibiting many from an education. The uniforms I viewed were often stained and worn with holes at the elbows and knees. I heard of siblings who had to share uniforms so that they took turns going to school. In other families the uniforms were borrowed or simply passed down from oldest to youngest.

K.C. Armstrong: How did the lesson go? How was this different from your experience in American schools?

Virginia Armstrong: After introducing myself that morning, I told the children a bit about where I was from and why I was visiting their country. I asked Ms. Sunguya for a map of the world or a globe to help them visualize the extent of the trip, and she seemed embarrassed as she shuffled through some papers, looking for a picture or map. It was then I realized the extent of the deprivation in the room. I had certainly noticed the tattered uniforms and shoes and also the bare, shabby walls with extremely faded, stained paint, but it hadn't dawned on me that there wasn't a teaching aid in sight. A small, cracked blackboard hung at the front of the room, but no bookcases or shelving lined the walls. No closets which could have enclosed writing paper, notebooks, crayons and books. No computers—and no light switches . . . No electricity.

So, I told the children about America and about the plane ride to Africa. They couldn't believe I had spent 18 hours in the air! I told them about going on safari and staying in a hotel and about my children and grandchildren at home. And they eagerly shared their own experiences and proudly sang a song they had learned together. We discussed many topics, but one thing overwhelmed me, and that was their passion and gratitude for being in school. When their teacher and I first entered the classroom, the entire group of 60 students rose quickly and silently to their feet. They recited in unison: "Good Morning, Teacher. How are you today, Teacher?" And then they respectfully stood in anticipation of an answer. Their teacher, Ms. Sunguya, modeled the routine for me and, after assuring the class she was quite well, gave permission for them to take their seats, two children to each desk.

The children were enthralled to hear about a different country and different customs. Hands waved wildly in the air by the smiling children, but no one spoke without first being recognized. They were charming, adorable, and hungry for information about a world outside their home. The importance of education to them was obvious and later many told me they dreamed of going on to higher education, even university.

These children were so motivated to perform with distinction on their National Exams, because this is how they could progress through school. They worried about how their parents would be able to pay their fees and if they would be needed at home before they were able to finish school. Most related getting up before the sun to perform their household chores before beginning their trek to school so they earned the privilege of leaving the family for the day.

Lunch time came, and I learned that the children were fortunate to receive a hot meal, which was included in their tuition fees. A small school kitchen was set up in a separate building with a wood fire over which hung a large kettle of porridge. The children were given bowls of this mash, which they ate while sitting in the dirt yard of the school. Three nearby latrines were enclosed by thin concrete walls: boys', girls', and staff, separated by a single panel of concrete. This was basically what we would call a three-seat outhouse with partitions. The mud and overflow from these latrines ran down an incline past the single outdoor water spigot where the children washed their hands and drank. The susceptibility for disease here was astonishing.

After lunch there was a short playtime before lessons resumed. Groups of girls gathered with fraying, knotted ropes to play jump rope and double-Dutch. Many of the boys played soccer, using wadded up tape or a plastic coke bottle as balls.

Since I had brought along a few deflated soccer balls and a pump, I quickly blew one up and taught the whole group to play dodgeball! The entire schoolyard was teeming with laughing boys and girls who had never experienced the game but took to it expertly. Although their English was quite good, they were confused by some of my expressions, so to make an outer circle I had half the kids join hands and keep backing up until they were in good striking position. The others got to be inside the circle and dodge the ball, which was being thrown energetically through the throng of squealing children. Somehow, they got the idea that when they were tagged by the ball they should grab it and run a lap around the schoolyard, but with the help of the other teachers, they learned to remain in position. What fun we all had! Even my flashback to a US school which had banned dodgeball as "too violent" didn't interfere with the experience, since every little face in front of me was absolutely joyful. Education here seemed so much freer with fewer restrictions and guidelines than I experienced at home.

Sadly, the day came to a close, and I promised the children I would never forget them. I would write letters for the teacher to read to them, and I would send them "the whole world" (a globe of the Earth) for their classroom as soon as I returned home. They could then better envision all the land, all the countries of the world with all their different customs waiting to be explored one day.

K.C. Armstrong: Continue with your description of the trip itself.

Virginia Armstrong: Well, the very next morning our expedition was transported to the Machame Gate, at the base of Kilimanjaro just south of the Equator, where we signed in and began our trekking adventure, wearing only shorts and light shirts and carrying our daypacks through the rainforest. These packs, which we tried to keep relatively light, held our individual needs such as our water, snacks, an extra layer of clothing, camera, journal and such. The extra clothing seemed unimportant until later when we began needing layers, as our heavy packs were only available to us in our camps at night.

K.C. Armstrong: I climbed the fence to get away from the police a couple of times, but as far as climbing that's as far as I got. Many of us have not had this sort of climbing experience. Tell us a little about it.

Virginia Armstrong: Well, I'm glad I never knew about that, K.C. We'll talk after the interview. Do you want me to continue the story?

K.C. Armstrong: I'm sorry, I keep interrupting with trying to make light of this. As you know, this was and still is very hard for me to hear, but this story needs to be told and from now on I'll do my best not to make my stupid jokes.

Virginia Armstrong: I know it was, and if I recall correctly, you had a great way of dealing with your concern and nervousness.

K.C. Armstrong: Alright, easy Ma, that's for another chapter, let's not talk about that and okay, we all know you're witty. Let's go on. Tell us about the first morning.

Virginia Armstrong: This first morning we watched for Colobus monkeys and identified olive and fig trees and gorgeous orchids as we nervously but excitedly picked our way through the gently ascending trails and lush greenery.

After an overnight at 10,000 feet at the Machame Hut, we climbed the following day to the Shira Plateau which was covered with exotic plants I had never seen before, even in pictures. The next few days were exhausting, with rugged hiking and scrambling, notably up the Baranco Wall, a vertical scramble up a steep rock face with a frighteningly shear drop, known in mountain humor as "the fast way down." This maneuver brought us to the Southern Glaciers at approximately 13,000 feet. We slept at Karanga Valley and then moved to High Camp at Barafu Hut at 15,000' following the mountaineer's adage, "Climb high, sleep low." From zone to zone we added layers, applied sunscreen, tightened our parkas, drank lots of water, took our malaria pills, and paced ourselves.

K.C. Armstrong: Did you have to carry your own provisions? Did you have help?

Virginia Armstrong: Our porters did the heavy work. At a ratio of two to three porters to each climber, the natives literally ran past us to reach each of our daily destinations with plenty of time to set up camp before our later arrival. Once we finally stumbled into camp each afternoon we were greeted with hot tea and popcorn served in a large dining tent. The cook-tent would be set up beside this and would provide the welcome sound of joking workers, clanging dinnerware, and delicious smells of dinner. The very first thing we spotted upon reaching each camp was our larger packs placed neatly in front of our expertly pitched tents. All we needed to do at that point was wash in the heated water our porters supplied, enjoy a tasty meal, and sit for a while under the vast and starry African sky, always gazing up—to the peak of the mysterious Great Mountain. The African skies are boundless and were lit by a pale full moon. No other light was visible, making the contrast of sky and stars with the outline of our Mountain always looming above so intense, dramatic and unforgettable.

In the morning we reversed the setup process; our porters brought warm washing water to our tents and greeted us at the dining tent for a breakfast of African coffee or tea, eggs, toast and more. Once we consumed the calories we knew we would require for the day, we set our heavy packs for the porters to pick up in front of our tents and put our immediate needs into our day packs. We left Camp first—with our experienced African guide, John Mtui, and our American tour director leading the way. The porters were left to take down and fold all the hikers' tents plus the "kitchen" and "dining room" tents, the latrine tent, and then load all the equipment, food, cooking utensils, water, and expedition members' heavy packs for the day's trek. All of these items were carried by the porters-on their heads with pots, pans etc. hanging from their belts—and yet these men passed us by noon each day, hurrying and yelling encouragement as they scrambled upward to prepare camp once again before we dragged ourselves in from the day's climb. As the days passed we noticed that some of the porters left the party. It made sense; as we ate and drank the provisions, less man-power was required to carry the load. But all the porters were so cheerful and so encouraging! As they passed us on the route or greeted us for our meals they gave us thumbs-up and a hearty "Jambo!"

K.C. Armstrong: How did the trip progress?

Virginia Armstrong: The days became cold and the nights frigid until we traded our zip-off hiking pants for lined pants, snow jackets, woolen hats and gloves. At night we left the dining tent with hot water in our thermoses to place between our feet or snuggle with in our warm, sub-zero sleeping bags. Getting up at night and venturing to the latrine tent became more and more dreaded as the temperature plummeted and we became more fatigued. We were glad to have been advised to bring a "pee jar" to relieve ourselves within the tent when necessary.

The extraordinary terrain changed each day and the view was becoming more and more dreamlike. Most every kind of ecological system is found on Kilimanjaro: cultivated land, rainforest, heath, moorland, alpine desert and, of course, the arctic summit. Although the snow caps are diminishing due to global warming, we could still see the white peak as we gazed at the mountain as we climbed. One of the most beautiful sights I encountered was the morning we first climbed above the clouds and actually looked down on a solid layer of white fluff that confirmed we had truly climbed above the entire world as we know it. It was then we realized that we were higher in elevation than when riding in the small plane that had deposited us at the Kilimanjaro airport!

But along with all the beauty was hard work. The climb itself was probably no more challenging than several mountains I had summited in the past. The difference was in the higher altitude. I remembered that even in the States, climbing the Rockies and Presidentials in CO, my headaches would begin at about 10,000 feet, and that held true on Kili. Most of the party was taking Diamox, prescribed to help us acclimatize as we climbed higher and followed standard mountain precautions. One does not summit in a straight vertical line, even if the trails were laid out that way. Paths twist, rise and fall, and each day the conventional wisdom for success is to gain elevation at a moderate pace and then come back down to sleep a few hundred feet lower so your body can adjust more gradually. Since higher elevations, particularly above 8,000 feet, have lower levels of oxygen and decreased air pressure, the body compensates by producing additional red blood cells for more effective oxygen transport. This, of course, takes time.

K.C. Armstrong: How did you feel physically during this long process?

Virginia Armstrong: Well, after 10,000 feet my symptoms progressed from headache to nosebleeds, nausea, and loss of appetite. This, I was assured by our tour guide, was normal. Then the swelling began—my lips were comically huge and my hands resembled baseball mitts. This did not disturb me though as I was again told by those with experience that this was simply my body adjusting. It is common to lose interest in food at altitude, but I vigilantly ate, knowing how important the calories were for the effort, and drank water continually, as this was also supposed to facilitate the process of building red blood cells to provide the body with increased oxygen.

It is difficult to determine who may be affected by altitude sickness since there are no specific factors such as age, sex, or physical condition that correlate with susceptibility. I didn't really understand this and felt confident that I was going through a normal process. After all, I was incredibly fit! I worked out several times a week and was no stranger to mountains or to physical challenge! Admittedly, I compared myself to other members of the expedition, some of whom did not lead nearly as active a life as I did. I trained hard for this, and I was going to see the top of this mountain. I really believe I would have been sensible had our experienced tour guide felt I was not acclimatizing successfully, but since he thought nothing was amiss, I was very happy to agree. After traveling halfway around the world to accomplish a goal, turning back would be a huge disappointment.

K.C. Armstrong: I mean, to hear a story like this is so awesome, Ma, you're really making my job easy. Tell us what happened next.

Virginia Armstrong: Finally, we reached our last staging camp just below Uhuru peak. This was it, and we all could just taste the summit! This is the point in the climb where some expeditions leave camp at two am with headlamps so that they reach the Uhuru summit just before daybreak. They are then the first to see the sun rise that day from the highest point on the continent of Africa! Our group, however, planned instead to leave at first light to make a later assent so we could spend a bit longer at the top once the sun was at its peak. At over 18,000' we were already well into the

Glacial Zone where life of any kind is scarce. The oxygen levels are about half of what they are on lower portions of the mountain and with the solar radiation during the day and gale force winds, this part of the expedition can be brutal.

I left the camp with the others, and the steep ascent was treacherous and exhausting. I felt this was a test of my will, and I would give a full effort. I didn't feel endangered, but all my fading energy was focused on being and doing, with thoughts of the glacial summit and little else in my clouding consciousness.

Each step became a lifetime of concentration and effort. One step. Breathe. OK. Now another. Breathe. "Pole, pole" (*slowly, slowly*) Hours later my bowels let go, and I had no strength to step off the trail. Step. Breathe. My headache was no longer recognizable, nor was the swelling of my hands and lips or the itching of my entire body. Step. Breathe. Sip of water. Step. Breathe. Nothing left on the outside. Only the inside and the weak, stringy voice: Step. Breathe.

And then I saw myself on the ground. From somewhere came a raw, gasping sound as if someone clawing out of an enclosed tomb for a single breath. People. A mask over my nose. Nothing. The gasping was closer and louder.

I saw a beautiful multicolored backdrop to my thoughts . . . first and rapidly, thoughts of regret: my children won't have a mother. I won't see my grandchildren grow. Then, as quickly, a deep calm: a beautiful serenity impossible to describe.

"It's OK. All is as it should be. They no longer need you."

A peaceful thought of my mother who had left this life six years earlier. She was smiling, and I felt the warmth of her love and of my large, extended family in an all-encompassing embrace of pure and immeasurable bliss.

At the very same time I could see myself surrounded by porters turning dials on a machine with a nozzle ending in my nose. Something was supposed to happen, but it didn't. My mouth formed the word "Gamow," indicating the inflatable pressure bag promised by our tour director. He looked disgusted, shook his head and walked away.

At that moment I felt the comforting arms of John Mtui, our native guide, pick me up and lean me against his legs in a semi-sitting position. I watched as though I was a mere spectator as he tightened the mask from the portable oxygen suitcase on my face and switched a dial. I felt a sliver of air seep into my lungs. The beautiful vision and cloud of peace which had enveloped me began to fade, and I felt another breath of air, and another. That's when I realized that the gasping noises I had heard earlier had been coming from me.

John's expertise brought me back to where I had been—the final ascent of Kilimanjaro with a party of climbers who had been encouraged further along the path so as not to witness what was happening below. I was told later by one that when she looked back there was a rainbow overhead where John and I sat, my back resting against his legs, and his arms around me for support.

I climbed Mt. Kilimanjaro; I did not summit Kilimanjaro.

K.C. Armstrong: First of all, I commend you for doing something so brave, amazing and challenging, but I can only imagine someone who has been successful at anything she put her heart into, such as her family, her career and helping other people, the cards would say that you deserve to go out with this victory. It's almost unfair. How hard was the come-down? This was not normal for you not to be able to do anything you tried. Did it ever feel to you like an insult? Or a loss that you didn't deserve? Especially at the time where life is supposed to be celebrating you, this was supposed to be a gift to yourself and the one time you do something for yourself, you . . .

Virginia Armstrong: The distinction is without any importance. Sometimes life takes us by surprise, as does death. You know this. When we are focusing on the tree limb, the forest overtakes us. We set a goal not comprehending that it is only a piece of a greater lesson which swallows our myopia. The vision wasn't the mountain. Rather, like Hemingway's frozen leopard, or the snow caps on Kilimanjaro themselves, the vision was a symbol of something much greater. In my tunnel vision I never saw the implications of my self-imposed challenge.

The challenge was of discovery—of using all I had experienced and become to grow closer to my potential and purpose. The mountain was a vehicle, driving me to heights of global awareness and newfound dedication.

K.C. Armstrong: What were you feeling at the time?

Virginia Armstrong: As I awoke from the grayness of near-death far above the cradle of civilization, the epiphany struck in a forceful yet whispered breath:

"It's not about the mountain. It was never about the mountain."

And a picture of the yearning smiles, the waving hands, the intense eyes of those children reaching out to me the day before from an impoverished classroom in Moshi, at the foot of the Great Mountain, appeared in technicolor. "Teacher! Teacher! Teacher!"

K.C. Armstrong: How did you handle that?

Virginia Armstrong: Coming back was difficult; I couldn't decide if I really wanted to. But that knowing whisper implied that I *should.* There was, simply, more to do. I felt tears on my cheeks and a repeated phrase in my consciousness: *It was not about the mountain. It was never about the mountain.*

K.C. Armstrong: What were you supposed to learn from this experience, besides to never do this to your kids again, especially the real handsome one.

Virginia Armstrong: Both my children are handsome.

K.C. Armstrong: Okay ma, I said no more jokes, I'm sorry, this is a serious question.

Virginia Armstrong: Something had drawn me to Africa; I'm still not sure what. But the lessons from the Great White Mountain remain. We must climb to the heights of our best selves. Our visions, dreams and goals are fluid. I tried to help those beautiful children. I returned to Africa and spent more time at the Kibo School. I visited orphanages and street children there and stayed at a wonderful hotel staffed entirely by troubled boys rescued from the streets of Arusha. I helped one achieve a university education and exchange messages with him regularly. I have worked to improve conditions in education in Moshi and have hosted members of the Kenyan Maasai tribe in my home in the USA. I have run fundraisers and booked presentations for these modern warriors to raise money for education and safety in their villages. I have fed a single mother and her children in a desolate mud hut surrounded by treacherous desert. I've created pro-bono websites for African friends struggling in business and helped sponsor schooling for young Maasai girls who bravely reject early marriage and FGM. I have buried one friend's brother and sent money to the family of another's widow. I have supported John Mtui's eldest daughter through university.

K.C. Armstrong: As you've had time to reflect, what have you learned?

Virginia Armstrong: I have learned that poverty and need are with us always and everywhere. We all have so many opportunities to make a difference in the world. We do not have to travel to other countries. Sadly, there is also hunger and need in our own towns and cities. Wherever we are, we can feed the hungry, clothe the needy, educate those seeking advancement.

K.C. Armstrong: What is the lesson you might like to share?

Virginia Armstrong: *Self-knowledge. Passion. Self-confidence. Take care of yourself. Take care of your loved ones. But then, isn't each individual just as entitled to health, safety, and opportunity as you and I?*

Perhaps this is my true lesson from the experience. It was not about the mountain: it was about the children. But all children represent our collective future. There is nothing more important in the world and for the world than giving each child his or her birthright: safety, education and opportunity. This has become my calling, and I hope it will also be a priority of anyone who can hear us.

K.C. Armstrong: *How have you taken this lesson into your everyday life back in America?*

Virginia Armstrong: Since the African adventure I have continued to dust the milk bottles, so to speak. But it isn't only African children who are denied a chance to make their own choices without worrying about their basic human rights being met. Since Kilimanjaro, I have delivered a packed motor home of clothing to Native American children in South Dakota. Collected clothing locally for families struggling economically. And volunteered in soup kitchens across the US. According to the World Food Program, approximately *795 million* people in the world last year did not have enough food to lead healthy, active lives; that's about *one in nine people* on earth. Children in every corner of the world deserve safety, food, clothing, shelter, and education. And they need the love and concern of our entire global community to enable them to make sound choices that will determine the future of civilization.

K.C. Armstrong: What would you like to say to our listeners?

Virginia Armstrong: Compassion doesn't have to be reserved for the starving children and tortured animals you see on TV commercials. We've all done charitable acts—large and small—and know how we feel afterward. True accomplishment and inner peace come from helping those around us. This is what will create a better world, and each of us can profit immensely for being part of that change.

Just a reminder; sometimes we are so immersed in our own situation we forget to take the time to deliver the unworn clothing at the back of our closet to a local church, put some canned food into the collection bin, volunteer at our children's school, or sponsor a poor child who can't afford an education. Small acts can bring us together as a local and also global community and can foster understanding and embracing each other's individuality.

It is, first and last, about the children. For all of us.

You may visit www.leavingfootprints.org for information on booking Maasai tribal members when they tour the US or for other fundraisers, including setting up Lost and Found programs in your local schools. Contact Virginia at info@leavingfootprints.org.

CHAPTER 6

―――――――――― ◇◆◇ ――――――――――

Jeanne Beard

Phone: 1-800-266-7013 **Email:** jeanne@nationalautismacademy.com
Address: P.O. Box 5395, Wheaton, IL 60189 **Web**
Address: *nationalautismacademy.com*

Jeanne Beard Intro

Jeanne's story is special to me. I have a favorite aunt and uncle whose daughter was born, nearly 25 years ago, with an undiagnosed developmental disability. There were so many aspects to my niece's disorders, but I'm sure she was there somewhere on the autism spectrum. Sadly, Kelsey left us when she was only ten years old.

I can only imagine how challenging it must be as the parent of a special needs child. There must often be heartache and disappointment right there beside joy, acceptance, and gratitude. That's why Jeanne Beard has such a powerful effect on me. When I first interviewed this kind woman, I saw such obvious love of family and desire to help other parents who were going through what she had experienced. I once heard someone say that we are all born with a specific mission, either to teach something or to learn something. There is nothing in the world more amazing than this mother's love, and she is able to teach us a whole lot.

Interview

K.C. Armstrong: Alright, guys. This is WMAP, World's Most Amazing People, and you already love my next guest, as she has been on the program before. Jeanne Beard exemplifies the depths of a mother's love. Her interaction with her autistic son has affected not only her own life, but the lives of others she is now helping as a result of her experiences.

So, I'm psyched to bring back my friend who will talk about her experiences with the autism spectrum and her two sons, one whom has Asperger's and ADHD. This is such a devoted mom, and we can all learn a thing or two from her. So, it's my honor and privilege to introduce once again the inspiring Jeanne Beard. Jeanne, how are you today?

Jeanne Beard: I'm terrific. How are you KC?

K.C. Armstrong: I'm doing great. So, let's refresh our audience here. You have an organization called The National Autism Academy. What is your goal there, and what was your basic idea when you set it up?

Jeanne Beard: Well, the National Autism Academy is a parent and professional training organization designed to encourage, educate and support parents of children on the autism spectrum and also provide quality education and practical information to the professionals that work with these children but have not had much professional training.

The NAA is a resource that I developed because it provides answers to many questions I had when I was first introduced to the confusing world of autism. I couldn't find the kind of support I needed as a parent to validate my experience of raising boys that were a little bit different. There were times I wondered if I was crazy or if this was really happening—why does my child behave this way? One minute my son would seem so typical, and then the next minute he couldn't tie his shoes! I didn't have any resources to help me find the answers I needed. And so, I developed the National Autism Academy to make information available to support the understanding of parents and professionals as they live their life and work with individuals on the autism spectrum.

K.C. Armstrong: That's so helpful. And you really threw yourself totally into this pursuit, and I applaud that; I think it's awesome. It must be baffling to notice that your child isn't responding the way you expect but not know why. You referenced something called "the spectrum." What is that?

Jeanne Beard: The basic diagnostic manual, the DSM-5, came out in May of 2013 and has described autism in a new way. Everything is being lumped under a new umbrella called *autism spectrum disorder*, or ASD. And so, autism and autism spectrum disorder are general terms for a variety of complex brain development disorders. The impact on each individual is so broad they had to call it a spectrum; autism impacts each individual differently. There's a saying that "if you've seen one person with autism, you've seen one person with autism." So, the basic idea of a "spectrum" allows the room to interpret a lot of different behaviors under the same umbrella.

K.C. Armstrong: I understand. And did you tell me last time that people with Asperger's are toward the high end of function on the spectrum?

Jeanne Beard: Yes. Asperger's Syndrome is a common name for high-functioning autism. So that would indicate that the individual is verbal and potentially very intelligent. These people can appear very "normal" in many ways and yet they still have the social disability piece that comes with autism. My son falls under that category. When they changed the diagnostic manual (the DSM-5), in 2013, they actually eliminated that name as a diagnosis, but many people still relate to Asperger's as an indicator that the individual is very high functioning but on the spectrum.

K.C. Armstrong: Now are ADHD and ADD under the spectrum of autism?

Jeanne Beard: ADD and ADHD are not technically in the diagnostic criteria, but there are some characteristics that are very, very similar, and those diagnoses are frequently pre-cursors to the diagnosis of autism. I believe there are a lot of children on the autism spectrum that are also diagnosed with ADD, attention deficit disorder, or ADHD, attention deficit hyperactivity disorder. Those two conditions are relatively similar. My son was first diagnosed with ADD and then re-diagnosed with Asperger's Syndrome as he got older and it was clearer how he was being affected socially. For many people, diagnosis is a process.

K.C. Armstrong: Yes, I can see that. Now that we're seeing more and more information coming out about this, what can parents look for in their own kids that might give them an early warning that, hey, my child might be on the spectrum? I think you told me that lack of eye contact is a signal. Can you expand on that?

Jeanne Beard: Lack of direct eye contact is one of the most commonly recognized signals, but it is not diagnostic. Many people with autism can make eye-contact. There are a number of other indicators, especially sensory hypersensitivity on some or all channels. Having few or no friends, displaying extreme behaviors, and lots of anger are common, too. Also, if your child loses their language, just stops speaking at some point, that would be a giant red flag. If that's going to happen, it is typically between the ages of two and three.

K.C. Armstrong: Right. That's what happened to my little cousin. She was a bit younger than that when she stopped speaking.

Jeanne Beard: That's a huge red flag. You know, I think the easiest way for me to explain all this is to tell you the story of my own son.

K.C. Armstrong: Please.

Jeanne Beard: My son wasn't diagnosed until he was going into 6th grade, junior high school. For a long time, we couldn't identify exactly what was happening with him. It wasn't until that age that the autism really became apparent. As a young child, he had eye contact and some sensory hyper-sensitivity issues, but not a lot. If your child is always covering their ears because noise is too loud, or it's too bright, or clothes are too itchy, or if your toddler takes off their diapers because they don't like the feeling of them, these are things to notice. My son had some of that, but not really enough to raise a concern when he was young.

When he went to preschool, the teacher told me he didn't respond to her like the other kids. She would call all the kids together to do an activity, and my son would not respond to that request. He would just continue to play rather than join the group. Children not on the autism spectrum would see the other kids sitting down for story-time or a project and think, "Oh, everybody else is doing that. I better do it too." My son didn't have that reaction. He saw the other kids but continued doing what he wanted to until the teacher would specifically say to him, "Kyle, I want you to come over here and sit down." And then he would. It's not that he wasn't compliant; it's just that he wasn't able to pick up social cues like the other children.

As he entered first grade and had to stay seated at a specific desk, that was very difficult for him because there was so much activity going on around him. I remember the first-grade teacher saying to me half way through the year, "I lost my happy Kyle! I don't know what happened to him." That is not what any parent wants to hear. He became increasingly anxious and depressed during first, second and third grade. At that point he was treated for anxiety and ADHD since we had not yet gotten the diagnosis of autism. So, we limped through grade school. Kyle's academic performance was well below his capabilities, and he had very few friends. He didn't get invited to birthday parties.

Keep in mind that we could have a regular conversation with Kyle at home. If I asked him specifically, "Please take this over here and do that with it," he would do that. So, I wasn't seeing a lot of real difficulty at home in terms of behavior. But as he became older and started into junior high school, he became very angry and upset to the point where, in October of 6th grade, he wasn't willing to go to school at all. I couldn't get him on the bus. That is when we saw a big change in his behavior, and that is when the psychiatrist finally diagnosed him with Asperger's Syndrome. He was so angry because he just couldn't handle having a locker, changing classrooms, writing down homework assignments, and managing new types of social activity. It was all completely overwhelming for him.

K.C. Armstrong: That's where the anxiety came from.

Jeanne Beard: Right. He was trying to be like everybody else, but it just didn't work for him. He said to me, "Mom, I'm different from everybody else." And he was, but we didn't know why or how.

K.C. Armstrong: He was smart enough to know something was going on. He realized that something prevented him from acting like everyone else. That must've been so frustrating for him—and for you as well.

Jeanne Beard: Yes, KC, it was very frustrating and baffling, and it's painful to watch your child suffer and feel bad about themselves. Kids would bully him and tease him.

Sometimes kids on the spectrum don't even know they are being bullied which makes them even bigger targets.

K.C. Armstrong: That's horrible. Bullying is the last thing any kid needs. So once Kyle was in 6th grade and had a diagnosis, what happens from there? Therapy? Medication? How does that work?

Jeanne Beard: Different families choose different options for treatment. We did choose to include medication in our treatment plan. Our pediatrician said very pointedly that "a child with no friends is the real tragedy," and he went on to explain that if we gave him medication for the ADHD component, that would help him focus and concentrate, be better able to make friends, and also create a window of opportunity for him to be more receptive to therapy with a psychologist. It's really hard to do therapy with an individual who doesn't have the ability to pay full attention. That helped me get over the difficulty accepting medication as part of the treatment for my son.

K.C. Armstrong: I see, right.

Jeanne Beard: Once Kyle was medicated for the ADD and was able to focus better, we were able to engage him in social activities. After trying 3 therapists that didn't know how to help us, we were finally able to enroll him in private therapy with a psychologist who worked exclusively with autistic children, Dr. Tim Wahlberg. The experience level of the professional is so important! So many therapists don't have any training in autism and have little practical experience, so be sure to seek out someone with expertise in the area of autism or you won't see the results you are hoping for. That's one of the reasons we offer training to professionals at the NAA. Therapists that focus on treating anxiety and ADHD symptoms, but are not addressing the thinking and behavior that is part of autism, are putting a band-aid on the problem and not really addressing the main issue, which is teaching functional skills.

In addition to private therapy, Kyle participated both in social groups at school and in social groups with other kids in the private therapy setting. He actually learned to communicate better and to relate to what common social behavior looks like by attending these social skills groups.

Today Kyle is 22 years old and has an amazing group of friends he can relate to and who relate to him! If he came into the room when you and I were having a conversation, you wouldn't even know that he wasn't just another typical 22-year-old. He appears to be very "normal," which he is in many respects, even though he still has challenges that are related to the autism. Those challenges become apparent when he has to do new tasks or more complicated tasks, particularly anything that requires social interaction like driving, going to the drive-through at McDonalds, or going in to Walgreens and buying something. Those types of activities are still very difficult for him although I see him progressing all the time.

K.C. Armstrong: That's great! Now let me go back to when you were working with the doctor with therapy and medicine, I guess like Ritalin or Adderall. What type of changes did you see? What do you recall was the first change?

Jeanne Beard: The first change was definitely the increase in focus. I had held out as long as I could as far as medication goes. Handing your kid a handful of drugs in the morning does not feel good. It's not something I wanted to do. I kept thinking we could find a natural way—maybe with diet. None of the things I tried gave us any relief, so regretfully and kind of hesitantly I said okay to trying the medication.

Once he started in therapy with Dr. Wahlberg, we saw Kyle more able to manage his schoolwork. He could bring an assignment home and with enough prompting, could actually get the homework done. Many children on the autism spectrum feel that school work is for school, and home is not for schoolwork. They get upset with the notion that homework is schoolwork that has to be done at home. They like to keep home and school separate, and the majority of them hate school.

K.C. Armstrong: Yeah, I had the same feeling. I agreed with him 100% in school and still do.

Jeanne Beard: Yes, so the focusing was the first benefit we saw. Sometimes medication is necessary for people to live more comfortably in their own skin and be happy, and that was really the bottom line for us. That is every parents goal, I think, but when we are dealing with autism, we need to be more flexible about what that "happy life" might look like. It may not include a house in the suburbs, a spouse, family and a dog. People with autism may be more comfortable living in a small apartment, without any one else to complicate their lives. Thinking about our kids failing to fulfilling our dreams for them is a bitter pill to swallow for some parents – it makes us feel like we are failing as parents. My dream for my son is that he's able to be functional in the world and be comfortable with himself. I want him to be happy.

K.C. Armstrong: Right. That's the thing that every mother wants regardless if the kid is 2, 20 or 50 years old. One thing I always wanted to ask you is if there are unfounded stereotypes about people with autism and Asperger's. It seems many people think that people with Asperger's are brilliant at one thing and also very introverted and introspective. Are these stereotypes still widespread?

Jeanne Beard: Yes, absolutely! There are still stereotypes of children sitting in the corner rocking and drooling—that's a very old and outdated stereotype. Autism today is different.

K.C. Armstrong: Hopefully we don't hear that one much anymore.

Jeanne Beard: I agree! People on the autism spectrum aren't always introverted as the stereotype suggests. Experts report that the ratio of introverted to extraverted is about the same as the general population – about 50/50. There are a lot of very high functioning people on the autism spectrum, who want to have friends, but don't know how to do that successfully. Being in a relationship with someone with autism can be a lot of work, and those relationships can feel like very high maintenance, so they often don't last.

It's also not uncommon for someone on the spectrum to have an area of special interest. My son happens to absolutely love Pokémon and anime and Japanese drawings, and he's actually quite an excellent artist, although he doesn't want to share his art with anyone. Other kids have different interests. One boy I heard about was totally into stoplights! He knew how much a stoplight weighed, how high they hang, and how long the light lasts, and every other fact about stop lights.

K.C. Armstrong: Wow!

Jeanne Beard: People on the spectrum have different areas of special interests. Some of them have an interest in trains, some of them dinosaurs. It could be history, it could be any area. They can literally be savant-like in a certain area and have so much information that it's shocking but not be able to tell you what month of the year we are in!

K.C. Armstrong: That's so interesting. Do you think the best way to manage autism is to try to find a magic bullet that's going to cure it or to embrace it? What do you think?

Jeanne Beard: Well, this could be a controversial statement, but in my opinion, there is no magic bullet, nor should there be. I really think that the way to live our best lives, if they include autism, is to understand it, accept it, get as many tools and tips as we can, particularly as a parent. That's the way to be the most effective parent, and provide the best chance for our children to lead successful lives. Our greatest gift we have to offer is to nurture our child to be their best self. If we're spending all of our time trying a different diet or some other kind of solution to make the autism disappear, that's probably not going to work, and it's certainly not embracing the child for who they are, nor helping them to cope with life. I asked my son one day, "Honey, if there was a pill that could get rid of the autism, would you take it?" His answer was so sweet. He was probably 17 or 18 then, and he said, "No, mom, give it to somebody who really needs it, because I like me."

K.C. Armstrong: That's awesome. You must've melted when you heard that.

Jeanne Beard: I did! I loved that answer. And you know what? It clicked at that moment that, as parents of children with autism, we're trying to use therapy to make our children fit into the rest of the world, and the message that some children might get is that they're not okay the way they are. It's a very tricky thing to help coach a child into becoming a functional adult, but to also let them know they are loved for who they are—accepted as they are; they're not broken or sick or bad or wrong. These kids are smart, and they understand what you're saying. They know how to interpret if you're constantly correcting them or telling them they are doing something strange. I think that it's really, really an important thing for a parent to provide that deep acceptance to their child and that the child realizes that.

One day when I was completely frustrated, I called up Dr. Wahlberg and said, "I don't know what to do! I can't manage all the things he needs help with! I am overwhelmed. If I can only do one thing today for my son, what is that one thing I should do?"

And before I even got the question out, he shot back an answer I'll never forget. He said, "Provide your child with unconditional love." That's what they all need—to know they are accepted for exactly who they are, that's unconditional love. So as important as it is for us as parents to work with our kids to help them be functional, we also have to be careful not to give our kids the wrong impression about who they are and how much we love them. Autism is part of them, but it does not define them any more than red hair, blue eyes, or being left handed defines them. But because of the kinds of therapies and adjustments we're always trying to make in their lives, they could easily get the wrong idea.

K.C. Armstrong: That was such a thoughtful response by the doctor. That must have lifted you up a bit.

Jeanne Beard: It helped put all the challenges into perspective.

K.C. Armstrong: Thank you for sharing these personal and awesome experiences so others know they are not alone. Now, tell us about your book *Autism and the Rest of Us*.

Jeanne Beard: Well, the subtitle is *How to Sustain a Healthy, Functional and Satisfying Life with a Person on the Autism Spectrum*. I did most of the writing in 2014 and 2015; it was published in March of 2015. I'm proud to say we hit Amazon bestseller status last summer. It can easily be found on Amazon.com.

K.C. Armstrong: Nice! That's really awesome, Jeanne, and I hope our audience picks it up for themselves or someone they know who could benefit from your insight. I read that you said one time, "Having a child with autism requires parenting on steroids." That's an interesting statement.

Jeanne Beard: Yep, parenting on steroids for sure! Again, you know that all parenting is hard, but parenting a child with autism is ten times as hard. I talk to 20-30 new moms per week, and the number one thing they say is that they are exhausted from the constant demands and stress. It's not the same as having a child without autism. For example, we can try to teach our children with autism to brush their teeth, and it could take a whole year for them to learn to do that on a regular basis independently. They are not motivated socially the same way as children who aren't on the spectrum. You can simply say to a child not on the spectrum "Look, if you don't brush your teeth you're going to have bad breath and cavities, no girls are going to like you, and you're going to be in a lot of pain." That's probably enough to get them to brush fairly regularly.

With a kid on the spectrum, that approach may have no impact at all – they simply don't relate to the social pressures that motivate the rest of us. You can ask them every day, "Did you brush your teeth today?" And they may even say yes, but unless you saw them do it, you may not know if it actually happened. So, it requires a tremendous amount of persistence and patience, as well as compassion. We have to be really strong as parents, and really strong and emotionally healthy within ourselves to be able to sustain that kind of parenting intensity for the long term. As parents, we need to learn to sort out what is the autism and what is the child, which is very difficult to do until you have had some training in how the autism influences thinking and behavior.

K.C. Armstrong: So here you are, Jeanne, a very successful professional, working in sales for a huge company in Chicago, and raising two kids, one with demanding special needs. I'm sure you've met many challenges along the way. And you've mentioned several. Are there any other times you can recall being especially frustrated? I'm sure other parents who are experiencing similar situations would like to hear about this.

Jeanne Beard: There are just so many day-to-day frustrations. Of course, any child can be frustrating, but I think our kids can deliver even more worries. For instance, I cannot get my son to understand the value of going to school. I can't convince him that schooling, or lack of schooling, will shape his life. He doesn't put the pieces together to see the long term. Even today as a college student, he is moving at a very slow pace, but still moving. Of course, I'm happy with that, but it's hard for him because he doesn't see the long-term benefit. He still wonders why he has to go to school, why he should care what the teacher says or what grades he gets. Those are all social motivators that someone with autism doesn't naturally find motivating. I have to reassure him that graduation from college means he's going to get a job, which means he's going to be able to make money, which means that he's going to be able to support himself and so have some freedom to do what he wants to do.

Trying to explain all that to him in a way that he understands is very difficult. He is very linear in this thinking and doesn't have that kind of executive functioning ability to project long-term outcomes resulting from his behaviors today.

Another challenge that comes up and is incredibly frustrating is when you think your child has grasped a concept you've been working on for a long time and then, a month later, we're right back to where we started. This happens to parents with kids on the spectrum frequently; just as we start to think we are seeing real change, it suddenly slips away and we find ourselves right back in the same old pattern. Change is a challenge for people with autism to the point where they fight it, which is one of the reasons it is parenting on steroids.

K.C. Armstrong: I appreciate your honesty. Along those same lines, when you think of your son's future, what do you worry about the most?

Jeanne Beard: Well, I don't know if everyone is like this, but in those dark moments, my mind certainly goes to the extremes. Sometimes I sort of freak out and think of that guy that weighs 600 pounds and has to be taken out of his house in a crane . . . Or I think of a hoarder who's got stuff piled to the ceiling, or someone who is homeless and living under a bridge. Of course, that is just my crazy imagination, but it's driven by a very real fear of the unknown. I don't believe anything like that is really going to happen, but the fear of "what will become of him when I am not here?" is very real. There is a saying that most parents of children with autism want to "live one day longer than their child."

All of us worry about what's going to become of our children. But when you see your child not progressing like other children, it's scary and discouraging. We can't help but compare ourselves to others. For example, my neighbor's son recently graduated from law school. I am so totally thrilled for him; he's such an amazing young man! But at the same time, I recognize that my son is only a few years younger than he is, and we are still struggling to pass one or two college classes a semester. So, milestones raise our sensitivity and can make us sad. As much as you love people around you and love to see their accomplishments, it is a painful reminder that maybe I'm never going to get that kind of results with my kids. As a parent that's discouraging, sad, and frightening, and it makes a lot of us feel like we are failing as parents.

K.C. Armstrong: I appreciate your candor, Jeanne. Let's move on to great experiences you have shared with Kyle. Can you share some strong bonding moments?

Jeanne Beard: Yeah, you bet! One of my favorite memories which really showed me his true nature happened when he was two and a half. We had just moved into our house on a little cul-de-sac in the suburbs. Kyle was dressed up for Halloween, and his dad was going to take him trick or treating around the neighborhood while I handed out candy to the children coming to our door. So, Kyle had his little pumpkin bucket ready to go, but he had a major meltdown when his dad tried to take him out of the house. We couldn't figure it out! Kyle wouldn't leave until he could take candy from the bowl I had to give to our trick or treaters and put it in his bucket. I told him, "No, Kyle, you go out to get your candy from other houses." But he wouldn't leave the house until I finally put a handful of candy from our bowl into his empty bucket. Confused, I watched from our porch as he went to the house next door and they rang the bell. Our neighbor answered and reached over to put candy into his bucket. But Kyle backed away, took candy out of his bucket and put it into her bowl! All he knew is that Halloween was for giving candy away. He didn't put all the pieces together about what the customary way of doing that was.

This showed me the he has an absolutely loving and generous and wonderful personality. It was the sweetest thing. But it also helped me realize at the time, that he didn't have the ability to automatically process all the elements which make up social interactions. Autism is, ultimately, a social disability. I am proud to say that today he *knows what he doesn't know,* and he can ask questions to find out what knowledge he is missing! That's a huge accomplishment for someone with autism!

K.C. Armstrong: How sad to think his innocence and generosity could have been misunderstood if you weren't so perceptive!

I'm wondering if that naiveté prevents him from being aware of some of the dangers in the world. Do you worry about that?

Jeanne Beard: Absolutely. You're bringing up a really good point because individuals with autism often don't have a total grasp of a potentially dangerous situation, even though they may look like they do. I heard the story about a young man on the spectrum who was driving and got a flat tire. He took his car to the dealership and the dealer sold him a new car! They didn't fix the tire; instead, they sold him a new car because he was an easy mark. I don't know if the story is true or not, but this is the kind of thing that could happen.

K.C. Armstrong: There are always people out there who will take advantage of others. We know that.

Jeanne Beard: That's right. Another story is about a young man who was pulled over by a policeman. He was not paying attention the way the cop thought he should, and the policeman didn't understand that he was autistic or what that meant. The officer reached through the driver's window to turn off the ignition key, touched the kid, and totally freaked him out. The young man went nuts, and so the officer called an ambulance, and the kid wound up strapped to a gurney on his way to the hospital. There are many situations where individuals with autism can be misinterpreted, misunderstood, misled and cheated. And so, to answer your question about worrying about his naivety, the answer is yes, of course I do. The good news is that my son is somewhat cynical and doesn't easily trust anyone. So, I think that may work in his favor in some respects. But he can still be unaware in ways that can make him a target, which is true for many people with autism.

K.C. Armstrong: I see. Now tell me, if you don't mind, the effect having a special-needs child has on family dynamics. I imagine, for instance, that this could have a huge impact on a marriage. I guess it could either bring a couple together or do the opposite.

Jeanne Beard: Well, yeah, the statistics on divorce in families with special needs children are astronomical. I think the last one I saw was that 80% of those marriages end in divorce. I've noticed as I've been working with families that very often when there's a child on the autism spectrum in a family, there may be a parent also on the spectrum. That may contribute to some of the marriages not working. Being married to a spouse with autism has a whole different set of challenges attached to it, and I address that in my book.

The bottom line for all of us surrounding a person with autism is that we need to be very strong and practice a lot of self-care. We have to know ourselves and our needs and take care of ourselves while accepting the other person, whether that's a spouse or a child, even when they may not be able to connect with us emotionally in the way we want them to. And if our need for emotional connection is greater than our spouse's ability to deliver, that can certainly create a situation which ends in divorce. It takes a lot of knowledge, willingness and understanding to manage a long-term relationship with a person on the spectrum.

The stress and exhaustion of managing a child with autism that I mentioned before can really take a toll on the parents' relationship, too.

K.C. Armstrong: Well, I really have to applaud your honesty. You're very brave to put yourself out there like that, and we can all feel what a compassionate, amazing person you are. This concern for others led you to share your experiences and knowledge in this area. Beside *Autism and the Rest of Us: How to Sustain a Healthy, Functional and Satisfying Life with A Person on the Autism Spectrum*, I believe you also have another book?

Jeanne Beard: The first book I worked on was Dr. Wahlberg's book, *Finding the Grey: Understanding and Thriving in the Black and White World of Autism and Asperger's*. I was on the writing team for that project, and it was an awesome learning experience for me. Since his time was so in demand, it was my job to capture the content from his notes, talks, and asking him questions, to make sure that the concepts were clearly articulated for other parents and professionals. Dr. Wahlberg gave me hours and hours of his time when he was driving or late in the evenings on the phone to explain things so I could fill in the outline I had created from his notes. It was a world-class education for me, and it helped me to understand so much. Today Dr. Wahlberg is the Clinical Director at the National Autism Academy, and a good friend.

K.C. Armstrong: So, you worked on two books and now have set up the National Autism Academy. Let's talk about that.

Jeanne Beard: I'm so excited about the National Autism Academy! The idea is to provide a resource for parents and professionals that will shorten their learning curve and give all of us a place to create a hub of quality, clinically-based information, so we can benefit from each other's experiences. When I was first navigating the challenges of autistic behaviors, diagnoses and choices, I really felt that there wasn't an uplifting, encouraging, positive outlet for parents to share information. My hope is that, as the Academy matures and as we gather even more information, we'll have a body of knowledge that will benefit insurance companies, the government, other organizations, parents, pediatricians, professionals and ultimately benefit the long-term outcome for children with autism all over the country. Through the Academy, if I can help just one person be as successful as possible, I'm happy about that. But if I can change the world, then I'm *really* happy!

K.C. Armstrong: That's awesome, Jeanne. A great resource for everyone, no matter what the nature of involvement with autism, since we are all involved in some way, large or small: *www.nationalautismacademy.com*.

Hey, Jeanne, a little fantasy here. Say, considering all you have just told us, a genie appears and offers to grant you three wishes. What would they be?

Jeanne Beard: Hmmm. First, I would love every person on the planet to understand what autism is, how it impacts a person, and what the individual with it is going through. Instead of expecting the child to be force-fit into the social environment, I would like understanding people to help the social environment meet these kids part way. Just enough so they can be comfortable.

K.C. Armstrong: Got you. Number two?

Jeanne Beard: Well, I would like to help parents and children secure the knowledge and services needed to allow children with autism to create and fulfill their own individual dreams. To be able to dream their big dream and actually have all they need to make that happen. I do believe that parenting a child on the autism spectrum can be as joyous an experience as parenting any other child if we have the right perspective. Again, these kids aren't broken or sick, they're just different. If we can really embrace the difference and provide them with the tools they need, then we can really make a difference. And I just talked to a mother this morning who is having extreme frustration with the county and the state she lives in, trying to get some resources for her three-year-old daughter. So, I would love to see the resources provided that would help parents enable their children to live out their dreams.

K.C. Armstrong: Ok, that's two. A third wish for the genie?

Jeanne Beard: I think the last wish would go back to the housing thing. I would love to see what I call win/win/win housing. That's a housing environment where individuals with autism have their own private space, but with the support they need. So maybe that would be a condo environment where there are meals provided, or maybe laundry services provided. Whatever support is necessary to allow each individual to live their most independent life and would then allow parents to feel confident that the child would be safe once the parent is gone. I mean, that's a big fear for a lot of parents. As we get older, we're looking at what will happen to our child when we're not here anymore. That's a giant fear. So, I would love to see an international housing program happen that would satisfy the needs of children, young adults, and adults, as they grow on the spectrum.

K.C. Armstrong: Great answer, so I'm going to give you another fantasy! You get a donation of a million dollars to the National Autism Academy. How will you use it?

Jeanne Beard: I would start with the housing movement. I'd gather up enough parents with enough kids that we could come up with a solution together that would provide long-term housing and care for all the diverse kids as they age out of the system. I think we can create this in a way that serves other populations, too. Maybe graduate students at universities who want to understand the population, or widowed mothers that feel complete when they have someone to care for and so would not have to be alone.

Another thing I would love to see is respite services for parents who have children who can't be left alone for even five minutes because they might injure themselves or cause major problems, like set the house on fire. Parents of those kids need an opportunity to step away from their children long enough to have an adult conversation or even just take a nap. I'd also like to set up some sort of longer-term respite care for families, so they could leave their child for a weekend and go away or be able to participate in activities that aren't well-suited to their children's needs.

K.C. Armstrong: I understand. But, Jeanne, here's the reality. You don't need the genie's three wishes, and you don't need a million dollars from that anonymous donor. You just need to keep doing what you're doing; learning, researching and helping others to understand the big world of autism. By creating the National Autism Academy, parents and professionals now have a resource that didn't exist before to share their questions and concerns. That's a really great contribution. What is your primary advice to parents with a newly diagnosed autistic child?

Jeanne Beard: Thanks, KC. To answer that, I would say that if you suspect your child has autism, acknowledge the fact. Nobody wants to think that their child isn't like everybody else. It's a tough suspicion to face. But it's so important to find out early, the earlier the better. If it is autism, ignoring it won't make it go away. The more intervention you can provide, the better chance your child has of living their best life, and isn't that what it's all about as a parent of any child? If your child has a problem using his legs, you'd get him a wheelchair, right? Because children with autism most often do not have physical disabilities, it's a little bit harder for many people to accept that something is legitimately different about them. But these kids are wonderful human beings, and my hope and prayer is that each one of them finds a way to live safely, happily, and fully. It is very, very rewarding to watch your child grow and become the person he or she was meant to be in spite of any challenges.

We don't hear it very often, but there is a ton of hope. Many of these kids are very able to find their way in life. We have many very successful people in the world who are on the autism spectrum. Jim Henson, Thomas Jefferson, Albert Einstein, and the list goes on and on –Google it!

So, I just want to encourage people who are living with autism to take care of themselves. Find a bigger purpose, find a spiritual way to make peace with the autism and then enjoy watching a flower bloom because that's really what can happen with kids on the autism spectrum.

K.C. Armstrong: Amazing, Jeanne. In just a few words, what have you learned from your son?

Jeanne Beard: Oh, I've learned an immense amount. I've grown in patience, acceptance, openness, and willingness to honor each individual for who they are. You know, the list goes on and on of personal attributes that I have gained from working with a child with special needs. There is such a gift in it for a parent who is willing to accept and embrace that gift. And I so love both of my children and completely honor my son for his strength and his willingness to get up and face the day—every day—in spite of the difficulty he lives with.

K.C. Armstrong: Well, you and your children are obviously blessings to each other, both teaching and learning together, and that's beautiful. Jeanne Beard, thank you for a great interview and for being, without a doubt, one of the World's Most Amazing People.

Jeanne Beard: Thank you, KC. I loved it, every second of it.

CHAPTER 7

Lito Mason

Lito Mason Intro

I was always impressed when I saw my Western Kentucky University teammate, Lito Mason, touch the football. This wide receiver had acceleration and speed like a Ferrari attached to a rocket! As a rookie quarterback, I remember Lito being so fast that if he ran a Go route, by the time I dropped back to pass him the ball, Lito would already be in the end zone with his hands on his hips—waiting like he had been there all day.

I'm just fooling around, but Lito's story is as spectacular as his athleticism. As a teammate and friend, I saw that if Lito was determined to do something, it would get done.

He took this attitude into one of the toughest social problems many inner-city kids face across the country. Lito could have done what most of the young men did in the projects he grew up in. He could have been another underprivileged kid swallowed up by gangs, drugs and the streets.

Instead, he made a promise to himself to take the road less traveled.

After seeing people shot in the back of the head running away from a crime scene, after his father was beaten to death by police, and after growing up way too fast, Lito found a way to get a college football scholarship, and now he dedicates his life to being there for at-risk kids. He sets an example for them that, just because you may start off on your own 1-yard line, if you avoid getting pulled to the ground and tackled for a loss—you will see an opening that you can follow Lito Mason through—to the goal line.

Interview

K.C. Armstrong: I've known Lito for about 10-12 years, and we're going to hear his story today. This interview is a very, very brave thing for this man to do, and I have nothing but respect for him. Guys, with no further ado, it's my honor to bring to the program Mr. Lito Mason. Lito, how are you today buddy?

Lito: I'm getting through it, fresh off neck surgery. Tough surgery, but I'm getting through it.

K.C. Armstrong: Yeah, so are you laid up now, or are you home?

Lito: I'm home now. They removed two discs from my neck, took some bone off my chest, and put it where my discs are supposed to be. Too much of that football.

K.C. Armstrong: Is that where it came from, Lito?

Lito: I think it was. It started out with one disc, and it started creeping up my neck so four of the seven discs in my neck are screwed up. They fixed two of them, and then in February I'm facing back surgery for the third time. But I keep fighting, Life's a journey, you know what I'm saying, not the destination.

K.C. Armstrong: That's true, and that's what Lito is here today to talk about. And like I was saying in the intro, Lito, I think you're so brave for doing this, and I really appreciate it, man.

Lito: Oh, absolutely. You know, everybody goes through something. One of the things I live by is, I never judge a man by the way he chooses to survive because I'll never walk one moment in that man's shoes, not one. So, how can I judge him when he goes on to be a doctor, dope dealer, pimp—I don't care what he does. I can't judge him. It's left up to God to judge him.

K.C. Armstrong: That's true.

Lito: So, to me, I treat everybody the same—and that's with respect.

K.C. Armstrong: That's the golden rule right there. So, Lito, let me take you back a little. You were born early 70's, and you were named after a character from an old Western. Who was that?

Lito: Yeah. It's kind of interesting. They didn't quite have a name for me. I was born one of four children, two brothers and a sister, and it's weird—because their names are really simple. Kevin, Ian and Joy. Some real simple names, right? Well, we don't know where Montelito came into the picture. So, from birth, it was a challenge, and coming to find out, Montelito means "little mountain." And it seems like my whole life all I've been doing is climbing little mountains. That's all I do. Seems like I got to work ten times harder than the next person to achieve a simple good, but it never stops me. I mean, just like the predicament I'm in now, you know, I wasn't expecting this. I knew something was wrong, but I wasn't expecting to have major neck surgery.

K.C. Armstrong: You're no stranger to procedures like this. Isn't it true that when you were born you were bow legged? It seems so strange to me because Lito in college could run like a 4-2-40; he was one of the fastest guys I've ever seen. But you were born bow legged. Talk about that.

Lito: Okay, so, yeah. Basically, I was born with my legs so bowed that the doctors wanted to break both legs to straighten them out, that's how bad they were. But my mother wasn't going for that; I guess she just could not see anybody breaking her child's legs. So, I'm sure you have seen the movie Forrest Gump and those little braces he had to wear on his legs, right? Well, I had to get fitted and wear those braces for a little while when I could first walk, plus some weighted shoes. And eventually I just kind of grew out of it; they straightened out. So, from the time I could walk it was a challenge; however, I came through it. One of the legs stunted my growth, messing with my growth plate. So, I am the shortest person in my family. I'm not supposed to be this short, but I am. Everybody else is 5'10" and above, while I'm 5'8." Even my mother is 5'7" and my father was about 6'1."

K.C. Armstrong: You're saying that from the start you had a lot of these little challenges, and this was no different than anything else?

Lito: No, no. I was what they called or considered a "free bleeder." Like I would just go outside to play, and my nose would bleed as if somebody punched me. It was crazy! So as a child I used to have to drink this thing called liquid Sudafed to stop my nose from bleeding. It tasted like dishwashing liquid with some sugar in it, so it was gross—you can't even imagine. It's crazy because I overcame all of that, and I kept on fighting and thought everything was going to be pretty normal.

But when I was about five years old, five or six years old, I'm going through life, you know, thinking everything is all right, and I remember being down at my grandfather's house, and there was a lady down there. I never told anybody this story, so this is kind of a first for me. That lady molested me.

K.C. Armstrong: Who was this? What was her relationship to you?

Lito: She was a friend of the family. And, you know, some people would think, that, being a boy, that would just be a rite of passage.

K.C. Armstrong: Not at five years old, it's not.

Lito: Right, so it's something I never speak about. But let me tell you, I can still visualize the lighting in the room, I can still tell you what it felt like and I remember who it was—but I never spoke of it. Never, ever, ever spoke of it. I just let it go or whatever because it's like I said, nobody was going to believe me. And then people would've said, "Well, that's good. You got your first little piece of P."

K.C. Armstrong: Yeah.

Lito: You know at a young age, well, that's not cool. And it led to some other things. I started acting out a little bit when I was around ten years old.

K.C. Armstrong: Lito, before you get there, let me not gloss over this. I hate to do it to you, but it might even be cathartic for you to get it out. This was like a Christmas party or something, right? Talk to me, how this person gets to you. Be specific about what happened, if you don't mind.

Lito: Okay, so basically it wasn't a Christmas party, it was just kind of routine to go down to my grandfather's house. And my grandfather was like a modern-day Robin Hood, right? I hate to put it like that. I don't want to throw my grandfather under the bus, but he was kind of a John Gotti of my little town, I'll just put it like that.

K.C. Armstrong: Okay. So, he ran things in your town.

Lito: Right, right, right. It was no secret to anyone down there, but he took care of people. And this lady just so happened to be staying up in one of his rooms. And, I mean, I knew her; she was not a stranger to me.

K.C. Armstrong: How old was she, you think?

Lito: I was only about five or six years old, she's about, I think, eight or nine years older.

K.C. Armstrong: Okay, so she was like a high school kid?

Lito: Right. Basically, I was up there running around, playing, and I can remember her calling me over to the side of the bed. She's laid up in the bed, and she just told me to stick my hand under the covers. You know what I mean? I didn't know what I was doing. I didn't know what that was all about, didn't even know what it is. Do you understand what I'm saying?

K.C. Armstrong: Yeah.

Lito: But I remember being told don't tell nobody.

K.C. Armstrong: When this is happening, you're only five years old. Did you know that she was having you do something wrong?

Lito: I knew any type of secret at that point wasn't a good secret, but I didn't say anything. I mean, you kind of got to understand the environment that I grew up around, which I'll get into with you. You got to understand—like when I started school, every morning when I got up. My granddaddy owned a liquor store right in front of the apartments that I grew up in, so when I walked out the door to get on the bus, there'd be five or six winos sitting outside waiting for the liquor store to open up.

So, these old perverted dudes would be whistling at my mom and, you know, there wasn't any role models around there. There just weren't. I grew up in the housing projects, and so you would think, "Aw, that girl let you do that. Hell, I wanted to do that." You know what I mean? So, it wasn't like they don't view child molestation toward a male the same as they did a female, especially back then. Today they take that more seriously, but it definitely led me down the wrong path. I mean, to the point where in 5th grade I got caught with condoms in school. Didn't even know what a damn French tickler was, but I had one. Ended up losing my virginity at 12.

K.C. Armstrong: Yeah, because you were sexualized at such a young age. When these horrible things happened to you at five years old, you had nobody to tell. Did you think about telling your brothers?

Lito: I didn't tell anybody. I kept it to myself and I don't know why. I knew the lady, I still know her. She's still alive. She wouldn't admit it to this day if I said anything about it, but I'm telling the story, and so I'm not going to throw her under the bus.

K.C. Armstrong: Of course not. As a five-year-old you didn't understand what was happening, though you said you knew that it was wrong because she said not to tell tell anyone. Lito, how did it make you feel when you thought back on what happened? What did you take away from that whole situation as a five-year-old?

Lito: I took not to be alone with adults like that anymore. When you grow up around the street and things like that, it's not a Third World Country, but you learn things fast. You don't have time to slow down, and there wasn't such a thing as going to counseling, especially when you're poor, and we were the worst kind of poor. My mother worked; we didn't get public assistance and stuff like that.

K.C. Armstrong: Was that just a pride thing for your mom?

Lito: I don't know what it was. I know we could have used it. So, she worked a full time job, but so did other people in the projects. People on public assistance would pay like, maybe $50 a month for rent, but we had to pay the full price.

K.C. Armstrong: And there were four kids.

Lito: Right, it was four of us. Me and my older brother have the same father, and my younger brother and sister—they have the same father.

K.C. Armstrong: Okay.

Lito: So, we never lived with my father. I loved the man to death though. Don't get me wrong.

He was just doing his own thing.

K.C. Armstrong: Okay, so you didn't have a male role model, a male living with you guys growing up. There was no father figure.

Lito: The streets kind of raised you. Back then it really took a village.

And so everybody, including criminals, were part of your village. You'd be surprised at what you can learn from someone who may look like they have a disparaging life, but you don't know what led that person to get there. That doesn't mean they're stupid. That doesn't mean you don't listen to them; they were still elders. So, regardless, you didn't disrespect them. I mean, it was weird. You come up around this and you still learn to have respect for your elders, so you didn't pick on them or whatever. They kind of looked out for me. They weren't necessarily good role models, but they were real quick to tell—like when I'd skip school. You know, somebody was looking out for me when my mother had to go to work.

K.C. Armstrong: That's interesting, Lito. Now the neighborhood that you grew up in—was there a lot of violence? As a young kid, did you see a lot of the underbelly, as they say, of society?

Lito: Yeah. I spoke about my grandfather and that juke joint, right? That was a place he owned behind the projects. Also, the liquor store in front of the projects, right? So, you grew up, and it was kind of weird because you know how you might say this person's role model might be a fireman or a policeman? Well, we looked up to criminals. Who was the best criminal in the neighborhood, you know? Who would fight the best? Different things like that. Those were the things you admired. And, unfortunately, it's a vicious cycle. Fortunately for me, I knew where I didn't want to go after getting in trouble a few times.

K.C. Armstrong: Yeah, you were in elementary school. And how far apart were your brothers?

Lito: My little brother is ten years younger than me. My little sister is four and a half years younger, and my oldest brother is just a year and a half.

K.C. Armstrong: Okay. So, you and your older brother went to the same school?

Lito: Yeah. Our middle school was from the 6th through the 8th grade. When I got into middle school he was in the 8th grade, and I remember they used to have a running joke about me, him and his buddies, to see if I was out in the hallway getting a paddling.

K.C. Armstrong: So, you were a troublemaker?

Lito: Yeah. I didn't want to be there, and a lot of it stems from not being watched. No one was paying attention. I was that second to the oldest child, so I'm maybe the child that's supposed to know better, but here I was, kind of the black sheep. You know, everybody else is doing well, but nobody was paying attention to me, so I got away with a lot of things.

K.C. Armstrong: Got you. But what was that like growing up? Did you feel less-than because, as you said, you looked up to people who could fight the best and who . . .

Lito: Well, for the most part I got along with everyone in the neighborhood and we looked out for each other. I just had to fight a couple of bullies to gain respect so people left me alone. For instance, one guy kept picking on me so I picked up a horseshoe and was ready to hit him with it. When he saw that I would stand up to him, the bullyinging stopped. That's basically what happened and then I didn't have to fight no more.

And I started break dancing. Well, that led to some other things that weren't necessarily good. Running around with the wrong crowd—like I've told you, my granddaddy owned a liquor store. So, you know, we started drinking some gin . . . no we started out with Wild Irish Rose. And if you let the winos take a couple sips of your liquor, then they would go get you a bottle from my grandfather's store.

K.C. Armstrong: Were you around ten at that point?

Lito: More like 11 and that's when it really started hitting me. Once I was 12 and going into the 7th grade, the streets were more important to me than school. I just felt like teachers didn't care, so I quit going. I'd skip school two to three times a week. And I had a neighbor whose handwriting was just like my mother's, so she would write my excuses.

K.C. Armstrong: When you were skipping school, were you out break dancing or were you just hanging out?

Lito: I was out break dancing, I was out stealing, I was out doing everything I wasn't supposed to have been doing. We kind of got into a little criminal activity. Things that juvenile delinquents with no guidance do, and it's crazy because I hate a thief. I really hate that. I have no respect for a thief. I was once that kid, though. But I have to look back and say I was that kid with no guidance. Nobody was paying attention to me. I'm 12 years old, I'm walking in the door on a school night at midnight. You know what I mean? I was all over my little town. I knew so many people and . . .

K.C. Armstrong: And you grew up quick, even lost your virginity at 12, right? You want to talk about that?

Lito: Oh, yeah. Yeah, I lost my virginity at 12l, and when I look back on it, it's disturbing because she knew exactly what she was doing. She was only like a year and a half older than me, but I didn't know what cumming was; I thought I had to pee. You know, so I had no idea what was happening. When I didn't know what I was feeling, I jumped out the window! So, later on in life it dawned on me that this young lady was probably molested herself. There's no way she was supposed to know so much at her age.

K.C. Armstrong: Yeah and there's a direct correlation of that experience for her with the one you had, being sexualized at such a young age yourself.

Lito: Absolutely. And she knew, and she invited me and my partner over to do that. So, after that it was interesting. I ended up, like I said, break dancing. I was fortunate enough to break dance and get in a nightclub and things like that. So, at 12 years old I saw my first stripper, butt-naked stripper. This lady she had these big ol' whomp whomps, boy. I'm talking big ones and she lit two cigarettes on them and balanced them on these big long nipples of hers.

K.C. Armstrong: Oh my god.

Lito: It was crazy. I hope I can say nipples on your show.

K.C. Armstrong: Yeah, you're alright. This is informational so, it's alright. (laughing)

Lito: Okay. So, she's on the stage and you know me—I'm 12 years old I'm looking up like I ain't never seen nothing like this before in my life. Once again, you tell your mama you saw that? So, I never told my mama. But about that time I started getting caught doing stupid things by the police.

For instance, we needed a ride home from a skating rink one time; we couldn't find a ride and we lived really far. On the way home we ended up breaking into this little store. We were hungry and had no money, so we stole a bunch of candy and dumb stuff like that, you know, juvenile stuff. On our way home, the police tried to stop us and, well, we took off running. The cop chased us all down and said, "What are y'all running for?" Now, understand our pants legs are stuffed with candy and things we stole from the store. I mean *stuffed*!

The officer said he'd give us a ride home, and we made him drop us off on the backside of the projects. Anyway, I know the next day when he got the report because we left candy all in the back of his squad car! That was sort of the turning point for me, plus we got caught stealing a bicycle. That's when I was done running around the streets.

Unfortunately, through all of that, I ended up failing the 7th grade and had to repeat the grade. And I was really trying. I really tried to avoid the street. So, I went out for the football team. Well, I'm a street kid, don't know anything about football camp, never played organized sports. When I went out, the coach told me that I waited too late, I couldn't play football. So, here he was, not knowing anything about my life, but pushing me right back to the streets.

K.C. Armstrong: Right, and then the other thing, Lito. Didn't you also need $25, but your mom just didn't have it to give to you?

Lito: Oh, that was when I tried to play Little League. She wouldn't give me the $25 to play Little League Football. She wouldn't try to find it, but she didn't understand either what I was doing. Throughout that time I wasn't getting caught doing anything. If she's listening to this interview right now, some of this information is brand new to her because I never got caught, alright? So, I went back to the streets, hung out, break danced, and still had a little popularity.

But the next year I wanted to go out for the football team. I ended up managing the team my second year of 7th grade, but they put us in this classroom for delinquents. It was like an experimental class-room—like something you see on "Lean On Me" or something like that. I don't even know if it was legal to do this, now that I look back on it. But the kids were too smart to be in learning disability classes but too much of a disruption to be in a regular class.

K.C. Armstrong: I see.

Lito: So, they corralled us all into this one class, and it was embarrassing. That's when I started learning my lesson. This was when it was too late to go out for the football team, but I swallowed my pride and became a water boy. Well, it wasn't the coolest thing in the world to be a waterboy.

K.C. Armstrong: Yeah, I was going to say that. Were you looked down upon by the guys on the street because you weren't around, and you weren't playing; you were just a water boy?

Lito: Well, it wasn't a cool thing, but I stopped hanging around those guys who started really getting into some serious trouble. I really wasn't ever much of a follower, I was a leader. And when the crew started doing stuff that I wasn't interested in, that's when I started to do my own thing.

At that point I felt like my mom didn't even care about me anymore, so that's when I decided to try something different. I wanted to be a part of something, so that's where football came in. The Coach wouldn't let me play, not knowing the talent that I had, so I thought I'd get on his good side by became a water boy. Washing jocks, getting the guys water, you know, was a humbling experience. Then I tried to go out for the basketball team. The way it worked, if you played football for the coach then you were automatically expected to play basketball.

K.C. Armstrong: Right, right. Same coach for both sports.

Lito: I wasn't given a chance to play, so I sat on the bench for two weeks. But the next year was a clean slate. I showed up at camp. Well, here I was, a freshman with raw talent but I didn't know how to run a play, didn't know positions. I loved football but didn't know a single thing about it.

K.C. Armstrong: Right.

Lito: And I got to play against the former coach, who had switched schools. I ended up having two interceptions and two touchdowns against that coach that wouldn't let me play.

K.C. Armstrong: That must have felt good!

Lito: I wasn't showing off against him, but I had raw talent. He came to me the next year and said, "You should come out to the county and play for me, and I'll make you a star."

I looked at the man and said, "I'll be a star right here. I don't need to go to the county." The same man had almost pushed me back out to the streets where I would have lost my life, and things were changing too. That's when crack cocaine started moving into the area. So, I went on playing football. I ended up quitting my sophomore year for a week because I got tired of walking to practice twice a day. Turns out the coach was looking for me though I had no idea he was paying any attention to me like that. I mean, hell, that was my first year. I wasn't nobody.

Anyway, he got me into the classroom and asked me what I was going to do with my life.

I told him I was going to join the military, but he said, "You're going to go to college and play football." Now, you gotta understand, I was 5'1" and one hundred fifty pounds. So, somebody you never played a down for tells you that you're going to go to college and play football—you really going to believe that?

K.C. Armstrong: No, no, no! That must have been like the guy was speaking another language.

Lito: Right. And I'm from the projects, so I know nobody that played college football and did all of that. But I believed him. First guy that ever believed in me, and he was right. First of all, I played enough quarters my sophomore year to actually letter. By the time I was a junior I started getting these recruitment letters out of nowhere, and it was really shocking. And, you know, lights are on the road, things are starting to turn around for me, looking good.

K.C. Armstrong: Lito, let me stop you right there for a second. Where was your father during all of this? Did he go to your games?

Lito: No. My dad was a former drug head and an alcoholic. He was kind of a spoiled child so, like I said, imagine the Gottis and their children. You know how spoiled they were and how they lived off the image of John Gotti, so to speak. I'd hate to put him up there because my granddaddy wasn't that big, but he was pretty big.

K.C. Armstrong: Yeah, I know what you're saying.

Lito: He lived off of that image but he was around. He always called me his number one son. That's where I get number one from. People thought that I wore number one because I thought I was good. No, it wasn't that; it's because my dad called me his number one son. He had seven children. He was there for me. Matter of fact, when I decided to get serious about football, he gave me $25 to go to Wal-Mart for a set of those concrete 110 pound weights. Remember them?

K.C. Armstrong: Yeah, of course.

Lito: Listen to this: so I bought those weights.

I had to catch the bus to Walmart, get the weights, put them in a basket and push them home. When I got home I didn't have a weight bench; so what did I do in the middle of the night? I went down to the playground, and you know those big old park benches they have—like picnic benches? My uncle had some tools over at my grandmother's house, so I took the bench apart, took the wood to my grand-mother's house, and I build a weight bench out of that bench from the park.

K.C. Armstrong: Incredible!

Lito: I wasn't going to let anything stop me from this goal of going on. I lifted weights all summer long by myself. I stopped running with people; I wasn't with the crew anymore. When I showed up at camp, they all were trying to figure out why was I so much stronger than everybody else. I had dedicated my life to changing, and I got to that point of change. I was about to make my dad proud. He finally did something for me that was worthwhile, buying those weights, and I wanted to make him proud. And then I got a knock at my door from one of my neighbors telling me that my daddy had just gotten killed.

K.C. Armstrong: Oh no.

Lito: They took my daddy. He had gone to jail on a DUI, and back then you were only supposed to be kept in the drunk tank for 24 hours—until you sober up.

My daddy told me a long time before that if anything ever happened to him I should get this tape to the FBI, but I just thought he was drunk. I didn't know anything about that. I thought, you know, he's just drunk-talking or whatever.

K.C. Armstrong: What, like a cassette tape or a videotape?

Lito: I don't know. I never got to the tapes because I didn't believe him.

And I didn't realize how much the police were messing with my father and whatever the heck was going on.

K.C. Armstrong: What do you think happened, Lito?

Lito: They beat him to death. I got a letter from a girl in jail that was there at the time. They kept picking at him while he was in there, and they kept telling him he's supposed to get out, he's supposed to get out. And the girl said they kept messing with him. And they started beating on him and they dragged him down to the basement. They beat him to death and hung him with a belt.

K.C. Armstrong: Oh my God.

Lito: Yeah, so, you know, here I am. Things are starting to turn around in my life, and the person who called me his number one child is gone. You know, they just took him away from me like that. It was kind of incredible. I didn't really know how to think about it. I didn't know how to deal with it. I was about to walk into something, uncharted waters, that nobody in the family, nobody in my neighborhood had been down. And so, I just looked at it as God calling him home. Like I said, my dad was an alcoholic, so I had to look at it as if, well, what if he had stayed alive and I would have been in a car with him? We would have been in a car wreck which might've left me a vegetable. So, God doesn't make mistakes. We do, you know what I'm saying?

K.C. Armstrong: Yeah.

Lito: When you get called home, you just get called home.

Yes, it's a horrible thing to happen from an earthly standpoint, but it's a beautiful thing that happened when God said, "No more." So, I relied on my faith and I didn't let it beat me down. What's interesting is I had to take off a couple days for grieving and going to the funeral. Well, I ended up losing my starting cornerback position. I lost my position just because I had to go to my father's funeral. It was like one thing after another just kept on trying to push me back out onto them streets. I mean, it was just kind of crazy.

K.C. Armstrong: But Lito, looking back, where did you get this determination and perseverance? Where did you get that from? Did you get it from your mother, or did God give this to you? Was it just inside you? What do you think?

Lito: I think it was God-given and also my grandmother's strong influence. She was a very, very, strong woman, my grandmother. She never let you see her sweat, and she never gave up. It seemed like there was nothing ever too big. She used to wash clothes for rich folks and different jobs like that. She took care of her father up until he couldn't walk and see anymore. She was just a strong woman, so I would always listen to her, even when no one else was listening. She was very wise. Hell, she used to think she was psychic. You know, I think that's where the determination came from. And my grandfather was a no-nonsense kind of man. So, I don't know, I just wanted something different.

I saw so much bad stuff—like I could remember as a child this dude getting shot in his head and running through the projects. Dude got shot in the head and he's still running. He ended up dying on this lady's porch, right? So, you see this kind of stuff around you and you got to think that, man, this can't be life. So, I knew from the time I was a freshman in high school that that wasn't going to be my life. I couldn't stay there, I could not stay in my town because I knew too many people, and I was going to get sucked in the wrong way. And that's what ended up happening, so I was just determined after I started getting in trouble not to go back down that road.

But I can tell you, I always try to follow through with things, you know? So, that's kind of how my life has gone. Because when you quit one thing it makes it much easier to quit something else. So, I just stopped quitting. I just started persevering and overcoming. I don't mark dates. I couldn't tell you the date my grandfather died. I quit marking things in my head because I don't want to relive it. I wanted to keep moving on. The people that mark things are looking for a moment in their life to hang on to. I don't want to hang on to those moments because they just set you back. So, I kept pushing, so I'm terrible with dates. If you ask me, well, when is such and such's birthday, I couldn't tell you.

K.C. Armstrong: Well, that's a great way of thinking. It's really, really an intelligent way of looking at things.

And thank you for that. But, Lito, take us through this now. You had worked your butt off all summer. All of a sudden you get the news that your father died, that he was beaten by police. How do you view police after that?

Lito: I didn't have a problem with police. I had a problem with the men that killed my father.

K.C. Armstrong: Good point.

Lito: The police didn't kill my father; that badge didn't kill my father. It was some bad people with a badge that killed my father. So, I didn't have a problem with police. I wasn't scared of police. I didn't white knuckle my car every time one got behind me or anything like that because I wasn't doing anything wrong. I did worry at times when I was with family.

I just kept on doing right and had the right people around me. My high school coach became like my father figure and ended up saving my life actually. Because I found somebody that believed in me, that gave me a chance instead of pushing me right back out there where it was easy. It would have been easy to sell dope out there in the streets. Who couldn't do that? So, that's always going to be there. It would have been easy to stay at home and get a job at one of the plants. Who couldn't do that? Everybody did that. I was always different from birth.

K.C. Armstrong: You were destined for something else. You always thought there was something big for you. So, you started doing great in football, you're going to class when you can, your coach put it in your head that you could do it and you're getting all these letters— and then you get offered a scholarship.

Lito: Right. I actually ended up getting offered ten Division One scholarships.

And that was crazy because I couldn't pass the ACT! So I thought well, shit, I guess college won't be the thing, but I kept working with my school teachers. Once again, I wouldn't give up. You gotta understand when I was doing all that skipping school I wasn't learning what I was going to see on the ACT. I didn't have that in my mind, so I had to overcome that obstacle. I scored like 5 points below passing the first time. I started hanging after school with my geometry teacher and she prepared me, and I ended up passing that bad boy! At the top of my list was UCLA, University of Kentucky, and Memphis State University (now the University of Memphis). And those were the schools that I was really, really interested in going to.

I ended up signing with the University of Louisville. They really had me. My host, Earnest Givins, liked me. I'm in the first round, you know. He's riding around in a drop top Mercedes Benz saying you can be this guy right here. And I was like, well, shit, I guess I can.

You know what I mean? If he can do it, I can do it.

K.C. Armstrong: That's true. Now, Lito, check it out, so you're in school and you move around to a bunch of different places and you finally get that piece of paper, a college diploma. What do you do after that, and how are you feeling to be the first person in your family, in the community with people that you grew up with, to have a college degree?

Lito: Well, this was interesting. You know, I ended up going to Western Kentucky University with you guys. Western football meant more to other people than it did to me. All it meant to me was just to get that paper.

K.C. Armstrong: Right.

Lito: I had a chance to play in the NFL World League or whatever it is before college. But I turned it down because while somebody else was paying for school, I needed that paper more than I needed to play some more football. And I was tired. People didn't understand my story enough to know that I had nothing to go back to. Say I played in Europe and got hurt. I would have to come back home and try to figure out a way to finish and pay for school. And so, I got that paper, and it was like nothing could stop me. I had overcome the odds because I didn't think I was going to live to see 21. That's kind of how it was with me. I grew up around enough stuff that said, "Hmm, you go back home, you going to be wrapped up in the wrong thing." So, I got that paper and got a job at a psychiatric and addiction ward for the next eight months.

K.C. Armstrong: That's awesome. That's giving back because you know what it's like to have just one person believing in you.

Lito: Absolutely. After eight months I packed up because I met my future wife, my ex-wife now, at Western and told my mother I was leaving town. She didn't believe it until I pulled up with a trailer, packed, and left. If I say I'm going to do something, trust me, I'm going to try to do it. I might have a lot of things get in front of me that stop me from progressing as fast as one might think I would. But trust me, I'm working on it. Just like getting you this story. I knew I had surgery the next day, but I wanted to get you the story that I promised I would.

K.C. Armstrong: That's right. You're going under the knife and you wanted to make sure that you hit the deadline. So, this is something you carried through your whole life. And then how does it happen that you move to Idaho, working in, what, law enforcement?

Lito: Well, actually, I moved out there and worked at a psychiatric and addiction ward, and at the same time coached high school football. Then I moved on to work with developmentally disabled sex offenders. Very, very challenging work. Again, I didn't judge the guys so I excelled in the work. I went on to become a qualified mental retardation professional. In time I kind of burnt out on that. My wife wanted to stay at home with the children (I had my first child at 30). And she wanted to be at home for the first five years, so I gave her six years. I ended up opening a nightclub out here, actually. So, here I am in a state which is 2% African American, and I was able to open one of the biggest nightclubs in the area.

K.C. Armstrong: Sounds like your grandfather talking right there.

Lito: Right. It was the dream, so I did that for a few years until I decided it was time to get out. The state was messing with me, running kids up in there, trying to take my liquor license, and all kinds of crazy stuff that goes along with that life. Then I got into a car wreck, another setback, and I had to have back surgery. A young girl was on the telephone, smashed into the back of my car, and screwed my lower back up so bad I needed two back surgeries.

It seemed everything that I could think of was trying to hold me back, everything. But I fought back and got the back surgeries I needed. I moved and I ended up filing for bankruptcy on my business. I still didn't let it hold me down. Finally I got to working in juvenile detention, so I'm still giving back to the community. I want to work with people; all I know is people. If you put me in front of a forklift or something I couldn't tell you what to do. But put me in front of a group of people, and I can inspire them to do better. That's all I know. I don't know anything else.

K.C. Armstrong: There seems to be a theme throughout your story. Are you saying that in life you're going to have setbacks, and to get through you basically have to endure and keep going? This seems to be what you did your whole life. And now that you're a huge success story, how do you tell a kid who is in the same situation that you were that things are going to be alright?

Lito: The first thing you have to do is you have to have faith in something that you can't see, and that's God. When you have faith in God, you will see Him work. You won't understand how He works; you won't understand why He works. I'll give you a prime example. I remember one time I decided I was going to pray for a music studio. I had this little group and I was the music producer. I wanted a studio and I prayed about it. You know, they say be careful of what you pray for, but I wanted a Puff Daddy studio. God gave me a studio, but it wasn't a Puff Daddy studio. When I look back, He gave me the particular type of studio he did because I didn't know how to play an instrument, I wasn't going to be able to

213

dedicate my time, and the people around me weren't going to be any good.

He saw things that I didn't see. So, what good would it have done me to have a hundred-thousand-dollar studio? So, you gotta have faith and understand that things will work out. God will give you want you need. Say you ask for a million dollars. He might give you that million dollars, but he just might not give it to you all at one time. Now your income may change so over the next 20 years you get that million dollars.

K.C. Armstrong: I get it, Lito.

Lito: And so, you've got to have faith that things are going to work out. In order to learn something, you have to go through something. You've got to have faith in yourself because, at the end of the day, you're not going to lie to yourself. You'll lie to everybody else, but when you look in the mirror you ain't going to lie to yourself. And that's how you overcome: you keep on pushing. You can't let things set you back. I mean, I've had everything except the kitchen sink thrown at me to set me back. I mean, my ex tried to have me locked up over something stupid she knows good and damn well I didn't do. I'm a single father, I'm still a positive role model in my kids' lives, I'm having surgeries; I thought I was going to die a year ago. I was diagnosed with what they think is Lupus and so, you know, you just keep fighting. It's like you as a quarterback. You know how you're supposed to forget the last play?

K.C. Armstrong: Yeah.

Lito: You know they tell you that, but it's hard to do, isn't it?

K.C. Armstrong: Yeah, totally. You've got to forget the last play.

Lito: This is what I look at. I say at some point in your life you have to do a real self-evaluation. And what I mean by that is you have to look in the mirror, you have to look at yourself, and you have to say, "Am I doing the best that I possibly can?" If your answer is yes, then you're lying to yourself. And if you're going to lie to yourself, then you're going to keep on carrying excuses around. I did a self-evaluation because there was something going on with my children and when I had to ask myself was I doing everything I was supposed to do, I was doing a good job, but I wasn't doing *everything* I was supposed to. And when I got to that answer of what was wrong, that problem straightened out with my children. We think that because we provide food, we provide shelter, we do this, and we do that, we ain't running around here doing it the wrong way and we think that's the best that we can do, but it's not. A lot of times we forget that you gotta protect the emotional status of your children too.

So, I would say to any kid, just don't give up no matter what. There's always a hustle out there that you can do, and you don't have to do it illegally. It was so easy for me to turn back to the streets, but I didn't do it. I didn't go to the streets and start slangin dope. I can go to any city in America and find something wrong. I can find drugs and alcohol, but it's hard for me to go to any city in America and find a job, which is the right thing. So, doing the right thing doesn't always come easy.

I talk to a couple of my buddies that have been to the penitentiary and they talk about, "Man, I'm happy

215

to get back out here in these streets. Man, you know, things ain't coming away." I say to them, when you were sitting in that jail cell I guarantee you prayed to God to let you go and you was going to do anything he asked of you if he let you out. Now listen to you. He let you out, but he didn't say the road was going to be easy. See, we want the road to be easy. We want to dictate our punishment. Because you went to jail, okay, you think that that was it. No. It's up to God to dictate that punishment.

That punishment might last for ten years. You might go through a storm for ten years, you know, but what about the families you destroyed when you were selling them that dope, and what about those Christmases and birthday parties you've taken away from their children?. So, you know, you can't dictate your punishment and you just need to keep going. You can't give up, no matter who is in your corner. The best person in your corner is you. You can lie to everybody else, but you're not going to lie to yourself.

K.C. Armstrong: Yeah, Lito. We went a little bit over an hour here, but you were terrific, and you have so many inspirational insights that make sense. You're a tremendous interview, you're a tremendous person and you definitely are one of the World's Most Amazing People! And, by the way, thank you so much for sharing your story. I know you are helping a lot of people right now. And when this book comes out you're going to be helping even more. So, is there anything else that you want to say in closing?

Lito: Yeah. Life is a journey not a destination. Trust in your journey no matter what comes before you, no matter what obstacles. I mean, life does not stop happening because you got a problem. Just trust in your journey, and you'll get through it.

K.C. Armstrong: Great advice for all of us, Lito. Where can people get a hold of you?

Lito: Facebook, *Lito Mason*, I don't hide from nobody. I'm right there. WKU all day long.

K.C. Armstrong: That's right. Lito was one of my teammates and he's a great guy. And, dude, thank you so much for coming on the air, man

Lito: Hey, thank you bro, I appreciate it. Thank you for including me. I love you, bro.

K.C. Armstrong: Love you too man. Alright guys, that's Lito Mason. What a great guy, and what a great story. That was really uplifting. I hope you guys felt the same way.

CHAPTER 8

Laurene Hope

Laurene Hope intro

Laurene Hope is a beautiful, talented artist and performer from the United Kingdom, one of our very first guests in the new studio. I remember we were having technical difficulties the day she first called in, and I actually had to hook up my iPhone to the board to complete the interview. Laurene was such a good sport—patient, understanding, and above all, entertaining!

Beside her incredible vocal talent and community station Moving On TV, Laurene has accomplished what few have; she has overcome BPD (borderline personality disorder) without the use of prescription drugs. While this approach may not work for everyone, Laurene devoted herself to the Aylesbury Therapeutic Community and worked relentlessly to learn about her affliction and to come to terms with the many setbacks in her life. She has been so successful in taking control of her own health, that she speaks and shares information to help other people do the same.

Laurene has even flown to the US to visit us here at WMAP—twice! She is a favorite at the station and a WMAP ambassador wherever she goes. Our listeners especially love her ethereal rendition of "Danny Boy" and the mash up we made of her original "I Wish You Peace" with a piano rendition of Rammstein's "Weiderwine."

I think, above all else, I admire Laurene's courage. She battled and overcame the sorrows of abuse and abandonment to find her own health, happiness, and creativity. And she sacrifices her own privacy to tell others about her complicated illness, so they can learn from her ongoing journey.

Interview

K.C. Armstrong: Hey guys, this is WMAP, The World's Most Amazing People. I'm so excited, man. I've got to tell you, I get some great guests here on WMAP, but there's one person that very quickly became a fan favorite because of her honesty, the challenges that she overcame, and her motivation. I'm talking about Laurene Hope, an inspiration and a friend. Laurene is a bestselling author, artist, life-coach, speaker, and founder of *Moving on TV* and *Moving On Theatre*. She has extensive training as a classical singer and is a great proponent of the Therapeutic Community and shares her experience of meeting the challenges of Borderline Personality Disorder without medication. We've got so much to talk about here, Laurene. Are you ready for this?

Laurene Hope: Hi, K.C. It's half past one in the morning in England. So, after a crazy, crazy day with the weather here, I'm ready to pass on details of my recovery with hope and compassion so people know they aren't alone with their problems.

K.C. Armstrong: I can't wait to share your story here because it's just so incredible. And what you've done with your life, with your career, and your views towards other human beings are all just amazing. I think you're awesome!

Laurene Hope: Thank you. It takes one to know one, K.C. Armstrong!

K.C. Armstrong: Thanks, Laurene. Well, let's get some background and then discuss your healing within the Therapeutic Community and how it changed your life completely. To start at the very beginning, you were born in Israel?

Laurene Hope: No, no, no. I was born in Ireland—in Dublin City where the girls are so pretty.

K.C. Armstrong: But you moved a lot, didn't you? Tell me about that.

Laurene Hope: Well, I was born in Dublin as a third generation Jew. My family originally came from Russia, but then we moved to Israel when I was seven. I suppose my parents wanted to bring up their children as good Jews in Israel, but the move was a terrible shock to my system because I was a very, very sensitive child.

K.C. Armstrong: You were very sensitive, but maybe part of that was because you had borderline personality disorder—or is it bipolar disorder?

Laurene Hope: K.C., bipolar and borderline personality disorders are completely different illnesses.

Borderline personality disorder (BPD) is actually referred to as *complex needs disorder* now because it incorporates so many different types of mental illness. It's like a mix of every condition: a bit of OCD, a bit of depression, and more. Anyway, to answer your question, I wasn't diagnosed properly until about ten years ago although subtle signs, like the sensitivity, were always there. I had never heard of it before. I just knew that I was getting very very sick. My mother had died, I couldn't perform anywhere, I was feeling lost. I didn't know how to get on with people and work with them. And bit by bit my whole life just fell apart. My husband started working lots of difficult shifts, and I couldn't cope. I don't have children, I'm not performing, and I'd lost my mom. That was a big hole to deal with.

K.C. Armstrong: Didn't you tell me she was unloving toward you?

Laurene Hope: My mother, bless her, was a very unhappy woman who wasn't capable of giving much love. Unfortunately, when we went to Israel she became increasingly difficult. But quite honestly, I forgave my mom. I think she had serious BPD.

K.C. Armstrong: OK. And that can actually include bipolar traits, like the extreme highs and lows, right?

Laurene Hope: That's right, K.C. BPD is a mix of many different mental conditions so it doesn't fit a specific limited profile. You know, the rage I experienced drove people away from me. I was actually arrested on the street once while having a panic attack because the police didn't have a clue what to do with me. I was crying, and they said, "If you don't stop, we'll cuff you." And that's what they did! They threw me in a cell and told me I was mad and that I was going to kill myself. I didn't know what they were talking about. I was panicking, and I was scared. So, this was my life before I went into the therapeutic community. I was getting very sick, but I've never tried to self-harm. I developed an eating disorder as a child after my molestation, which was awful. But I've never ever tried to commit suicide . . .

K.C. Armstrong: Laurene, let me stop you for a second because there are so many things we need to discuss. We can't go forward until you explain what you just mentioned about your molestation. Can we talk about that? You told me off-air that it took place at a dentist's office.

Laurene Hope: Yes, K.C. I was between the ages of 11 and 12, and this happened at my dentist's office.

Mom and dad were working all the time. They neglected my sister and me, but I'm not blaming anyone. As I said, things were different then; they were very poor, and they didn't know any better. They just sent their daughter to the dentist.

K.C. Armstrong: Right. A parent doesn't think a child would be harmed there.

Laurene Hope: Of course not. But this dentist stuck his tongue down my throat and touched me all over.

Thank God I wasn't raped. But I did go through a lot, and as I said, I was very sensitive to begin with. At some point I left the office, but I went back. I had to do a lot of work on that to try and figure out why a child would go back to her molester. It was because I thought I killed him.

K.C. Armstrong: Did you know what was happening to you and that it was wrong?

Laurene Hope: I didn't understand what was going on. I was in total shock. I tried to explain to mom and dad. I told them the dentist kisses me. But, you know, in Israel everyone hugs and touches, and my dad didn't understand what I was telling him.

K.C. Armstrong: So, you didn't go into more detail—just that he kissed you?

Laurene Hope: Yeah, but it is very important to understand how a child's mind works, OK? This lunatic, this dentist, was having an orgasm, and as a child I thought he was dying! I ran out, and I thought I'd killed him, K.C. And I remember living with that fear, so I went back. And the minute he opened the door and I saw he was okay, I felt trapped. I felt like I had to stay because my parents told me I had to go there. Can you imagine they just kept sending me back? I carried the guilt of those experiences in my little heart for years and years. It wasn't until I started training in reiki with my husband and doing a lot of work on myself that I jumped up suddenly one day and thought, "Oh my God, I was abused."

K.C. Armstrong: Laurene, this happened when you were 11 or 12. Did that affect how you related to the opposite sex? That's about the time school dances and boy/girl socializing start: were you able to trust the boys around you?

Laurene Hope: Oh, I couldn't. See, I couldn't deal with my horrible experience. This is the thing. I numbed it completely. When my parents realized something was wrong they took me away from it, but then we never talked about it. My dad would say to me, "We're not going to say anything to upset your mother." That's how I grew up. You mustn't upset the dragon in the house, which she was. Bless her heart; mom was a wonderful teacher, but an absolute lunatic! Dad was like a mouse around her. He just said, "We've taken you away from him (the dentist) now. End of." Nothing else, K.C. There was no therapy, there was no talking. I had no one, so I turned to food.

K.C. Armstrong: You turned to food and blocked out the whole painful experience. I don't know if I've been watching too much Law and Order, but I've heard if you block something like that out, it could lead to borderline personality or other mental disorders. Is there truth to that?

Laurene Hope: Of course. Because I had blocked this all out, the Therapeutic Community later had to make me feel like a tiny child again; that's the process. They take you back, and that's when the magic happens. Suddenly I felt the pain that I had never felt, and I realized that it had nothing to do with me. My mom and dad were the idiots that sent me back there. I finally found inner peace because I had thought it had been my fault; everything was my fault, especially since I upset mom and dad.

My dad used to say, "You're giving your mother a heart attack." You're not allowed to be unhappy, you have to be a good girl, you mustn't cry because you're going to give your mother a heart attack. You know, my mother died of cancer at 80 and no one ever had a heart attack! And I was dad's aggravation. It was all me, everything was me.

K.C. Armstrong: Terrible. You thought everything that went wrong was your fault. And yet you had to put on a happy face for your mother or risk displeasing your dad. What a painful way to grow up.

Laurene Hope: K.C., my parents weren't cruel people. They were just very tired, very drained, very stressed out and very, very confused. Dad had PTSD from WWII and from growing up in an orphanage, and mom grew up in a very, very cold household. So, all my family are mad, you know. They're all screwed up, bless them!

K.C. Armstrong: I love that you're able to talk about all this with brutal honesty but also with your great sense of humor. Apparently, you've done a lot of work. I would assume that was really hard, when you had to go back and relive these things?

Laurene Hope: Well, the work I did was nearly two years in the Therapeutic Community. It was a nightmare because I didn't know I was doing anything wrong when I started there. Everyone comes in with their problems and starts triggering everyone else all over the place! A lot of them got into groups, and they pushed me out. It was like I was the scapegoat. But I was also creating my own pain. I mean, there were scenarios where I would say something cruel and everyone would run out crying. I didn't know what I said to make everyone upset because I had no empathy then whatsoever.

K.C. Armstrong: Well, nobody showed you any, so how could you understand empathy or compassion?

Laurene Hope: Exactly. I never experienced unconditional love from my parents or my family. My mother used to actually make fun of me for my eating disorder. She didn't have a clue, and there was no empathy at home. I felt completely alone with only food, singing, and my accordion for comfort.

K.C. Armstrong: Music was your creative outlet. Do you think that's why you're such a great performer today? Maybe performance is your way of communicating with people you don't know, a way of gaining acceptance. Does that make any sense?

Laurene Hope: I will tell you why I'm a good performer now. It's because I got sick. Without that I don't think I could have gotten the level of feeling to put into a show like Piaf in *Love Conquers All* [Roger Peace]. You can't show all that emotion without having gone through the depth of pain I've gone through. And I could do the breakdowns on the stage instead of on the street, and people would applaud me for doing the same thing.

K.C. Armstrong: I know you have received much praise for you work. Didn't you have a standing ovation on the very day your father died?

Laurene Hope: Yes, I did. I was notified that my dad had fallen, and my family was just allowing him to die. You wouldn't believe what I had to look at, what I watched. They took all his medication away from him. When my husband and I went to see him, there was no food. When I went to Israel to take care of him. I sat with dad, got him out of bed, and sang to him. I taught him how to talk again. It took me a long time to understand him, but by that time I loved my dad so much. He thrived because I gave him continuous love. He used to Skype me in England and cry sometimes. Martin and I celebrated his 95th birthday with him. And a few days before we returned to Brighton from Israel he said, "When you go, I'll die right quickly." I told him I loved and forgave him and gave him my blessings. He went within a few days.

K.C. Armstrong: I'm sorry to hear all that, Laurene, but you both found love and peace with each other in the end. How did the ovation come about?

Laurene Hope: What happened is dad died that morning while I was in Brighton, UK, and I just didn't know what to do. And then I thought, what would Maria Callas do? In the show *Maria* [Alma Bond], she performs the night that the love of her life, Marcel, was killed in a plane crash. And I thought to myself, well, Maria could go on, so I'm going on. And, dad always told me the show must go on. He told me that many times.

K.C. Armstrong: He guided you in that decision.

Laurene Hope: He always said that. And so, I went on, and I did the show of my life because I was raw. My dad had just died that day. When I cried it was for real. And when I sang . . . well, I got a 5-star review, the strongest review you can get in Brighton. And at the end the people were cheering, and I got a standing ovation.

K.C. Armstrong: It's kind of funny. I should tell the audience that Laurene and I have a personal relationship, and we talk all the time. Right before this interview I wasn't really feeling well, and I said to Laurene, "You know, the show must go on!" I didn't know that saying has such an important place in your life. Laurene.

Laurene Hope: Yes, K.C. It's amazing you should say that!

K.C. Armstrong: So Laurene, so far it seems like you had an awful lot of adversity growing up. Your mother didn't know how to show love, your dad and mom both put you, although unknowingly, into danger. Not only did they not get you help for your terrifying experience, but it sounds like they just wanted you to be quiet and move on like it never happened. So, you developed an eating disorder and eventually lost both your parents. So much more than anyone should ever have to go through! But you keep mentioning this "therapeutic community" which gave you your life back. Please tell us more about that.

227

Laurene Hope: Well, it wasn't until I entered a mental health group called the Therapeutic Community that I began to learn how to work with people, and just so much more. I knew I was mentally ill, and a psychiatrist offered me the opportunity to join this fabulous community when I told her I refused to be medicated. I was put in a group of about twenty seriously mentally ill people, and we were pretty much supposed to help run the group ourselves and support each other. We actually used tough love to deal with each other. There's a terrible stigma about BPD. People say we're liars, thieves, psychopaths, even murderers! And when I entered, the staff treated me the same way they would someone who actually was all those things. I thought it was going to be really easy, but it wasn't.

But the beautiful thing is, you don't have any medication. You're not allowed. The Community was a place where they took your medication away from you to get back to what made you the person you are. The only way to find out what's wrong with you is to have to sit with your pain and acknowledge it. We had a bell which we could ring every time we were in distress. I used to ring it all day until Mel, one of the staff members, asked me if I could try just sitting to face my pain. And I did. I was overwhelmed with panic, fear, nausea, everything you can imagine, but I didn't die. You know, nothing bad happened. I came through it, just sitting with it.

I started to learn how to live in the world and that every single person that you look at is your mirror image and your teacher. Slowly, instead of blaming everyone and feeling that they're punishing you, I learned they are actually giving you a gift.

At first, I felt like I was bullied. People there were unkind because they were suffering themselves, and I just couldn't fit in. But it was exactly what I needed. I was reduced to being a tiny child. And I think that was the only way that I could let go of the problems of my childhood. It was like growing up again and being re-parented all over again

Even though I felt bullied in the beginning, I can't express my gratitude for the tough love and the suffering. Without it I would have been finished. Now when I had my awakening, I was being pushed and pushed and pushed; some members of the group tried to get rid of me, but there was also a 24-hour support system. At first, they said I wasn't conforming. I was too much of an individual, and they wanted to get me a little bit more balanced, you know.

K.C. Armstrong: Sounds like they thought of you as a troublemaker.

Laurene Hope: Yes, I was. But finally, I thought, "Hang on a second, why does everybody hate me? What's wrong with me?" I'd been there for a year and I cried for six months on the floor, and they put up with it because you go there to get your pent-up emotions out. And so, you get to a point where you look in the mirror and say okay, what's going on here? People don't like me. Maybe I'm doing something wrong. And then one night they snapped at me, "Laurene, you're on thin ice. We're going to keep you, but this is your last chance."

K.C. Armstrong: How did you feel?

Laurene Hope: Hopeless—I didn't know what to do. I remember waking up the next morning and grabbing hold of my husband Martin and pleading, "Don't let me go back." And then I realized it was what I had said to mom and dad about the abuse. You see how this connects? I had asked mom and dad not to go back to the dentist, and the minute I realized that, K.C., I had this huge feeling of . . .

K.C. Armstrong: Hang on a second, Laurene. The abuse was your mom and dad's fault, nothing to do with you. You didn't need to hold on to guilt for that.

Laurene Hope: It's true, K.C.! As soon as I made that connection I felt total inner peace. Do you know, when I left the Community they told me they didn't believe I would make it. "My God, Laurene," they said, "you must have the skin of a rhinoceros the way we treated you." And then the magic started to happen. I had another eight months to go. I promised them they would see a changed Laurene, and every time they bullied me, I said, "thank you" and "what did I do wrong?" I started asking questions and they couldn't bully me anymore.

K.C. Armstrong: Did you have faith? I know that you were so alone with so little to hold on to. You probably didn't think anyone was rooting for you, but what was your faith like? I mean, did you believe that there was something bigger, even when you were going through the worst of it?

Laurene Hope: Yes, I always believed there is something. I love the teachings of Jesus and Buddha. I've always been a searcher from the time I started singing, K.C., and my voice started soaring in a quest for spirit. I couldn't put my finger on it, but I always knew there was something more. But in the Therapeutic Community, when I had my awakening, I started to work. I started to look at everyone and send them love and peace. And I took a course in miracles which is all about love versus the ego, and I started using that. Every time someone would be horrible, I'd be nice to them. Often, they didn't get it; they thought I was messing with them and it would upset them even more.

K.C. Armstrong: Did they finally realize you weren't screwing around?

Laurene Hope: Yes. The people who had bullied me started to realize that I had some kind of awakening.

They said things like," Oh, I quite like sitting beside you. You're quite peaceful." I became an elder because all these new people came in, and I was suddenly important. I was recognized as the person who was getting well, but I tell you a wonderful thing about the Therapeutic Community was that Martin got his space. In the Community you're not allowed to pour anything onto your family. They put you on contracts, and if you break them they can throw you out. So, my husband got some relief from carrying my burden.

K.C. Armstrong: Wait, Laurene, hold on, I'm not sure I understand what you mean.

Laurene Hope: You can't put more stress on your family. If you get panicky or upset, you ring someone in the Community. They are your support system 24 hours a day rather than pouring out your heart to a family member.

K.C. Armstrong: So, when you finally finished your stay in the Therapeutic Community, what happened next?

Laurene Hope: Well, first I would like to recommend the Therapeutic Community to anybody who has a diagnosis of borderline personality disorder.

K.C. Armstrong: Yes, please do.

Laurene Hope: OK. If you are diagnosed, ask immediately for the Therapeutic Community. I'm going to push this time and time again because I do not believe that there's any other way to manage this condition. It's just mind blowing, K.C. You get 24 hours a day support. Where do you have that in life? You get behavioral contracts, and everyone's an individual. So, for example, if you're someone that doesn't give enough to others, then you'll be put on a contract to support more; if you're someone who gives too much, you'll be put on a contract to protect and support yourself more. You're given discipline by having to help run the Community. You're given authority by having to chair some meetings. You're given continuous therapy, and you're given a bell to ring when you feel overwhelmed.

K.C. Armstrong: Laurene, now tell us the truth: did you take advantage of the bell?

Laurene Hope: (Laughs) Well I did annoy some people! But seriously, this is your biggest opportunity to heal if you have BPD, and remember, that's a blanket term for many types of mental illness. Your first step is to say to your doctor, "Look, I understand that these places exist. I've heard from Laurene Hope that the Therapeutic Community saved her life and made her a peaceful, happy person that can survive in our world. So, I want to get in there even though I know it's not going to be a piece of cake." And people can email me through my website; I'm allowed to support people since I'm a former member of the Community. I do not believe for one minute that you can medicate BPD because it's a complex needs disorder, and you can't medicate 100 different conditions at the same time.

K.C. Armstrong: Right. There's no wonder drug that can handle it all.

Laurene Hope: People should know they are not on their own. There are thousands of people out there like you. There are forums on Facebook. Joining the Community is a step towards a new awakening. I believe you go through a metaphorical crucifixion where it's the most painful thing you can go through, but then you have your resurrection. You come alive again; you're reborn. Obviously, they need to create more therapeutic communities. It would be good if they put money into it, you know, rather than spending the money on more and more medication. As it is now, there is no funding for continued support once you leave the Community, which is unfortunate.

K.C. Armstrong: Yeah, they should keep you in touch with these people.

Laurene Hope: There's just no money for that. We used to have something called the Moving On group, and that's why I call my theatre company "Moving on Theatre." But anyway, after I came out of the Community I had to figure things out by myself. I'd lost my whole support system, but I started implementing everything I learned in the Community. And people can learn more about this because it's all going to be on Moving On TV. I'm creating a program called *The Recovery Toolbox*, a series with every little episode another tool that I learned. These tools can save people's lives, and they're so simple.

K.C. Armstrong: That's one reason I'm interviewing you, Laurene. I know you've been there. You've been to the bottom. You've had so many challenges. Just speaking for myself, I would have folded ten times over, but somehow you got out. So, I want to help you get your experiences out to other people.

Laurene Hope: If people want to learn more about the tools of recovery, it's all free on Moving On TV. I do what I can. I've learned to be a person of solution. You have to sit with your pain and brainstorm, create solutions. What is the tiniest thing you can do today that's going to make you feel better? So, for example, if I'm not able to do anything big because I don't have the money, or I don't have the people, I can still set up a camera in my house and talk about something that I think can help other people. Small steps to a goal.

K.C. Armstrong: Let's hear more about your Recovery Toolbox which people can find on your TV channel for free.

Laurene Hope: OK Here's a sample from my toolbox: HALT! This is the acronym for Don't get too Hungry, don't get too Angry, don't get too Lonely, and don't get too tired. If you get too hungry your blood sugar will go all over the place and you won't be able to deal with your head. If you get too angry you'll need a rage room. You know, you'll need to be able to get into a room and throw some stuff around and let it out. Otherwise your anger builds to such an extent that it's not going to be good. And then, don't get too lonely. You have to get out of the house, mix with people, spend time with friends. Finally, don't get too tired. Get sleep! Get your seven hours or you won't be able to function. Use HALT and you will be able to cope a lot better. The other thing I say is you've got to have a dream. You need a passion. With you, K.C., it's WMAP. With me it's music and rehearsing and building a band for my Piaf show and singing and doing Moving On TV. You have to have a dream, right?

K.C. Armstrong: Of course.

Laurene Hope: Whether it's painting or whatever, it gives you grounding and an identity. It gives you a reason to get up in the morning and then you take tiny little steps towards achieving your dream.

K.C. Armstrong: Wait, Laurene, let me stop you for a second. When you say you've got to take little steps toward that dream, how do you do that? There's always going to be some days when you don't think you can do it. What are some little things that you can do to get there?

Laurene Hope: Well, for example, you want to lose weight, okay? But let's say you can't face going to the gym and doing lots of exercises. What you do is go to a gym and you just walk around. Just get to know the gym or even just stand on a machine. The minute you're doing that you're starting to create a different reality. It works, K.C.! Little steps. There's always a way to do something.

K.C. Armstrong: You're incredible, you know that right, Laurene?

Laurene Hope: I trained as a life coach, K.C. I wanted to be able to understand how to set goals. Another tool that is very helpful is to make a list of all you do have. I listened to one of your interviews, I think it was Virginia Phillips, and she said you can always find five things you are grateful for. List them! Other things are very important to me and others that are diagnosed with BPD in particular. Learn about your condition. Go on Google, get books, read, understand it, educate yourself and all the personalities that are in you. That's what I did. And then teach your loved ones because you have to have their support. Martin and I went to counseling together and I explained everything to him. He understands how my head works, and we've been together twenty-four years.

K.C. Armstrong: That's awesome!

Laurene Hope: And after I came out of the Community our marriage got better because I was able to educate my husband on how to talk to me. It's called Stop, Think and Listen. You have to treat everyone as a vulnerable, sensitive human being that deserves respect, and you have to really, really listen to what they're saying. And sometimes you have to repeat back to them what they said because they need to be validated. So many of the people in the Therapeutic Community were never validated. We weren't allowed to be ourselves or to say, "Help, I'm suffering." With many of us, our parents wouldn't listen because they couldn't deal with our pain, like my molestation for example. We learn to express how we feel and to say to others "Oh, I'm so sorry you're suffering, and I understand your suffering." Do you understand what I mean?

K.C. Armstrong: I do. Seems like good advice for any relationship. Would you be the person that I'm speaking to right now if it weren't for Martin?

Laurene Hope: Well, I went into the Community partly in order to save my marriage. When I came out, that's when Martin and I started to get to know each other. He is very accepting of me. Martin never tried to change me, ever.

K.C. Armstrong: That's awesome. That's love.

Laurene Hope: His compassion was unbelievable when I lost my father, and I'm very, very lucky. When I broke my leg he was my caretaker for a while, and that's how it is in a relationship sometimes. Your partner picks you up and holds you—they heal you. And yeah, he's been absolutely incredible, but without the Therapeutic Community I wouldn't have a marriage now.

K.C. Armstrong: Got you, OK. What else has helped you maintain your peace, Laurene?

Laurene Hope: There's something called the "violet flame" meditation which I discovered and researched on YouTube. It's all about beautiful visualizations, and to me it just feels like I'm connected to God. I use that, and a book called *The Healing Code* by Alex Lloyd. I use a positive affirmation like "I am peace" or There is only love" and I ask everything but love to leave my life. The visualization is really very beautiful and very calming. I used this meditation after the loss of my dad. Before I do the meditation, my problems are right on top of me, and it's like being pushed down by this heaviness. Then, when you do this violet flame meditation with the mantras and the Healing Code, it relieves the feeling of anxiety and depression. It's like magic so I'm passing all this on.

K.C. Armstrong: You're amazing. And what else are you up to?

Laurene Hope: I'm writing a book called *Standing on My Own Two Feet*. I can see everything that I need to teach about mental illness. I want to show the progression of traits from childhood that you may not even notice. I see my own progression. One of the traits of BPD, for example, is risk taking. When I was little I was always climbing up cupboards and swinging the highest on the playground to show off. I didn't have any fear or thought of consequences. If I had been lucky as a child, my problems could have been picked up earlier.

    Another part of recovery that I would recommend is not to watch TV. There's so much violence! Watch Moving on TV which has no violence and is very respectful. I feel physically sick when I watch mainstream television.

K.C. Armstrong: How do you have time to watch TV anyway? You're helping people, it seems, 25 hours a day!

Laurene Hope: Right. I have learned so much from my experiences in the Therapeutic Community that I want to help others who may feel somewhat like I did. It was there I started using a course in miracles, which is free on the internet, and teaches you on a day-to-day basis to choose love and happiness. Everyone is connected to you so what you give you receive. If you smile at someone they're likely to smile back at you and vice versa.

K.C. Armstrong: What else did you learn that you'd like to share?

Laurene Hope: I learned that it's absolutely ok to be a bit selfish. Not to the point that you're hurting other people, but you have to take care of yourself. Self-nurturing and self-compassion are necessary. And also, structure.

K.C. Armstrong: You know that's something I completely agree with. The Japanese believe that even in your living quarters structure is all important. If in your bedroom you've got clothes all over the place and your living space is out of whack, then your life is going to be out of whack.

Laurene Hope: Exactly. With BPD you can't have too many choices, and if you're very vulnerable you need to give yourself a clear structure. So, the Therapeutic Community is like a job. Three days a week you're at your job. You're up at eight in the morning, you're there at nine to start your job, and you finish at three. And you're able to cope after that. You give yourself structure. Do you know what I mean?

K.C. Armstrong: I sure do, Laurene.

Laurene Hope: Also, I found, and this is mind-blowing, K.C., that you aren't always upset for the reason you think. Someone could say something to you and you may think you're bothered by that. It may actually be something your mom and dad or a friend said or something that happened to you as a child. In the Community we learned to sit with this feeling and ask yourself, where did I feel like this before? Then, as you think back, you may touch that real incident that is the core of your unpleasant feeling.

And then you won't be angry or whatever anymore. For example, after I came out of the Community, Martin and I had a row and I was really upset. I don't remember what it was, but he became very shut off from me. I thought it was him that was making me feel that way. So, I sat in a room with my journal and wrote about it. And do you know what I discovered?

He was bringing back the coldness of my mother. That's what she would do; she used to shut off. And I thought Thank God for that, it wasn't Martin. He was giving me the opportunity to heal more stuff around my relationship with my mother.

K.C. Armstrong: Now that's really self-awareness.

Laurene Hope: It really is. I mean, it takes a long time to get to real self-knowledge.

K.C. Armstrong: Great, Laurene.

Laurene Hope: You know, K.C., I came out of the Community with such inner peace that I knew I had to stay well on a daily basis. And, by the way, the Therapeutic Community is free on the NHS in the UK. So, with all the work I've done I can say this really works, and it's affordable, as well! People with BPD are highly sensitive, creative people, but it's harder for them to function in this world. They're special human beings with amazing talents.

K.C. Armstrong: To read your story, Laurene, is to see that the Therapeutic Certainly did work for you, and you are able to share what you learned there. I think you're going to touch the lives of so many people.

Laurene Hope: Thank you. Well, my job is to go out there and tell everyone about recovery, and I don't even think about mental illness as such. It's all about recovery. It's like the twelve steps. You come out of your denial, you recognize that you've got something you're not coping with. Whether that is a mental illness or not, K.C., is a big question mark.

K.C. Armstrong: I think everybody is mentally ill, so we might disagree.

Laurene Hope: You know, there's nothing really wrong with us, and I'm talking about those with BPD.

We just struggle a little bit more with life because we've had difficult experiences. We're more sensitive in some ways. But, you know, everyone is codependent. If you take away someone's children, they'll be diagnosed with a mental illness because they won't be able to function. You take someone's job away, and that leads to becoming mentally ill.

K.C. Armstrong: Is there any other advice you'd like to offer? Perhaps more from your toolbox?

Laurene Hope: Forgiveness. You can't function without it. I'm not talking about when you've been hurt or abused; you don't forgive what that person did because what they did was not okay. But you forgive their soul because you don't want to be lying in bed churning and feeling sick because of them. So, you're forgiving them in order to move on. One of the best techniques and programs I know about this subject is *The 13 Steps to Self-forgiveness* by Colin Tipping.

K.C. Armstrong: You know, people can sometimes do horrible things to each other. You're saying don't forgive the act, but forgive the person?

Laurene Hope: You forgive the soul of that person. Because what they did was not okay. You can't tell anybody that abusing a child, for instance, isn't a horrible act. But if that happens, you must let that person go and move on. You've got to take your rage out in some way. Do some kind of visualization. I put my abuser in a big mincer and I minced him up like minced meat! You can do all that in your mind, and you can change yourself. So, you forgive the soul of that person and you let it go. And you forgive yourself because we're all connected. A lot of the time we're holding stuff against ourselves and don't realize. It's very hard to forgive yourself.

K.C. Armstrong: Yes. The mind is very strong in both good and bad ways.

Laurene Hope: That's right. We can heal ourselves but also punish ourselves by holding on to guilt. Guilt is a complete waste of time, but we love to hold on to it.

K.C. Armstrong: I've heard a lot about the visualization thing you were talking about. Athletes use it to picture themselves winning, and the mind adapts to that and creates added motivation and confidence.

Laurene Hope: Absolutely. Let me tell you a story about the power of the mind to heal.

After my dad's funeral I was completely alienated from members of my family who had been so cruel to both my dad and myself. So, I decided to find an Al-Anon meeting to understand their alcoholism which caused much of their behavior. I parked in front of the building, got out, and boom—smashed my tibia plateau, a really serious break. I didn't know if I would ever walk again. I didn't want the operation my doctors told me was necessary, and I wanted very minimal medication. So, I wasn't allowed to put weight on my leg and was confined to a wheelchair. It was horrible, K.C.! But you know what? After four months in the wheelchair my leg healed naturally!

K.C. Armstrong: Amazing, Laurene. The power of the mind, right?

Laurene Hope: That's right, K.C. And you know, when I was in the wheelchair, I asked myself, "If you can never walk again, Laurene, what do you want?" Well, I want my life, I want my singing, I want my dream, I want to campaign for everyone to learn how to be happy regardless of all the pain in the world. I want to support vulnerable people. And I thought, wouldn't it be so cool to have a TV station where everybody could go on just because they're talented?

K.C. Armstrong: And so, there we are, back to Moving On TV. You can perform and also highlight others who have inspirational stories to tell and talents to share. I hope all our listeners and readers will check out your many programs on *www.movingontv.uk.* This is where they can check out *How to Stay Sane in a Crazy World,* contact you, and also link to your YouTube Channel. You can also be contacted there for singing and speaking requests, right, Laurene?

Laurene Hope: That's right. You can also purchase my daily cards that go along with

How to Stay Sane in a Crazy World by contacting me there or going to my Facebook page *How to Stay Sane in a Crazy World Cards.*

K.C. Armstrong: I should also mention that at movingontheatre.co.uk you can see Laurene's upcoming shows and also purchase her angelic vocals, also available on YouTube.

Laurene Hope: Right, K.C. And, please, check out *https://www.therapeuticcommunities.org/*

For more information about the Therapeutic Community including their contact information and locations world-wide. There's so much opportunity and help out there!

K.C. Armstrong: Absolutely, Laurene. Thank you for sharing your journey so openly. Your hard work and determination not to give up and to find a better life for yourself is not only amazing but also an inspiration to others who want to do the same.

Laurene Hope: Thank you, for this opportunity, K.C. If it wasn't for all those people doing what they did and the experiences I went through, I wouldn't have been on WMAP! All roads led me here today.

K.C. Armstrong: And if I hadn't encountered many of the people who brought challenges into my life, we wouldn't be talking right now, so it's all relative. And I'm so glad we're both in this place at this time, because I am proud to call you my friend and to share your information and wisdom with my listening and reading audience.

CHAPTER 9

---- ◈◈◈ ----

Dr. Elizabeth Rodger

 After Hours Veterinary Emergency Clinic
We'll treat your pets in times of need!

Phone: (907) 479-2700 **Email:** AHVECI@alaska.net
Address: 8 Bonnie Ave, Fairbanks, AK 99701
Web Address: http://www.ahveciak.com/

Dr. Elizabeth Rodger Intro

I truly loved interviewing Dr. Elizabeth Rodger because she has this amazing ability to know what an animal is thinking and feeling. She knows how they greet each day thinking it's the greatest day ever, and she appears to do the same.

It's so cool that Dr. Rodger followed her heart from Texas to Alaska and opened an emergency veterinary clinic to provide the type of care where it was so desperately needed. A vet who is so loving and caring and who truly understands our four-legged friends is extremely hard to find.

This is one of my favorites because I hear her passion in everything she does, and she does it all with an appealing sense of humor. Most amazing vet ever!

Interview

http://www.ahveciak.com/

K.C. Armstrong:	Alright guys, WMAP. We are the World's Most Amazing People! And speaking of the world's most amazing people, I am about to get on the telephone with one of my favorite guests, Dr. Elizabeth Rodger. What do you say about someone who has the courage to go on a life of adventures? How you doing, Dr. Roger?
Dr. Elizabeth Rodger:	Oh, I'm doing well. That's quite the intro, thank you.
K.C. Armstrong:	Well, it's the truth; it's what happened! Now there are so many things I want to ask you, but let's just refresh the audience in case they're not familiar with your story. Tell us how you opened up your wonderful emergency clinic for pets in Alaska. I know you didn't grow up there.
Dr. Elizabeth Rodger:	Well, I was born in St. Louis and my family moved to Texas. I grew up in Texas, went to school at Texas A&M, yee-haw! I've worked jobs from the Midwest to the East and decided that I wanted to be somewhere northwest. I got the best job offer up in Fairbanks. So, I moved there, and moving from Texas to Alaska was a trip. Literally and figuratively.
K.C. Armstrong:	I bet.
Dr. Elizabeth Rodger:	But the people here in Alaska are wonderful. The weather, as long as you dress accordingly, is really not that bad. Even 20 below is not awful, if you can believe it. I did regular practice

for four years, but this is before there was an emergency service so we had to take our own calls. I'd be woken up at 2 o'clock in the morning, have to get up and drive into town to see emergencies. I'd have to open up the clinic, see the patient, check them out; I had to do everything. And then, of course, close up the clinic, drive back home, get a few hours of sleep, come back and work all day. Within two years I managed to have two major car accidents and thought, "Okay, this is not good. Something needs to change." Interestingly enough after talking with some of my colleagues, I realized that I tended to attract a lot of emergencies.

K.C. Armstrong: How so?

Dr. Elizabeth Rodger: I don't know, it was just crazy. I would have eight to ten emergencies a month working only ten or eleven days a month. Most other people had one or two, maybe three, not that many. But I either was a sucker and came in more, or I just had the luck of getting more calls. But I decided to start looking into what it would take to start and run a small business. When I did that I was smart enough to talk to a very good lawyer and a very good accountant. And they both gave me sound business advice. I also had a friend who was a computer guru who helped me set up the computer system so I could be virtually paperless and didn't have to have a whole lot of supplies. Plus, I knew a veterinarian who had a clinic that he could let me use nights, weekends and holidays until I built up enough money to buy my own place. So it was a combination of timing and people who were there to help me start out, and I have been going ever since. It's been over 21 years now.

K.C. Armstrong: That's incredible. And, you know, you're a great guest not only for having the courage to take something on like this, but also for having stories of some wild stuff after being there for 21 years. Can you share some funny animal stories?

Dr. Elizabeth Rodger: Well, we certainly see emergencies, whether real or simply perceived.

Some of my funnier stories didn't turn out to really quite be emergencies; rather the animals were acting so strangely that the owners were freaked out. One of my favorite emergencies is puppies with hiccups. If you've never owned a puppy before you don't realize that sometimes they just get hiccups, and if you've never seen that in a dog it can look like they're having a seizure or something. And so they come in, the puppy is having hiccups, and I can reassure the panicked owners that it's not a catastrophe.

K.C. Armstrong: It's okay for a puppy to hiccup.

Dr. Elizabeth Rodger: It's just a lovely little taste of puppy cuteness. And it's always nice when we can see a puppy that's not really sick or injured. It gives us a little charge because we get to have puppy-cuddle time. Every so often we'll joke, "Oh, no this is really serious. He needs to be hospitalized for at least 3 hours so we can play with him."

K.C. Armstrong: That's funny.

Dr. Elizabeth Rodger: The other thing that gets to be fun is a cat in heat. The first time somebody witnesses a cat in heat, they think it's possessed by a demon. The cat will yell, roll around, race around the house, and act completely crazy. It's all sheer hormones.

K.C. Armstrong: And you were telling me one time about the people like me who will bring their pet in if it has the sniffles or if one hair is out of place, the overprotective parent. You see a lot of that, right?

Dr. Elizabeth Rodger: Actually, we love people like you because you bring in animals when they're still potentially fixable. Some people don't understand how sick their animal is and they wait and keep thinking it's going to get better as it gets continuously worse. It's frustrating when we're presented with an animal that a day or so earlier could have been treated but now it's too late and there's nothing we can do. We try to educate people like that so that they know what to watch for in case they ever see it again. But there are some cases where timing is critical. But people like you we jokingly refer to as "preeners" because you know everything about your animal. You know when there's something not right. And when you bring them in, we can figure out what's going on sometimes. Sometimes they're just strange.

K.C. Armstrong: Especially cats, right?

Dr. Elizabeth Rodger: Right. Usually we can at least make sure there's nothing big and scary going on and start implementing some kind of treatment so that the animal feels better, and the owner feels better, and they feel like they have a handle on what's going on.

K.C. Armstrong: The other day, I was doing an interview with a gentleman in L.A. who is running a mobile vet business. I said to him, "You know, I have a friend in Fairbanks, Alaska and she's looking for people to come up there. Would you ever consider doing that?" And I almost had him going on the adventure; he was almost ready to call you. But then after thinking for a minute he added, "Well, but then I'm thinking about buying a house . . ." So, this goes back to why I think you're so special. It's that you actually grabbed hold of a challenge like this. You really committed. Were you always someone who would, say, gamble on something or take a chance?

Dr. Elizabeth Rodger: I'm what some people would call an "old soul" in that, the new souls or the young souls are the ones that will just boldly go into something new. I tend to sit back, and I calculate the pros and cons and figure out what it's worth. It doesn't necessarily mean I'm going to be daunted by a challenge, but usually I do put a fair bit of thought into it and figure out how things are going to go. I do admit that my trip to Alaska I did a little bit more blindly than I might have done otherwise. But I like to have at least an idea. In fact, some of the staff members I've had working with me for many years used to joke around that when I first started the practice if I wanted to make a big decision about the clinic I would talk to my lawyer, talk to my accountant, mull it over for about two weeks and then do it.

K.C. Armstrong: So, you are normally very calculated. But how important is it to take risks? Do you think you'd be as successful as you are now if, say, you decided to open up in Detroit?

Dr. Elizabeth Rodger: I don't know that I have the personality to handle Detroit.

K.C. Armstrong: Maybe not a good example.

Dr. Elizabeth Rodger: One of the things that's nice about Alaska is that we don't' have a big population. And I don't have a lot of competition so I can practice how I want to. I don't necessarily have to follow anybody's mold. My clinic doesn't really run the way the big city emergency clinics do because we don't have the same volume of patients. Not to say we can't work on five patients simultaneously, but we just have to work together as a team, and we don't have nearly as many people. So, we have to work well and communicate clearly and be efficient. It's more of a camaraderie type atmosphere here in Alaska. It's less of that clinical tension that you can get at some of the clinics in the lower 48.

I have visited emergency clinics in Anchorage and in St. Louis and, while they're nice people with a good setup, they don't have that cohesiveness that I really like about my place. Here everybody works together, they care about each other, they help each other out. The point is, if we can work together, then we can do much for the animals and for ourselves.

K.C. Armstrong: I think part of the reason you're one of the world's most amazing people is because you know as well as I do how much people value their pets. They become part of the family and it's like they're kids. People are trusting you with their kids and if you're taking care of them, you know how happy you make your clients. That part of your job is really amazing because you're making a lot of people happy.

Dr. Elizabeth Rodger: Sure. One of the other things that we talk about at the clinic is that a lot of times when people first come in (or even on the phone) they're very upset. They're very concerned, and we call it talking people off the ledge. Because if they're that upset over what's going on, you have to get them calmed down to be able to find out what needs to be done and how we can help them. For example, if you don't have a car, you're homebound and you have a dog that's got a bloody nose, what do you do? We've found that there are actually a number of taxis in Fairbanks, and even in other cities, that will pick up people with animals and take them to vet clinics.

K.C. Armstrong: Oh, they better. That's only fair.

Dr. Elizabeth Rodger: You wouldn't think a taxi would do that but there's a fair number that will. And it's interesting when people can find friends or neighbors that will help them load up the 180-pound dog that can't walk.

K.C. Armstrong: That's a good friend right there. I was thinking of you because—you remember me telling you about Mr. Beakman, the bird that I found at just one or two days old? Well, my girlfriend is worse than me, so when Mr. Beakman started walking like he was drunk, she took him straight to the vet. I tried to be tactful when I said, "Hon, I don't know if the vet needs to look at the bird who just is walking a little strange." I mean, is that a little bit much?

Dr. Elizabeth Rodger: No.

K.C. Armstrong: It's not?

Dr. Elizabeth Rodger: That was actually a very good move. Birds can go from just fine to hell in a handbasket very quickly. If you get them to a vet, especially one who has experience with birds, and they get a chance to examine them and maybe do some blood work, then often times there's a chance. If you wait until they're acting really, really sick you can have a lot more problems, just like with any other animals. You know birds are prey animals. There's a mindset that these animals have, if you show signs of weakness and you don't get taken out by another predator, your pack members may turn on you. Because in a flock situation, a weak bird, a sick bird is a liability and that could potentially draw predators to the rest of the birds so, it's dangerous to act sick.

I've seen cats that will hide sickness. If you can see the subtle signs and get them in, then sometimes you can treat them. But sometimes they'll just be acting a little off and the next thing you know they're terribly sick. And I've seen on more than one occasion when people have multiple dogs, especially the mushers, if there's one dog that's just not quite right, their own teammates will actually turn and attack the dog.

So if you can pick up on an illness early it's so much better. If an animal in a household has other animals acting strangely toward it, there's usually something going on. Other animals can pick up on subtleties that we can't. Sometimes it's a smell, sometimes it's body language. Animals are much more aware of body language, even birds.

K.C. Armstrong: And when Mr. Beakman went there, the vet said that they had to do some blood work, but there's a chance that he might kill the bird by taking blood from it. Is that accurate?

Dr. Elizabeth Rodger: Well, if they've got a lot of experience with birds there are ways of taking blood to minimize risk. Birds can stress out too and on occasion they will die just from shear stress and panic. It's not that often, though. I used to do a lot of bird and reptile work when I was in regular practice. And you learn how to restrain them. It helps if you have staff members that are really good with birds. I had two staff members that I worked with that could hold them better than I think almost anybody I've ever run across. And a lot of it is understanding the behavior of the birds and knowing where their mind tends to go. Then you can minimize the stress and their level of agitation.

In fact, when I used to do a lot of bird work, the first thing I did when I got into the room was talk to the owners to get a history, find out what was going on, and let the bird get used to me being in the room before I ever even reached into its cage. It's always kind of worrisome and, like I said, sometimes an illness can be real subtle. I remember there was a little budgie that I worked on many, many years ago that had an overgrown beak, which is sometimes a sign of liver disease. And while I was doing a nail trim and a beak trim on this bird it just died. I did an autopsy on him and he did have an enlarged liver.

K.C. Armstrong: That's crazy. I'm sure the audience would love me to ask you this: How do animals show pain?

Dr. Elizabeth Rodger: That's very interesting! Sometimes if you can imitate what the animal is doing, you can empathize what is going on. But a lot of times animals don't show pain for the same reason they don't' show illness. Because if you're in pain and you can't keep up with the rest of the group, then you're a liability. So, a lot of times their signs can be subtle. For a cat, sometimes a sign of pain is just laying quietly crouched in the back of a kennel or somewhere where they are laying down, but they're not really relaxed. A relaxed animal that is breathing comfortably and dreaming when they're asleep is not in pain. Laying really still without moving much can be a sign of pain.

With older dogs a lot of people say, "Well, you know the dog's a little older. And we notice it takes him a little longer to sit and stand." Well, that can be hip and/or lower back pain. We've had people insist that their animal is not in pain, but it moves with really short strides. When you walk with real short strides, isn't that usually when your back hurts? This is what I meant by imitating what the animal is doing to figure out what's really going on.

Sometimes the pet doesn't want to jump on and off the couch. Or they don't want to go up or down the stairs. It can be a little frustrating trying to convince some people that the animal is actually feeling pain, even though he's not whining.

K.C. Armstrong: Right.

Dr. Elizabeth Rodger: They just don't necessarily recognize that. When birds are feeling out of sorts they'll sit all fluffed out with their feathers all poofed out like somebody inflated them.

K.C. Armstrong: Yes, Mr. Beakman does that.

Dr. Elizabeth Rodger: They'll do that sometimes to warm themselves up. Sometimes they'll do that when they just don't feel good. You know, even birds can be painful. They can tear off a toenail sometimes on the side of their cage or sometimes get caught and can actually break a leg or break a wing. And so, we do try and address pain control for all species.

K.C. Armstrong: Got you. And along the lines of sick animals, what are some tips, Doctor, about giving medicine to your pets?

Dr. Elizabeth Rodger: Some animals are great cooperators. I've got a dog that has a tendency towards being a bit gassy. We jokingly refer to him as the toxic avenger. And I have discovered that Gas-X works great in helping make that less of a problem. He'll take the raspberry flavored Gas-X chewable tablets just like kibble, like a treat. But if you have to give medicine to a dog or cat that's not quite so cooperative there are three tricks that I've learned over the years. They don't always work, but sometimes they can make the difference in animals that like to lick all the peanut butter off of a pill. Or the ones that can take the pill in their mouths and somehow magically hold it in their cheek and then spit it out later. One of the tricks that we do at the clinic is we'll tempt the animal with baby food because it's mushy and they tend to like it. So, we'll give them two or three bits of baby food and then get them all excited and think, "Oh, baby food is great. We really like baby food." And then we'll stick the pill in the baby food. And they're so caught up in the game they're not taking the time to check for the pill.

K.C. Armstrong: So, it's a matter of using a little chicanery.

Dr. Elizabeth Rodger: Yes, K.C.! That we call "the switch out." They get unadulterated treats, and this works for peanut butter, low fat cream cheese, whatever you can use that the animal likes, as long as you can completely cover the pill so nothing is sticking out. The next trick is a little more complex but tends to work on the animals that are still good about getting the pill out of whatever you have covering it. This one works best with something that is sufficiently sticky and soft. Now, what you do is you put the pill in, and I usually recommend low fat cream cheese or peanut butter, and then you put in on a piece of wax paper, a very important part because then you stick it in the freezer. If you don't put it on the wax paper it will stick to the freezer. So you freeze the medication, but first you have to make sure that's okay to do. Some medication is temperature influenced.

But if you can freeze it, then that covering is like a little frozen shell around the pill. And then you go back to that same technique I used in the first method. You give them several pieces of unadulterated treat and then you give them the frozen one. And it's frozen but tastes about the same. They can't lick all the peanut butter off. It would take longer, so they just eat it.

K.C. Armstrong: Good tips right there. Do you have any others?

Dr. Elizabeth Rodger: Another one I've heard works with cats is, you know what I mean by "squeeze cheese"?

K.C. Armstrong: Like what you put on crackers? Cheese Wiz?

Dr. Elizabeth Rodger: Yeah, that's it. If you put a line of this squeeze cheese on a plate, then a dot of of cheese, a line of cheese, a dot of cheese and then a line. In the second dot you put a pill, and make sure the pill is covered by the dot of cheese.

Take a minute to picture what I'm saying. So the cat starts licking up the cheese wiz, and he gets distracted by the time he gets to that second dot. He's all about the cheese—and that's the way to get a pill into a cat!

K.C. Armstrong: I think you've helped a lot of people right now because cats are so difficult. You know, they do what they want pretty much.

Dr. Elizabeth Rodger: Yes, they do.

K.C. Armstrong: I was reading somewhere that you have an example of your dog's philosophy of life?

Dr. Elizabeth Rodger: Oh, yes.

K.C. Armstrong: I've got to hear this.

Dr. Elizabeth Rodger: I've got a pit boxer named Wedge. And Wedge is either really brilliant and differently motivated or not quite the brightest bean in the bucket. But he has this attitude about so many things that whatever he's doing is like the best thing ever. If we're going for a walk, it's the best walk ever, it's the best car ride ever, it's the best nap he's ever had.

I decided that's just a great way of approaching things. I do a variety of different dances. It's my stress relief and one way that I try and keep my brain going. And so, somebody asked me, well, what's your favorite kind of dance? And I said, "Well, whatever I happen to be doing at the time; that's the best dance ever!" So, if I'm in a class and its Middle Eastern dance, then it's the best Middle Eastern class ever and I'm having a great time and I can just enjoy that moment. And then when I go and do a Salsa class, then that's the best class ever, and I can just Salsa the hell out of it. It takes out the whole comparison factor because I'm not comparing it to anything else. I'm so focused on what I'm doing that I can just enjoy the heck out of it. So, even though best is a comparison of sorts it's a comparison to itself. I decided that's not a bad way to go.

K.C. Armstrong: It really isn't.

Dr. Elizabeth Rodger: Just enjoy what you're doing in the moment and don't worry about what the next class is going to be or what you're going to be doing later on. You just enjoy what you're doing at the moment. Whenever things get a little crazy, I go for a walk with my dog and have the best walk ever.

K.C. Armstrong: The best walk ever. That's right. I love it. Let me ask you some more about animal behavior. For example, when a dog winks at you, are they trying to communicate with their face? Do they give signals like that?

Dr. Elizabeth Rodger: I'm sure they do, but it's very easy to misunderstand animals.

We may think he's upset because he pooped on the floor. But actually, they don't tend to feel guilty because they pooped on the floor. They're more likely to be upset because there *is* poop on the floor, and poop on the floor means mom's upset or dad's upset. They're not as consequence driven by their actions because they tend to live in the moment. They don't contemplate for hours, "Huh, what can I do that could really make my owner take me for a walk?" When they want to go for a walk, they'll go over to the leash, start poking the owner in the elbow repeatedly or such. There are a lot of behavior facial expressions that you can read from an animal and you can get an idea of what they may want. But they're not necessarily trying to communicate the same way as a human would.

So, if they wink at you is it because they like you, or is it because they're looking at you and they blinked one eye? That gets to be a little more difficult to interpret. But just take time and watch how animals interact with each other, how they play, their ear position. You can see the little wrinkles on their forehead some-times or the heights of their tail and how bushy their tail looks. I don't know if you've ever seen a cat that's been agitated, but their tails gets all poofed out and looks like a big old bottlebrush.

K.C. Armstrong: Yeah and they whip it back and forth.

Dr. Elizabeth Rodger: Right. Just because a dog's wagging his tail doesn't mean it's happy and it's friendly. A dog will wag its tail and still bite you, but you have to read the rest of the body language. How high are they holding their head; are they holding their head down a little bit? Are their ears back or are they forward? Are their eyes real tight and tense? If their face is all relaxed and they're wagging their whole bodies and doing a little tap dance, then odds are you're going to get a friendly reception. If they're walking to you very carefully and their tail is kind of up and tense and their face is kind of tense, then you want to be careful. You don't want to just reach out and give that dog a big hug—and definitely don't kiss it on the nose!

K.C. Armstrong: Got you. Doc, you've got a great sense of humor, but let me ask you a couple of serious questions. We all know how successful you are, and we know what you put into this place to see your dream come true. Now, if someone could look down and see your whole life from start to now, what's the first thing that person would say about you?

Dr. Elizabeth Rodger: I would probably expect to hear something about independence, that I'm an independent, intelligent, compassionate person. I think the thing that's most helped me along is compassion. Compassion doesn't necessarily mean I'm going to do what you want me to do, but I can certainly understand or try to understand and appreciate where people are coming from, where the animals are coming from. And it can help me make a decision as to what types of things I want to do to try and help out. Like I've said before, I'm not a fixer; I'm a facilitator. I will do what I can to give individuals the resources to get better, but it's up to the individual to be able to—be it a human, animal, whatever. And they have to do it within their limitations. But being able to appreciate the point of view of others helps me to be able to figure out how I can best facilitate.

Some of it is because, I admit, I'm a bit lazy. I don't like to put forth a whole lot of effort, especially when the gains are going to be kind of questionable. Sometimes when you help somebody out, they end up pissed off at you. So, if I can figure out what they want to do, then if I can give them the resources to use and still accept that not everybody is going to do what I think they should. They're going to do what they need to do.

K.C. Armstrong: That's a very good answer. Another thing, your career has always been about helping or paying attention to either animals, the owners, or your workers. You've had all these different relationships and social elements. By working with animals, have you learned anything about your relationships with people?

Dr. Elizabeth Rodger: Hmmm. Yes. Working with a variety of different animals has helped me learn to be more flexible in my way of thinking and my approach to different people. When you live with a snake you can't take it personally if the snake doesn't come slithering up to you. Okay, if it slithered up to me, I'd be scared. But it's taught me to be a little more flexible in how I deal with people and, well, other animals. Sometimes what works for one person when you try to communicate with them doesn't work at all with others. And I'm sure you've noticed that what motivates our grandparents won't work with some of the younger people today. We have to adapt.

K.C. Armstrong: Right.

Dr. Elizabeth Rodger: If you try to make everybody fit into a certain mold, then you're not getting anywhere with communication. If I talk to a client and I can tell they're just not getting it, I have to come up with a different way of explaining things or of approaching the situation. Once I realize that,

263

okay, they do understand what's going on, we can move from there.

Sometimes if you get upset with a dog, you can reprimand them and they're like, oh, oh, okay. But that doesn't necessarily work on birds. You can shake your finger and gesture all you want, and the bird will just mimic you. It's not that they're being spiteful, but they just don't understand what you're trying to do. If a flock mate is upset with them and they've done something wrong, they get their ass handed to them bird-wise. We can't do that, so we have to figure it out. If we want to train a bird, we have to figure out how to motivate them to do that. And figuring out the motivation of anybody or anything is how you can help them do what you want them to do. It's all a matter of figuring out what works.

Some individual's motivation can be as simple as the opportunity to learn something new. I know with some dogs, especially herding breed dogs, one of the best things you can do is teach them a new trick, a new game, just something new and interesting. Other dogs and many cats are food driven. If they get a treat it's amazing. Others just want attention. I think I'm most proud of my being a facilitator, being a mediator, being able to recognize that for me being able to help out is good without having to control everything. Knowing the limits of where my responsibility is and still being respectful of those I'm trying to help.

K.C. Armstrong: Was that a hard lesson to learn?

Dr. Elizabeth Rodger: It's something that I think got hammered home later. I had a friend that was in a really stressful situation. I had this strong urge to help him, but there was really nothing I could do. I had one of those amazing epiphanies where I realized that sometimes, even though I think that I can help or protect somebody, given a chance they can do an infinitely better job than I ever could. They know more of what's going on. On occasion I might be able to do a better job, but more often than not, you have to let someone else figure out their own problems. I mean, you can help them and support them and cheer them on, but not only does solving difficulties themselves empower them and make them more confident to be able to handle further challenges, but it also shows them respect. It gives them that acknowledgement that "you are an intelligent being, you can figure this stuff out, you can make things work." And that was really an interesting lesson for me to learn. Trying to help people do what I think they should do actually is disrespectful.

K.C. Armstrong: Well, doctor, I love your take on these things because of your sense of humor, your ability to take the path that's less travelled, and your willingness to learn from everything that you've done. It's really a great thing, a great lesson, for people to read.

Here's my last question for you: you set out to do something and you achieved it. You're running things, you're doing things the way you want to do them and where you want to do them – you've made it happen. A lot of younger people are listening to the program and reading this chapter and aspire to do something like that. They would love to walk in your shoes, set a goal, achieve it, and become successful. What advice would you give to younger people who are just starting out and want to excel in any field, not just being a vet, but in anything?

Dr. Elizabeth Rodger: My best advice is to do your research with a sense of humor, adventure, compassion and independence. Look into what you want to try. Find out as much as you can so you know what you're getting into. If you want to try a certain field, see if you can work in that field. If it's the veterinary field, for instance, work in a vet clinic. If it's in a bank, work at a bank. Get an idea of what that field entails because sometimes what you see on TV and movies is not reality. But if you know what you're getting into, you can not only gear your education towards that, but it also will help you integrate into that field as soon as you get all the education, skills and training you need. Some people say that if you never try, you'll never fail, but you'll also never succeed. And sometimes successes aren't what you expect; sometimes they're better than you could expect!

K.C. Armstrong: That's great. Doctor, give yourself a plug. Where can people get ahold of you?

Dr. Elizabeth Rodger: The best way to get ahold of me is through the clinic in Fairbanks, Alaska: ` *After Hours Veterinary Emergency Clinic*. We do have a website: www.ahveciak.com and a FB page: After Hours Veterinary Emergency Clinic in

Fairbanks, AK. If any veterinarian out there is feeling adventurous, I'm still looking for help. But if somebody wants to just experience a few months of living in Alaska, it's definitely worth checking out, because Alaska is a different kind of place. It's still part of the United States, just not as closely attached. And you're going to meet a lot of interesting people and see a lot of interesting wildlife. You have opportunities to do things you may never have done before, like climb around on a glacier or watch moose crossing in your front yard. I've had a moose actually look in the window of my clinic. I've had a porcupine walk across the street next to my clinic. You can sometimes see animals that you would never expect to. At times it's a little disturbing; sometimes it's just plain out fun. And when you watch a raven taunt a bird, it's quite hilarious. They're very clever animals.

K.C. Armstrong: Dr. Elizabeth Rodger, A veterinarian, a doer, a compassionate adventurer with great stories to tell. Plus, you made me laugh a bunch of times and I appreciate it!

Dr. Elizabeth Rodger: Well, thank you. This was a fun interview.

K.C. Armstrong: That's Dr. Elizabeth Rodger. What a great guest and what a great way to look at life. Just having the guts to do something and seeing it through. Love it. And even her dog Wedge has an upbeat way of looking at the world! Nice!

CHAPTER 10

―――――――――― ◇◈◇ ――――――――――

Daniella Cippitelli

Phone: 516.882.6109 **Fax:** 516.882.6129 **Email:**
info@magichappensfoundation.org
Address: PO Box 1030, Bethpage, NY 11714 **Web
Address:** *magichappensfoundation.org*

Daniella Cippitelli's Intro

I hope it comes through in her interview, but Daniella is the epitome of
what we stand for here at WMAP. She has this contagious laughter that
makes you smile. She's warm, tough as nails, thoughtful, creative, and
has the determination of an Olympic athlete. Daniella not only overcame
a potentially fatal diagnosis, she did it while running a business and
raising a family and then used that experience to find ways of helping
others who are going through something similar.

Interview

K.C. Armstrong: Alright, guys, WMAP, the world's most amazing people. I am tickled pink today because I have a very, very special guest. Someone who is a friend of the show, is a personal friend of mine and everyone loves her at the station. I'm talking about Ms. Daniella Cippitelli. We're going to stop here for one second. She has the *Magic Happens Foundation* that empowers people that are battling cancer because Daniella herself is a survivor. And it helps to enrich the mind, body and spirit through fitness and nutrition. And basically, she's helping educate the families of cancer patients. This organization raises money mostly through donations, and of course it's such a great activity for people with cancer to get into fitness and yoga. So, that's the *magichappensfoundation.org*. Get on there and donate!

And with no further ado I can't believe I'm sitting here next to Ms. Daniella Cippitelli. Daniella, how are you?

Daniella Cippitelli: I'm good, thank you. How are you?

K.C. Armstrong: Great. Perfect. Alright, so, Daniella, we are going to be speaking here today because I was so psyched that you're going to be a member of the lead writers in the book, *Simply Amazing*. So, have you ever written a book before?

Daniella Cippitelli: I have not written a book, no. I have written for magazines and newspapers before, but never a book.

K.C. Armstrong: Okay, so hopefully you're just as psyched as I am, and this is going to be terrific. We're going to go through your whole inspirational and incredible story. I want to get you started here by asking what happened in 2010? Something life-changing happened to you. What was that?

Daniella Cippitelli: 2010 was when we discovered that I had a tumor on my rib. I went through surgery, a chest wall resection with reconstruction where they cut out the tumor and the surrounding intercostals muscles. I had a positive attitude going into surgery since they were convinced that the tumor was benign. But it ends up that the tumor was malignant, so I had to go to radiation after that.

K.C. Armstrong: Well, you had just given birth. I mean, about six months prior to this, right?

Daniella Cippitelli: Yes! In 2009 I gave birth to my daughter. My son was about three and a half when she was born. Well, a few months after she was born, I went to the hospital in the middle of the night thinking I was having a heart attack.

K.C. Armstrong: Was the pain in your chest?

Daniella Cippitelli:! Well, yeah, it was in the chest, in that whole central upper body region. It was so intense! I was a trained martial artist, so I started controlling my breathing the way a martial artist should.

K.C. Armstrong: That's incredible.

Daniella Cippitelli: You know, I was always good at pain management. I was always one of those people who just stuck through the pain.

K.C. Armstrong: How was your breathing? Could you breathe at this time?

Daniella Cippitelli: No, it was hard. That's why, at first, I thought I was having a heart attack. But then once I got my breathing under control I was like alright, I'm breathing. I'm not having a heart attack because I am breathing. It's painful, but I'm breathing.

K.C. Armstrong: Wow.

Daniella Cippitelli: So, I was still married at the time, and when my husband woke up I told him what was going on. He decided to call my mother who lives a couple of towns over to watch the kids while he brought me to the emergency room. I'm thinking, you know, it's going to be an embarrassing situation. They'll tell me I have a gas bubble. Give me some Tums, send me home. I'm thinking, "Do I really want to go through this humiliation?"

K.C. Armstrong: Right.

Daniella Cippitelli: This is what I'm thinking. "Oh my God, I'm going to be so embarrassed!

It's nothing." But we went, and the next thing I know the doctors are standing in the room telling me that they're not releasing me, that they're removing my gallbladder! I was feeling really sick and they couldn't let me go home because they said I would end up back within 24 hours. I broke down hysterical because I've got an infant and a toddler at home.

K.C. Armstrong: And didn't you have a bunch of ventures too that you were involved in?

Daniella Cippitelli: I was a creative director for Hearst Business Media at the time. I had texted my manager that morning going into the hospital. I was like, "Oh, you know, I have to go to the hospital; I'm having some pains. I'll be late for work," is what I tell him.

K.C. Armstrong: You figured you were just going to be late.

Daniella Cippitelli: Right, so he laughs, like, "What now? Just take care of yourself." But later I had to text him that I wasn't coming in at all.

K.C. Armstrong: Right, right.

Daniella Cippitelli: Well, the surgeon took me to do the laparoscopic gallbladder removal, which is supposed to be a standard procedure. That in and of itself is not a huge thing. It actually happens to a lot of women after giving birth.

K.C. Armstrong: That just happens sometimes. But you're clearly not one for hospitals. I got you. I can only imagine.

Daniella Cippitelli: So, he cancelled his previously scheduled surgery to fit me in so that I could get home that night. But it turned out that during the surgery they found a blockage to my liver. And the type of surgeon that they needed was not available. I think it was a holiday weekend. And so it was either cut me open and make it a regular surgery or just do the laparoscopic gallbladder removal and then I'd have to wait to take care of the liver.

Well, he chose to keep it less invasive instead of cutting me open but, needless to say, I ended up having to stay in the hospital anyway. Throughout the whole weekend my blood counts were coming back abnormal, and nurses kept coming to my bedside and asking, "Didn't you know that you were sick?" I answered, "Sick? what is sick? There is no such thing for a mother. Mothers don't get sick!"

K.C. Armstrong: Mother's don't have time to be sick.

Daniella Cippitelli: You know what's really weird? I remember they said it so many times that weekend that it triggered memories for me. I remembered one morning after my daughter was born, looking in the mirror—and my eyes were yellow. And my thought was, "I'm not as young as I used to be." I lost that childish white brightness in my eyes. I'm like, damn, it stinks getting old, you know? But that should have been a trigger, especially since my father had had cancer.

K.C. Armstrong: Bruno.

Daniella Cippitelli: Yes. I remember his eyes were so yellow at one point. It should have alerted me, but it didn't.

K.C. Armstrong: What type of cancer did he have?

Daniella Cippitelli: He had colon cancer which went into metastatic disease, his downfall in the end.

K.C. Armstrong: But his was later in his life, wasn't it?

Daniella Cippitelli: Yes. He was, I think, 64 or 65.

K.C. Armstrong: That's still kinda young.

Daniella Cippitelli: Yeah, he was young. So, there were triggers that I should have noticed. For instance, I never in my life used to get heartburn, but after they questioned me for a while I realized that recently I'd had a lot of heartburn. I'd started burning a lot of Tums and Rolaids and stuff. Certain things should have thrown me off, but as a new mother and with a toddler and working full time, there was no time to think about illness.

K.C. Armstrong: You were so busy and you seemed healthy, so you weren't going to complain about anything.

Daniella Cippitelli: Right, exactly.

K.C. Armstrong: And second of all, since you weren't going to complain anyway, you didn't even think twice about the possibility that something might be wrong.

Daniella Cippitelli: Right, right. Not to mention that not only was I working full time in publishing, but on the side a friend of mine and I had started a company. It was the beginning of what ended up being a fitness franchise with online marketing and development. But when we first started the project it was just the two of us working at our dining room tables at 2 o'clock in the morning. We would talk to each other on the phone at 2, there would be silence for about a half hour, and then one of us would say, "Are you still awake?"

K.C. Armstrong: Did the company turn out to be something that was lucrative?

Daniella Cippitelli: Yes, it did. So, after this all happened with the gallbladder they next went in and did what's called an ERCP. There was no blockage in the liver anymore. My levels had come back to normal. After that, things were fine. But at that point

I thought, you know what? I need to get back into fitness. I had gained some weight after my kids were born. So, it was time. I needed to take a step back and start paying attention to what was going on with my body. So I started working out and getting back in shape and paying attention to what I was doing. Over the course of that year I was also building the business. It was during that time that I resigned from publishing.

The fitness franchise was taking off. We were growing in marketing and web development. I had to make the decision of one or the other. I couldn't keep going with both. You know, it was just impossible. Not to mention, I was a creative director. And it's not like I was just going in and doing a 9-5 job.

K.C. Armstrong: A lot of people depended on you probably.

Daniella Cippitelli: Right, exactly. So, I made the decision to resign from publishing, which I had been in for about 15 years and went out on my own with my business partner. I had a brand-new company and little kids in 2009.

K.C. Armstrong: Did you make that decision partly because you could work from home? Was that part of your plan?

Daniella Cippitelli: Well, yes and no. The intention was to grow. And we were looking at having offices. The intention was also to make it more flexible. I was very passionate about the idea of what we had started and what we were doing. My business partner and I had a great dynamic, so it was fun working with him. Throughout my life I have been an on

275

again, off again, entrepreneur. When I was 15, for instance, I had t-shirts printed up of this stupid design I thought was cool looking. My father let me print a bunch of shirts. I was convinced they were going to sell. I never sold a single one, but hey you never know!

K.C. Armstrong: It was a try.

Daniella Cippitelli: Exactly. So, as I'm losing the weight during this year of building the business, I started noticing, when I was lying down in certain positions, that I felt a lump under my arm. So, of course as a woman you're thinking, "Oh, God, is it breast cancer?" As you know, my father had passed away from cancer and a lot of people on his side of the family also had cancer. A cousin of mine died when he was only 25 from cancer. So, now, feeling something like that lump was truly shocking.

K.C. Armstrong: You've got to get this checked out as much as you don't want to.

Daniella Cippitelli: Right. So, I go to the doctor, and from the mammogram they tell me no, there's nothing there. They're equating the lump to cysts, fibrosis, things like that. Okay, fine, they send me on my way. As time goes on I'm noticing the lump is not going away; it's not changing in density. It feels like it's getting harder.

K.C. Armstrong: And you were losing weight at the same time, too.

Daniella Cippitelli: Exactly. They didn't know what the timeframe was. The lump could have been growing for years and years. So, I went for another mammogram a few months later.

K.C. Armstrong: Did you think, "Hey, this thing is not going away. It's still here. I'm not crazy. This is something that shouldn't be here."

Daniella Cippitelli: Exactly. And, like you touched on when it comes to pain, I'm one of those people who is like, "I can't be bothered with this." When I had the gallbladder removal I actually left the hospital. This is funny—I left the hospital to get coffee and then went back to the hospital.

K.C. Armstrong: Not in a gown? Tell me you had a gown on!

Daniella Cippitelli: I did, I swear to God I did. I stayed in the car. My husband at the time went in to get the coffee. Obviously, I didn't get out of the car because I had all the tubes and stuff.

K.C. Armstrong: You took the bag of fluids with you?

Daniella Cippitelli: Yeah. I'm not joking you.

K.C. Armstrong: You are a character!

Daniella Cippitelli: I am so serious. We laugh about that because I spilled the coffee all over the car. When we got back, the hospital staff gave me dirty looks because they weren't really sure if I left or not. I mean, it was only a gallbladder removal that I had! They didn't know for sure, so they just let it be.

K.C. Armstrong: Probably didn't want to do the paperwork for having to kick you out because I don't think you're allowed to do that, you know. That's so funny. Anyway, at this point you had gone back for another mammogram.

Daniella Cippitelli: They did another mammogram and the tech left. Then the doctor came in and started with the, I don't know what they call it, the wand?

K.C. Armstrong: Ultrasound?

Daniella Cippitelli: Yes. It was an ultrasound. After the mammograms they do an ultrasound sometimes. So, the doctor starts slowing down then stops over a certain area and I see this look on her face. She looked almost confused so I knew something was not normal. And that's when she said, really slowly in a puzzled tone of voice, "There is something there, but it's not in your breasts." She said, "It's under the pectoral muscle."

K.C. Armstrong: Oh, my God.

Daniella Cippitelli: And that's when she sounded really confused. Like, how could there be, you know . . .

K.C. Armstrong: Like she had probably never seen something like this?

Daniella Cippitelli: Right. A lot of the doctors hadn't. There was a breast specialist they sent me to who ended up sitting in on the surgery because he was so perplexed with the whole case.

K.C. Armstrong: Jeez.

Daniella Cippitelli: At that point they start sending me for all kinds of bone scans. I remember one of the scans that they did; I had to carry around a card with me all week saying that I was radioactive.

K.C. Armstrong: Did they do most of these tests as an outpatient?

Daniella Cippitelli: Yeah, with the contrasts.

K.C. Armstrong: Were any of these tests painful?

Daniella Cippitelli: No, no, not at all. The bone scan was just like a full body scan, like doing MRI's and CAT scans. After doing all these tests, they found the tumor on my rib.

K.C. Armstrong: How many tests did they do before they found this tumor?

Daniella Cippitelli: Well, the mammograms were first, obviously. I think there were actually two or three mammograms before they finally found it. Then there was a series or two of cat scans. Then there was the bone scan because at that point they knew something was there, and it was just a matter of identifying exactly where it was. So once they found the tumor on my rib, I went to see the cardiothoracic surgeon who said the tumor had to be taken out. They had to cut out the rib area and the intercostal muscles around it. All right, great.

Funny story: my son actually predicted that they were taking out part of my rib before we knew.

K.C. Armstrong: Really?

Daniella Cippitelli: When we were in with the surgeon and he said what he was going to do I thought my ex- husband was going to pass out in the room. Everything got really foggy after that because I kept remembering my son in the car crying that he didn't want anybody to take out mommy's rib. And we asked him, "What, what are you talking about Rob?" We didn't know what was going on at that point.

K.C. Armstrong: That's weird.

Daniella Cippitelli: And we told him, "Rob, nobody's taking out mommy's rib." So, when the surgeon told us that they were cutting out the rib, I looked at him, he looked at me, and I swear he almost passed out.

K.C. Armstrong: Wow, that is crazy.

Daniella Cippitelli: It was. It was so crazy, right.

K.C. Armstrong: After the interview I'm going to contact Robert to see what horse I should bet on tomorrow.

Daniella Cippitelli: (Laughs) So, as we're going through all this and they're making the plans for the surgery they're convinced that the tumor it's benign because I don't fit certain profiles they have wacky names for. Turns out my tumor was a *chondrosarcoma*. Going into the surgery everybody was convinced that it was just a benign tumor. They were going to go in, they were going to take it out. After I had the surgery it seemed to take forever to get back pathology. Weeks went by. We didn't get results back until over a month after the surgery.

K.C. Armstrong: Did they hint that it could be cancerous after they took it out?

Daniella Cippitelli: No. They were convinced that it wasn't.

K.C. Armstrong: Alright, so here it is, a month later.

Daniella Cippitelli: It was right before Christmas, too. The surgery was October 8th, 2010. So, now it's already November, and we're calling every day asking are there results yet? Finally, the call comes in.

I'm standing in my kitchen and the surgeon tells me that it was malignant—a low-grade stage one chondrosarcoma.

K.C. Armstrong: Oh, man. So, does that mean the thing they took out was cancerous or that there was still cancer in you?

Daniella Cippitelli: The tumor they removed was cancerous. Thank God it was a low-grade. It was stage one and it hadn't spread, which is key. We were told at the time that chemotherapy really doesn't work on bone cancers, so they sent me to radiology. and here's another kicker to the story. The angels were with me, you know.

There is no way in hell anybody can convince me that there is not a God up there: some being, some force looking out for you because I shouldn't have even found the tumor. Even today when other doctors see my medical history, they have to ask, "Wow, on your rib. How did they find that?"

I tell them, "They didn't. I did." I found it when it was still stage one, low grade. That in and of itself is like, wow. We asked the surgeon at one point why they didn't do a biopsy first because then we would have known going into the surgery if it was cancer. His answer was that the size of the tumor was so big that it had to come out anyway. They couldn't leave it there. So, why do a biopsy when they knew they had to do the surgery? Plus, if you biopsy a cancerous tumor, it's possible that the cancer cells could leak out. Had they done a biopsy first, they possibly could have "seeded" the cancer, and it would have spread.

K.C. Armstrong: So, you're getting all these breaks here.

Daniella Cippitelli: Oh, yeah. I was getting a lot of winks from God during that year. You know, it was just one thing after another. And it was funny because the doctors were so convinced it was going to be benign. People told me, "Don't worry, everything is going to be fine, everything is going to be fine." There was never a doubt in my mind if I had cancer that I was going to kick its ass and be okay.

K.C. Armstrong: Yeah, I love it.

Daniella Cippitelli: Right. That's not happening. You know, like, I don't have time for you.

K.C. Armstrong: I love your attitude.

Daniella Cippitelli: But I kept thinking if it is, I need to do something to make sure that I'm a positive influence number 1, for my kids, and number 2, for other people. I wanted to show other people that you can deal with things in positive ways, and I knew there was going to be a lesson in there for me somehow. And, low and behold, it turned out to be a malignant tumor. But I didn't start the foundation right away. That came a year later.

K.C. Armstrong: Let me ask you a question, though. After they took the tumor out and you were home waiting for the results, how were you feeling then? Were you feeling better?

Daniella Cippitelli: Oh, my God. No, are you kidding me? Have you ever broken a rib?

K.C. Armstrong: Yes.

Daniella Cippitelli: Okay, do you remember what that was like?

K.C. Armstrong: Yes.

Daniella Cippitelli: Okay, you can't breathe. Literally, you can't breathe.

K.C. Armstrong: Right. If you have to sneeze it's the end of the world!

Daniella Cippitelli: Every breath was so painful, but at the same time, I'm a mother. I've got no time to lay on the couch. My surgeon actually would joke with me since I was obviously one of his youngest patients because he was a cardiothoracic surgeon. He would laugh, "Usually I'm begging people to move. You I want to chain to a chair!"

When I first woke up from surgery, I looked up at my surgeon and asked, "Can I sit up yet?"

"I tell you what," he answered. "How about you just lay there tonight?"

K.C. Armstrong: Yeah, just relax a little bit.

Daniella Cippitelli: He said, "You can get up and move tomorrow. I promise you can get into a chair tomorrow."

I was the youngest person in that cardo ward and I wouldn't wear the gown. I had my sweats on, and every day I walked, once I was allowed to move. One night, one of the nurses came up to me to tell me the visiting hours were over, and then she saw that I was a patient. "Oh my God, I'm so sorry," she said. I was hysterical.

K.C. Armstrong: What a great attitude that you maintained through all of it!

Daniella Cippitelli: Well, you have to. You really do. With something like that it comes down to going one of two ways. You either get angry and feel sorry for yourself with the "why me, why me, why me?" Or you, "say F-you. We're going to do this my way, and if you're going to take me down I'm going down fighting."

K.C. Armstrong: There you go. So cool. You're fearless in the face of cancer that has taken so many people down. Did you feel you had to be strong for your kids and yourself, or is it something you did more for other people?

Daniella Cippitelli: You know, I don't think I was thinking about myself. My ex-husband actually got a little bit upset with me at one point. He probably wouldn't even remember if I told him this now, but I remember when we first found out he said to me, "I don't think you understand how serious this is." I did understand, but we had two little kids. I couldn't go cry in a corner. I had to keep going. Of course, he was just looking out for me. He wanted me to take it easy, and I think everybody was waiting for me to have a meltdown.

Don't get me wrong, I had thoughts of my own mortality. When a doctor tells you that there's cancer in your body and "hopefully" they got it all, it is certainly a serious thing. You're faced with that moment of holy shit, really? Did I hear that right? Somehow I knew, and I had made my decision before the surgery that if it was malignant, I was going to use the lesson to somehow do good.

I had watched my father go through cancer, and he was so dignified through the whole thing. He didn't stop. He kept doing what he enjoyed. Just two weeks before he passed away I had taken the day off from work to spend some time with him. We were sitting at the kitchen table and he was so green, oh my God. It was horrible. He wanted to go to his collision shop in Jamaica, Queens to check on things. My brother was running the shop by that point. My father didn't want me to have to drive him all that way, but I told him, "I took the day off from work to spend with you. I'll bring you there." He was active right to the very end. He was just not going to waste any second of breathing.

K.C. Armstrong: And I have a question that I think I know the answer to, but was it more painful for you to have cancer in your body and have this whole experience, or was it more painful to watch your father have to deal with it? And I think I know the difference.

Daniella Cippitelli: Oh, definitely more painful to watch my father have it.

K.C. Armstrong: Yeah, that's what I thought.

Daniella Cippitelli: Definitely, definitely. Because in my mind I'm always like "screw that!" I feel invincible. So I have some aches and pains. I joke with people sometimes: at the end of the world it's going to be just me and the cockroaches left. You guys are all going to be gone, and I'm going to be crawling out from under the debris with the bugs.

K.C. Armstrong: So, Daniella, once they got the cancer out and you're home, what happens next? You go back periodically to check to see if the cancer had come back, I guess.

Daniella Cippitelli: Well, once the pathology came back, then I had to move on to an oncologist. I went through radiation that lasted about 19 weeks, maybe less. In the meantime, though, I was out there doing my kickboxing.

K.C. Armstrong: How was the business going?

Daniella Cippitelli: It was going great. I wasn't letting anything stop me. I was doing my thing. By this point we had offices, so I would leave the office to go for my radiation and then go home, get my kids off the bus, and you know—do what I normally do.

K.C. Armstrong: Doesn't radiation make you nauseous and sick?

Daniella Cippitelli: The radiation, not so much. The radiation burns. And that was hard because you get these sores and they open up. Yeah, that was like really rough.

K.C. Armstrong: Does it make you tired? I mean, you're going to radiation and you're being a great mom to your kids and all the rest. How did it affect you, being the super mom that you are?

Daniella Cippitelli: You know, I don't remember being any more tired, but you have to remember I was always very active. Being active physically and having really clean nutrition really makes a difference in how you feel, even if you are kind of sick. And I mean mentally, too. I was just blocking it out. Like, no big deal. I'm an idiot, right? I actually healed faster because I was so active. As I said, in the hospital I was always walking around. They told me to be prepared for around eight days there. but hey let me out in three.

K.C. Armstrong: They were probably pushing you out! At this time, were you worried at all that the cancer might not totally be gone, or it might come back? Had that crossed your mind?

Daniella Cippitelli: Yes and no. On a daily basis, no. When I did think about it, I always thought, "I kicked your ass once, I'll kick your ass again." It's like I'm the reigning champ here, not cancer. I hold the belt. Once in a while, though, it does cross my mind. Especially when something is wrong, and I go for tests. Now, when something seems suspicious, they want to send me for tests right away. And when they don't find anything, that sometimes makes me nervous because they didn't find that tumor originally, but it was there. So, on a daily basis, no, I don't think, "Oh, my God it's going to come back," with every little ache and pain. But when something is wrong, I stand up and take notice.

But I also can't spend time and energy letting it get to my head. I guess it's like a fighter's mentality. You can't let the opponent psych you out. Cancer is my opponent. I've been in the ring with cancer and I've got that title belt to hold on to.

K.C. Armstrong: It's amazing to have an attitude like that. So, after all this, and I assume that you're re-tested a bunch of times, have we heard the end of the cancer? Is it now a thing in your past?

Daniella Cippitelli: I go for routine testing for the first ten years, and so far nothing is there. But then you know what they told me? I went for a regular gynecological visit and they asked for the date of my last mammogram. I said, "Well, you know, back when I was doing the surgeries and everything." The doctor told me to go for another one because the radiation I had could actually *cause* breast cancer. I'm thinking, "Thanks, thanks for that information. Like, come on!"

K.C. Armstrong: Daniella, because of your experience, you're someone that could answer this question: Do you think that when someone is told that they're sick or have a life-threatening illness that it's important to have the mental attitude that you had? Do you think if people don't have that attitude they run a greater risk of the disease progressing?

Daniella Cippitelli: Well, I'm trying to be really sensitive with my answer because I know that there are plenty of people out there who get cancer or something else and they insist that they are positive, but it's killing them anyway. So, I want to be careful how I answer that because I don't want to be insensitive to anybody else.

K.C. Armstrong: You're not. All you're doing is talking about you.

Daniella Cippitelli: OK. For me, yes. Personally. I think attitude definitely helped because for me it was just always about how I was going to use the experience to help other people. I honestly don't remember ever thinking this is it, this is the end. I never even made a will. In my mind it was just like, no. It was never an option for me that there wasn't going to be a positive outcome. I don't know why. It could be because going into surgery the doctors were so convinced that the tumor was benign. Maybe that had something to do with my mindset.

K.C. Armstrong: Not only the people that are listening to you or that are going to read this, but for your kids; what an amazing example you set at their early ages. Those kids must have learned such a valuable lesson. And, God forbid, if they ever go through anything like that, they have the best example to see how you're supposed to meet a challenge, right?

Daniella Cippitelli: You know, I really hope so. That was one of the things that I was thinking about the entire time. If something was going to happen, I needed to assure myself that my kids were going to remember it the way I remembered my father's ordeal. They wouldn't remember somebody who fell apart. I needed to make sure that they could look up to me always, and also know that their attitudes would greatly affect what happens in their life.

K.C. Armstrong: We don't know why these things happen, but maybe on some level this happened to you for a reason. Maybe it was written that you had to go through this because other people are going to learn something from you—your kids and people that you're touching right now.

Daniella Cippitelli: Oh, absolutely. I'm convinced that I was kept here because I'm supposed to be a messenger. I'm absolutely convinced of it because there's no other explanation for everything that happened. I was contacted by somebody shortly after my ordeal who wanted to interview me for a short article. She had lost her husband to a chondrosarcoma. After a very touching conversation on the phone, she was thankful that she found me because a lot of the times, especially where mine was, these tumors are found too late. So, I'm thoroughly convinced that there is a reason why I found it, why it was still in a treatable stage. The doctors never biopsied this thing because the story could have ended differently if they had. You know, just so many things in place that I'm convinced that there was definitely a reason for it. And I made a promise beforehand that I would positivity use whatever happened to me to help other people in whatever time I have here.

K.C. Armstrong: So, okay, now you have pretty much said goodbye to this thing. Your checkups are going fine and you decide that you need to help other people. What happens next?

Daniella Cippitelli: Oh, okay, well there is a story. I have a story for everything. I started my foundation in 2012 in October so it's about a year after the experience. I'm exercising and I had started running with one of the guys that worked for me. A girl that I know in Ohio wanted to run the Disney Princess marathon. She shot out on Facebook, "Does anybody want to run with me?" I had always wanted to run a marathon! I'm think, a half marathon? How bad could that be, right? Yeah, well, hmm, another story.

K.C. Armstrong: Yeah, right!

Daniella Cippitelli: Of course I agreed. My first half marathon at Disney World; are you kidding me? Hell yeah, I'm there! So now, mind you, there were only maybe eight months to train, and I wanted to raise money for a cancer organization. This is a few years ago, and I wasn't finding an organization that was really helping patients while they were going through treatment. A lot of the organizations are raising money for awareness; they're raising money for research. But what organization out there is actually helping people in it, going through it, you know—helping them stay empowered? I remember when I was going through everything, hitting that kickboxing bag was my empowerment. That was the one thing I knew I could control in such an uncontrollable time.

The entrepreneur in me now realized "find a need, fill it," right? And that's how it happened that I started the *Magic Happens Foundation* to raise money to help people going through cancer treatment.

K.C. Armstrong: That's awesome. Tell me about the foundation and exactly what it does, what it provides, and where people can get involved or donate.

Daniella Cippitelli: Donating and getting involved are easy because you can do that right on the website, *magichappensfoundation.org*. Right now we have a yoga therapy program for cancer patients. We're actually in the process of expanding that class. We just brought on a whole bunch of new Board members, so things are going to be changing with the foundation over the next year to expand on the things that we're doing. Our whole mission is to bring a unique, holistic empowerment to people going through treatment, whether that be through fitness, yoga or meditation. So, it's really about empowering the cancer patient through ways of keeping their body going and keeping their mind from sinking into that hole.

K.C. Armstrong: Yeah, I got you! Now for people to get involved with that, they would just go to the website to sign up?

Daniella Cippitelli: Right. If somebody wants to get involved they can go on to the website and fill out a form. Then we can contact them and let them know what we might have available in their area and ways that they can help.

K.C. Armstrong: Is it just Long Island, NY, or do you have other places that you can hook them up with?

Daniella Cippitelli: We're just on Long Island right now.

We do have contacts all over, so there are ways to connect patients, fitness experts and nutritionists.

K.C. Armstrong: Daniella, do you go out and give lectures and talk about your experience?

Daniella Cippitelli: Yes, I do; that's actually one of the things that I'm going to be getting more involved in. I brought on an Executive Director, and I want to pull out from the day-to-day operations so that I can go out and speak more. The form on *magichappensfoundation. org* about how to get involved is where someone could request a speaking engagement.

K.C. Armstrong: Great! so, guys, you've heard from Daniella Cippitelli and heard how amazing her story is. If you need a speaker to come in and really inspire people, I'm sure Daniella can do just that. You've heard how amazing she is, and her story and cheerful outlook would definitely bring everybody up.

Daniella Cippitelli: Thank you, KC. I always knew helping others was what I wanted to do.

K.C. Armstrong: That's awesome. So, Daniella, we're running toward the end.

But first, after everything we just heard and everything you've been through, do you have any words of wisdom or guidance to anybody who might be worried about a lump or something not feeling right in their body? What would you say to those people? And how would you encourage them?

Daniella Cippitelli: I would definitely tell them that you have to be persistent. Not that I don't believe in doctors, but nobody knows your body like you do, right? When you get that gut feeling that something needs to be locked into, you've got to pay attention. There's truth to the whole "go with your gut" kind of thing. And you have to be persistent. You really do. At no time did I ever think maybe I'm just imagining this. You have to have faith in yourself that you know when something needs to be looked at. You can't just pass it up.

K.C. Armstrong: Got you. That's important advice for everyone. Daniella, after the ups and downs of everything that you've gone through, what have you personally learned?

Daniella Cippitelli: A lot of things. I'm not going to say I learned everything happens for a reason because I think that's taking the easy way out. But I've definitely learned that giving back gives you a lot more strength than holding onto things. The fact that I knew that I wanted to use whatever lesson was being dealt to me for good helped me in my recovery. There was no question that there would be a positive outcome so I could help other people hold on and believe that they could have a positive outcome too.

Obviously not everybody is as lucky as I am, but how you deal with the situation is what you leave behind. I find a lot of people that I'm meeting now have the same mindset that they're still here, and now they want to give back. So many of the people getting involved with the foundation, even on the Board of Directors, are cancer survivors themselves who want to give back.

I was determined that there had to be something positive that people would remember. Even if I'm not here, there has to be something positive that my kids are going to remember, that my family is going to remember, that people will remember from what I went through. Even if I didn't make it to this point where there is a foundation, the stories about me and my legacy would have been like how I remember my father. He didn't quit, he didn't give up. He didn't say "why me?" He kept going; he kept loving the people he loved and doing the things he did.

K.C. Armstrong: That's remarkable and shows how we pass courage from one generation to another. Daniella, when that day eventually comes that you are no longer with us, what would you like people to have learned from your life and what it meant to them? What would you like people to say about you when you're gone?

Daniella Cippitelli: Wow, I don't know! I don't know what I would want them to say, but I know that I'd want them to remember that I was positive about things and always tried to help where I could. My son actually made a comment like that once. He said, "Everybody has a thing. Your thing is you like to help people."

K.C. Armstrong: That's your *thing*. Beautiful. You obviously have shown him the importance of helping others, and I'm sure he'll always remember and copy that quality. You're an amazing person and mother, Daniella.

Daniella Cippitelli: Well, if I die tomorrow and my son remembers my "thing" was that I liked to help people, then I accomplished what I was hoping to accomplish this whole time.

K.C. Armstrong: That's awesome. And we're wrapping up here with Daniella Cippitelli. Go to magichappensfoundation.org for more information or to book her on a speaking gig. Daniella, you are one of the world's most amazing people, and I thank you for letting me help share your story. In an indirect way I feel that my role here is to be able to get your story out to help so many people. So, thank you for everything that you've done, and—you truly are amazing.

CHAPTER 11

Shannon Knight

INTRODUCTION

What can I say about the great Shannon Knight? This is one remarkable woman and someone I am proud to call my friend. From the minute I first got her on the air, I was impressed and inspired by her spirit and her can-do attitude, and I can't imagine there's anything this woman cannot do.

Remind me sometime to tell you the full story about how I got a call from Shannon from the local emergency room when she was visiting the station in NY. Shannon was staying in a rented house and had fallen on a rock while trying to raise the American flag on the anniversary of 9/11. She fell only because she didn't want the edges of the flag to touch the ground. This is Shannon Knight.

Shannon's chapter speaks for itself. Not only has she been an inspiration to me and millions of people who hear her, write to her, read her books, or just exchange a friendly smile at the grocery store, but she has an ability to make anyone around her overcome feelings of helplessness or feeling like they are in a battle alone. She can bring you up because she herself has suffered, reinvented herself, and faced giant obstacles while retaining her dignity, grace and desire to help others in their own personal journeys.

In the short time we have known each other, Shannon has joined me on stage in Las Vegas when I was a keynote speaker, met my family, travelled to New York to help with the radio station and book promotions, and is always one of those people that somehow brings out the best in you. She doesn't stop—and doesn't quit.

I guess that's why I feel so blessed. I get to talk to and meet such genuinely amazing people, and many become family. Laurene Hope, Werner Reich, and Shannon Knight, as examples, have traveled thousands of miles or taken time out of their busy lives to spend considerable time at our station because they believe in what we are doing.

So it is my honor to introduce the last interview of our first book. I couldn't think of a better way to end *Simply Amazing* than with my amazing friend, Shannon Knight.

INTERVIEW

K.C. Armstrong: Welcome, Shannon. Your life experiences certainly haven't been ordinary at all. They are extra-ordinary and inspiring in so many ways! So, where does your story begin?

Shannon: Well, truthfully, it began when I was the victim of a dangerous stalker who physically assaulted me on two occasions. The second time was sexual assault in 1997 when I was a single mother with two children.

K.C. Armstrong: Who was he? An acquaintance? How did you meet, and how did it morph into something so dangerous? Take me through without saying his name.

Shannon: He was someone I dated, even though it was against my better judgement. Three months later, I realized he had a serious drinking problem and was violent. I told him I did not want to see him anymore.

K.C. Armstrong: You broke up with him.

Shannon: Yes, but he would not accept it and became obsessed with me.

K.C. Armstrong: When you told him it was over, how did he react?

Shannon: He got angry and started following me everywhere. He did crazy things like leaving letters rolled up like scrolls under the windshield wiper of my car. They were apology letters to God, asking Him to forgive me for breaking off with him. He wrote that I just didn't know we belonged together. It was crazy and frightening.

K.C. Armstrong: Of course, it scared you. Did you show these letters to any of your friends, family, or the authorities? Or did you just want people to think that you had everything under control?

Shannon: I think a lot of women are going to relate to this. I went through a denial phase of trauma, like someone does when they get a cancer diagnosis. I had kids and no time to make a big deal of it. I thought, *"Maybe this is just a one-time incident. Maybe it'll go away."*

K.C. Armstrong: I see. And after he left these scrolls, I assume it escalated from there?

Shannon: It escalated. He knew what flavored yogurt I was eating, what color pajamas I wore because he was using binoculars through a slatted glass window. He'd leave the information in a letter or voicemail, which terrified me. He managed to get the phone records from my phone company. He would say he was my husband and would change my password so he was able to call in and get all of my voicemails. It got so bad I had to stay in a hotel so he wouldn't have my address anymore. He'd find me and leave roses at the hotel I was staying at and pay for my room, just to show me that he had found me.

K.C. Armstrong: What was the final straw that made you contact the police?

Shannon: I actually had a paper trail of incident reports with several police department districts in two different counties—Los Angeles and Ventura. It was in the newspaper—March 7, 1999. "Shadow of a Relentless Stalker" is the name of the article; people can pull it up and read the story.

K.C. Armstrong: Take me back to the moment that you were attacked for the first time. if It's uncomfortable, I'm sorry, but I just want to ask because I'm sure there are other women who are just like you, who block things like this out. I'm sure it's going to be hard for you to talk about it, but you've helped so many people already with your honesty.

Shannon: I'm committed to talking about this because there are a lot of women, K.C., who feel like fools when something like this happens to them, especially when the stalking or the harassment happens on the internet, which is more frequent now. They minimize it: "Well, it's just the internet. It's not like he's at my house," but you can feel intimidated on the internet if someone is writing something that is threatening or just something that doesn't sit right with you.

The first time he attacked me, I got nine stitches and a dislocated jaw. This happened when I was trying to make peace. He said, "Just come talk to me." So I did. And the reason I'm talking about this publicly is because I hid it for so long. I felt guilty and foolish for being nice and going to talk to him, thinking there was a solution this way.

K.C. Armstrong: You were blaming yourself.

Shannon: Absolutely I blamed myself and thought, *"How can I tell people? They're going to think I asked for it; I never should have gone over there."*

When it happened, we had talked briefly, and I said something to him like, "Okay, so are we good now and everything?" I tried to walk towards the door to leave, but he grabbed me with such force. He was fast and threw us both down. My face hit the floor; the impact ripped my chin open and dislocated my jaw. I lay there bleeding and he would not let me get up. He said, "We're not calling an ambulance." Your head bleeds easily. I had a white t-shirt on. Blood was just pumping out onto my t-shirt profusely. I was terrified; I didn't know what part of me was bleeding. I was in shock and couldn't feel where I had been hurt. He wouldn't call 911. He just let me bleed. After some time, he finally said, "If you agree to say that you tripped over a box, then I will take you to the hospital." I agreed, so he took me there.

K.C. Armstrong: So, you were on the floor, scared for your life, and you agreed with him just to get him to take you to the hospital.

Shannon: My jaw was dislocated, and I could barely get the words out.

K.C. Armstrong: What a scumbag. So, he took you to the hospital, and I'm sure he was right there next to you the whole time, making sure you said what you were supposed to say, and he wasn't leaving, was he?

Shannon: No, they took me back and made him stay in the waiting area. The medical team asked me questions about what had happened. They questioned him, too. While I was getting X-rays, I had what's called a trauma-induced seizure. Once the seizure subsided, I was panicked and pleaded with the technicians to help me and keep him away from me. That's when they were alerted that I was attacked. The district attorney's office sent police officers to get a full report and photographs of my injuries. I received a subpoena later that week to appear in court as a witness which meant it was mandatory for me to appear. It was strange being a witness in the district attorney's court case "The People vs *perpetrator's name*." Even though I was terrified, I still had to testify.

K.C. Armstrong: Well, with good cause. This guy was looking in your windows with binoculars and he had physically assaulted you. And he was leaving strange notes and knew your every move. Who wouldn't be scared? Is this where a restraining order comes in?

Shannon: I got one, but it didn't matter. He was still dangerous because nothing stopped him.

K.C. Armstrong: What would you say to someone that is going through this right now? Because I'm sure you didn't feel safe when he kept violating the restraining order.

Shannon: Restraining orders are not walls. Don't allow them to give you a false sense of security. Exercise caution. As far as sharing what was happening to me, it was very difficult to tell family or friends. When I did start to open up about it, sometimes the responses I got minimized my situation. People would reassure me that it was only temporary. I found that people

K.C. Armstrong: That's so scary. So how does this lead into the second attack—the sexual attack?

Shannon: The sexual attack happened when I was at a celebration party for my recent promotion at work. I was at a crowded country bar, and I literally got carried out by him when I passed out. I got roofied. The stalker showed up, and he had his 18-year-old son with him. It was early in the evening, my cake had not even been cut, and I had only part of a margarita. I went to the restroom, and I know now it was during this time that he drugged my drink. What hurt me the most after the incident was when I realized how easy it was for him to explain away to my friends the need to call an ambulance. The detectives informed me that all my friends, when questioned, said he sounded so nurturing, and since they had seen him at my work they wanted to believe him. Everyone was having fun, and he was able to brush off the need for alarm because he told them it was not serious; I only fainted because of hypoglycemia. He acted very familiar with me and charmed my group of friends to the point where they were grateful for his assistance. I couldn't talk to my friends after that because I felt abandoned, hurt, and angry. I felt their lack of extra concern for my well-being and desire to continue on with their fun was how he was able to carry me away so easily. He took me to a motel room and raped me. I know there was another man, too, because I became conscious for a few seconds. I was aware of it all but completely immobile. I couldn't fight.

K.C. Armstrong: What would you say to women who might be going through something like this? Maybe it hasn't escalated to the point that it had with you, but they're getting a weird feeling, the person is showing up where they are, maybe something at work, or posting stuff on the internet. What are some signs that they should look for to suggest it's completely unhealthy?

Shannon: The signs are not very easy to see, because in the beginning it's that warm, fuzzy feeling that's romantic—like he really likes you. As I said, at first we were dating. By the way, it's called *simple obsessive stalking*; there's a term for it, and it's kind of like OCD—obsessive compulsive disorder. This kind of stalker stays fixated on his victim. So, when something like that happens, you're going to notice patterns. They're going to break every barrier. They're going to be parked out front of your work. They're not going to be worried about going to jail. He even called me from the courtroom payphone one time and left a message on my phone threatening me.

K.C. Armstrong: So, what'd you do after all of this?

Shannon: After the assault, I was one of thirteen people in a S.A.F.E. program in Ventura County. They gave the victims each a cell phone. They took us into dispatch and gave us a tour of what would happen if we dialed for help with that cell phone. All I would have to do is give my ID to dispatch when I was in danger. My personal ID would give dispatchers my exact location, and they would guide me to a safe area, talking to me until I got there. They could send the police without my actually having to find a payphone to call them.

Eventually, this man was found guilty and put away for the maximum sentence for stalking in the 1st degree and served time for battery and assault. When he was done serving time, I was told by the detectives it would be safer if I changed my identity and moved. Victims of Crime helped me through this process. I moved to Washington State with my daughter to start a new life. A week after we arrived in Washington, the engine blew in my car. I didn't have money or credit cards because of the complete identity change and could not afford the $4000 repairs. For two years we did not have a car and we didn't have family around to help. I had a new name and a new social security number. I was at a great disadvantage without my former credit, without college transcripts and work history, and with my new name. I felt like an imposter starting my life all over.

K.C. Armstrong: What did you do?

Shannon: We walked! Everywhere. We had to, and I had faith then. I did a lot of talking to God. If I didn't have faith in God, I wouldn't have gotten through anything. I don't know how people do. I couldn't have done it myself. So, I just kept believing that there was something better around the next corner.

K.C. Armstrong: My God. So, you've got no car, you're in a new place, you don't know anybody. You're trying to do the best for your family. You have to walk. How did you get a job?

Shannon: There was a delay to get proper identification to work. It took six months to get a new social security number. They process those victims of crime cases carefully. In the meantime, I was rejected over and over while looking for employment because of my lack of proper identification. I even asked to be hired working for cash under the table. That's how I got hired at my first job as a front office assistant working for a chiropractor. I was mistreated because of my personal circumstances so I did not last long at that job. I quit. It was humbling because some employers do treat you differently when they know your personal circumstances.

K.C. Armstrong: You mean because they knew your situation with your identity changes that weren't even your fault?

Shannon: Right. I had to trust them and reveal my story of what happened to me and why my name had no history attached to it. I was hoping they would be sensitive to what I was going through, starting my life over with a little girl to support. I thought they might overlook the lack of identification temporarily.

K.C. Armstrong: You were leaving yourself very vulnerable.

Shannon: I looked like a flake, and I'd go from one job to the next because of the mistreatment from employers. I worked flipping burgers, serving beer, and at a casino. All cash jobs without my social security number. I was paid far less than the other employees. Finally, I received my new social security number. I was ecstatic! I got my first legit part-time job working at Victoria's Secret. I knew that company so well since that was my last place of employment before I relocated. I had to start at an entry level position without a work history to show for Shannon Knight. When I was asked about my lack of work history, I pretended to be a divorced woman who was seeking employment for the first time. I had so much experience it was kind of awesome to see their expressions when they thought I was just a fast learner. I was promoted quickly!

K.C. Armstrong: Basically, so far—you've been dealt a bad hand. You worked at a casino so you know what a bad hand is. You did what you needed to do to have the things that every human is not entitled to, but should have the opportunity to have. What happened after you started working?

Shannon: Work was great; I started to feel normal again. When 2006 rolled around, I got my first cancer diagnosis: stage 3 breast cancer. Once again, my life was turned upside down.

K.C. Armstrong: Shannon, can you help me? What does stage 3 mean?

Shannon: My non-professional explanation of it is that stage 3 breast cancer means it's gone to your lymph nodes, which is a gateway to the rest of your body. At stage 3 you are now at risk for metastasis on your vital organs.

K.C. Armstrong: So, that's your glands; that's what's going to pump through the rest of your body. You're in big trouble. So, the first thing you knew about it was you were in stage 3. I assume stage 4 is considered lights out.

Shannon: Yes. I knew I was already in big trouble at stage 3, and yes, at stage 4 that's what the doctors will tell you in the United States. They will tell you that all you can do is manage your symptoms.

K.C. Armstrong: Now, tell me, when did you get the news? Did you go to the doctor? How did you find out that you had cancer?

Shannon: I felt a lump. The first time I went in, the doctor said, "I cannot biopsy that. You've got cystic breasts. You are going to look like swiss cheese." A year later, it grew to the size of a martini olive, and that's when I was in trouble. I had lumps under my left armpit and three other areas of my breast. That's when I got the stage 3 diagnosis.

K.C. Armstrong: Shannon, when you got the news that you had this lump and it was cancer, did the doctors say, "Okay, it's radiation and it's chemo?"

Shannon: Yes, the doctors recommended chemotherapy, radiation, and hormone blockers. So, to explore my options, I went to the University of Seattle, Washington, Cancer Care Alliance, and they put me in a room for an all-day experience where all of the interns and the students are practicing what to do when giving someone a diagnosis of cancer. They come in with a tape recorder while you're sitting there, and they're saying what they recommend for treatment. I had never heard of so many different drug cocktails. By the time I was done, I was confused, and envelopes were given to me for trial studies. When I made my decision, I only wanted the surgery, and I wanted to do alternative treatment.

I went to a little clinic in Arizona, which is no longer there, just for diet and stuff. I also had my lymph nodes removed, and then, later on, I got a staph infection and I was so sick. I had multiple surgeries. All of this was leading up to that perfect storm for my immune system to crash. The cancer was in remission, but it came back in 2010; I was symptomatic. It was stage 4, and it had already spread to my bones, my lungs, my lymph nodes—everywhere.

The doctors said to my family and my best friend: "We're just going to try to keep her comfortable, and no, she's not going to beat it." They gave me three months to a year to live. Boy, if that doesn't kick you in the butt and say, "You've got to start living and eating right." You're not on auto-pilot anymore. You are paying attention to every single second of life that goes by. I also thought, *"Why would you take me, God? I can still do so much."* Not to be disrespectful, but I knew there were people out there who didn't want to live. And I did.

K.C. Armstrong: Yeah, there are people that have pissed their lives away because they were unhappy with things. But here you are, you are a good person, and all of a sudden you get this diagnosis. Can I ask you something without sounding disrespectful? When they told you you're going to die in three months, where did you get the balls to say, "No, I'm not?"

Shannon: I guess that's part of the five stages of cancer grief, specifically, the denial part. I went into fight mode. "I'm gonna fight, and I'm gonna live, and I'm never going to give up until my lights are out."

K.C. Armstrong: You're incredible, Shannon.

Shannon: Thank you. There's a lot of us out there, a whole network of people like me.

K.C. Armstrong: You were told you were going to die and that the cancer was in your bones and lungs. I can't imagine how painful that must have been. Did they put you on a bunch of drugs? Tell us about that.

Shannon: Yeah. They put me on morphine for pain, which made me nauseous, but they can't control the pain any other way. Morphine messes with your digestive tract and your intestines, and it stops you up. That's not healthy when you are trying to fight for your life.

K.C. Armstrong: But the alternative, though, is you must've been in agony.

Shannon: It felt like my bones were broken. I had metastasis on my sternum, my ribs. I had to sleep sitting up so I had a bunch of stuff propping up my mattress. I was afraid of dying so I slept with nightlights on. I was like a little girl, so worried I would not wake up and die in my sleep. This terrified me.

K.C. Armstrong: I'm guessing that was at least partly because of the people you'd leave behind.

Shannon: Absolutely. I describe what that fear is like in my book, *Grateful Heart*. Fear affected me and those who loved me, but there is a difference. Loved ones didn't want to lose me if I died, but I was afraid of losing my life and everyone I loved, everything I had. I have an analogy of passengers on an airplane headed to Hawaii. Suddenly, the pilot announces the plane is going to crash. He says only 1 percent of the passengers will survive. The pilot allows the passengers to call their loved ones. Just like all the advice one gets from loved ones on which cancer treatments he or she should choose to survive, these passengers are getting all kinds of advice, like, "Oh! I saw something on TV. Hold your seat cushion like this." They're giving all their input and all their advice, but they don't understand that the passengers are in fight mode; they have tunnel vision. Whatever they do, it had better be right, because the pilot said only 1 percent would survive. Regardless of how much faith we have, when

309

it comes down to it, we are always going to be afraid in an event like that. Our loved ones are feeling fear as well. But it's different; if you die, your loved ones are going heal to some degree and go on living life, loving other people and being alive, whereas if you are facing death, you are afraid of disappearing.

K.C. Armstrong: Your story is incredible. So, was there ever a time when you said to yourself, "I'm tough and I'm going to fight, but what if it goes the other way?"

Shannon: Yes. The reality of what was happening to me would kick in when I would see my son or daughter and the fear in their eyes. My daughter would call me panicking, and I'd feel afraid. This feeling was particularly bad three weeks after I did radiation. I was only able to do 22 rounds out of the 40 planned because I developed a cough. Radiation is very difficult emotionally, mentally, and physically because you have to lay on a table with your shirt off and hold very still for the radiation beams to hit the targeted area. I saw the beams as they targeted on my sternum to stop the growth of cancer, which would have paralyzed me.

One day, I tried to lay still but because of a persistent cough I couldn't. The radiation oncologist said, "We can't do anymore if you can't lay still. We're done with you." I thought, *Now what?* I was scared. My twin sister came to my house after that final appointment. I will never forget that day because she saw me fall apart like a little girl. I told her in tears, "It's not like people say, that you're going to be ready to die when it's time." I sobbed and said, "I'm not ready!" She drove us to the beach, and my crying continued. As she was driving, she was trying to cheer me up by playing 80s music—Journey,

Eagles, anything from our high school days to make me feel anything except fear.

K.C. Armstrong: Did that work?

Shannon: Yeah, that music always cheers us up. Not to mention "the purple drink." Her friend was in the back seat and they made a grape Kool-Aid-type drink with vodka in it. It didn't taste like vodka, but it calmed me down. In fact, there's a picture of me on the beach Paradise Cove in Malibu from that day. I'm wearing a green maxi skirt and a long sleeve white shirt to shield the radiation burns from the sun. That picture is becoming popular on my social media pages. I was smiling and fearless in the photo because I was a bit tipsy! My sister loved me enough to do something a little crazy by playing our music. She didn't want to see me hurt.

K.C. Armstrong: That's called love!

Shannon: It was love. We had a good time. Once the sun was setting, I went for a walk under the pier to be alone. I lay down in the sand and I tried to make a deal with God. I said, "Why would you take me? Let me stay, and I promise I will work as hard as ten volunteers. Just let me stay! Let someone who is plotting suicide go in my place. Let me stay!" I just lay down. That's when I got to one of the five stages of grief called bargaining. That was in September 2010, and by August the following year, I was symptom free of stage 4 cancer. I was healed without ever using chemo.

K.C. Armstrong: Shannon, I have so many questions for you. I mean, the naysayers out there will say "Oh, this is a freak incident. This is something that should have never

311

happened. I don't believe it." What do you say to that?

Shannon: Battling cancer wasn't easy because I cared what people thought about me. I was a people-pleaser. Everyone had their opinions about what I should do. At this point, I don't want to waste a day worrying what people think about me. I'm just gonna be real.

K.C. Armstrong: Well, they told you to go to UCLA because they were experts. But instead, you went to CMN Hospital in Mexico.

Shannon: If I had to do it all over again, I would have gone to CMN from the very beginning when I had stage 3. Having the bilateral mastectomy came with the complication of developing a staph infection. My immune system was weakened, and cancer came back with a vengeance at stage 4. I had a PICC (Peripherally Inserted Central Catheter) line in my arm and a fanny pack type bag around my waist that contained my IV antibiotic on a timed drip. It had an alarm that would beep every three days when I'd have to get a refill of medicine at the hospital. This went on for a long time.

K.C. Armstrong: This is probably the stupidest question I'll ask, but why? Why, at the risk of cliche, were you saved? I mean, you're a good person, but good people are not always saved. A lot of times bad things happen to good people. Why were you spared?

Shannon: I think my fighting nature was the training for all of this. People talk about being positive, and I teach that in my life coaching. Life coaches teach positive affirmations and healing through forgiveness, which is great, but there is one strength that I don't think is talked about enough, which I know I have. It is a fighting spirit—tenacity and grit. I try to instill others with this attribute. When it comes to cancer and family support, I'm not discounting other people in the battle. Family and friends will have strong opinions about your decisions. Having a fighting spirit means you're willing to do what you believe in regardless of people who are angry with you. "I'm going to do what I feel I need to do." I wanted something better than chemo and wasn't going to give up.

K.C. Armstrong: But Shannon, most people don't have this strength. Where did you get this from?

Shannon: If you're thrown on a battlefield, and you know you need to pick up your guns and fire so that you can live, you don't get to sit in a recliner and think about it. I felt like I was thrown onto a battlefield. I felt like I needed to grab my weapons and start kicking ass. I didn't have the luxury of saying, "Oh, I'll sit back and read a bunch of books and research for five months and figure out where I want to go." This diagnosis was a call to action, so I took my chance, and I went where my intuition guided me, and it turned out to be right. I think everybody needs to listen to their intuition and trust it. It may say, "Do chemo." It may say something else. But you have to trust your God-given intuition; trust your instincts. That's how the deer know which bushes are poisonous to eat from and which are not. There is so much noise and commotion around us—life, technology—that we're not in touch with our intuition. We need to slow down and quiet our brain and let our soul do some guiding and leading in our lives.

K.C. Armstrong: Your story . . . it's just incredible . . . You touch a lot of people, and people tell you that, don't they?

Shannon: They do, and they are amazed that I am in such a healthy condition seven years later. But at the time, I didn't see it that way. It's like in those Middle Ages jousting tournaments when someone is thrown from their horse during the match. You are lying there in the dirt and being charged at by a dark knight. What are you going to do, just lay there?

K.C. Armstrong: Who really knows in advance how they will handle being given a death sentence?

Shannon: Right, you just know that you're gonna die. You have three months to a year, and conventional doctors are saying, "Do the right thing. Be smart." And they say it in front of friends and family. It was horrifying. I knew the reality of chemotherapy. If you're told that you're gonna die, why would you do the chemotherapy, which makes you so sick to your stomach? I thought, "*Why not go to God's pharmacy? Let's see what he's got.*" And that was in Mexico. They didn't have these natural alternatives in America.

K.C. Armstrong: Incredible. So, they told you to go get the standard treatment and wanted to send you to UCLA or a place like that. Something inside you said, "No, I don't feel right with that." Tell me about that. What exactly was the alternative to conventional cancer treatment? You went to CMN Hospital in Mexico, right? What was different about this treatment?

Shannon: Yes, the hospital is in San Luis, Sonora, Mexico. The first thing I noticed at CMN, though, was the compassion and care. And they provided healthy meals. It was a heartfelt, holistic approach. I used

IV treatments—IV vitamins and minerals. I chose intravenous B17, Laetrile, IV Vitamin C, Ozone Therapy, UVBI (Ultraviolet Blood irradiation), and hyperthermia, which is far infrared to raise your body temperature. When you get cancer, your body ordinarily doesn't get a fever, which is important because the fever is an immune response to fight off harmful pathogens. UVBI cleans your blood like a muddy river. It goes from a dark red to a lively cherry red color. That's a good thing. Far infrared therapy is one of the many different modalities used to create a low-grade fever to kickstart the immune system so your body starts to fight the cancer. There are all these different options, like ozone therapy—oxygen. Cancer hates oxygen! There's dendritic cell therapy and autologous bone marrow stem cell transplant. There are a lot of alternative options.

K.C. Armstrong: Shannon, why then does everybody take the traditional route? Why do doctors say this is the way to go, when you see cases like yours all the time, where you don't do exactly what they say, and here you are seven years later and you're helping other people?

Shannon: Well, from a business standpoint, chemo is a commodity and profitable. There is an informational website called *Dollars for Docs* where you can do a search on your doctor's name. You'll find out if they're getting paid to sell or promote chemotherapy. Pharmaceutical companies make a lot of money. I checked one of my doctors and found out that he was getting paid to do speaking engagements promoting Ibrance, which is one of the top chemo drugs for breast cancer. I talk to women who had a good response to the drug at first and others who did not. It is not meant to cure. It's got horrible side effects.

Often times, after patients go into remission, the cancer comes back stronger than ever. The doctors are salesmen, too, and they are good at what they do. Fear appeal is the way to get patients on the chemotherapy. They scare you so bad that you're afraid to try anything else. And if you ask what they think about you getting alternative cancer treatment in Mexico, they can't support you.

We trust our doctors in America because most of us already have established a good doctor-patient relationship. Suddenly, your doctor refers you to an oncologist, and your doctor's referral is like his stamp of approval. This oncologist will recommend the only thing that can be recommended: chemotherapy, radiation, hormone therapy, or surgery. We have to remember that this is the standard of care for cancer patients and that if we keep going to traditional oncologists in the United States, it always will be the same recommendation. If a doctor referred a patient to Mexico for the treatments I did, he would be at risk of losing his license to practice medicine. In fact, it would be considered gross negligence. At CMN in Mexico, their standard care is holistic, and their goal is different when it comes to treating cancer. Instead of just treating the symptoms, they are focused on getting to the root of the problem: *Let's fix your immune system. Why are you getting cancer in the first place?* It's like having a rose bush in your yard, and you see a bump on the stem on one of the roses. So you cut off the lump; that's like a lumpectomy. A bilateral mastectomy is like removing the rose bush completely from your garden. Well, why not get to the bottom of the problem and treat the soil? Cancer can still grow in the body. There is no guarantee that it won't still grow if you just amputate the part of the body with cancer.

K.C. Armstrong: Did you think that the conventional treatment would be worse than what you were going through?

Shannon: I grew up believing that when someone was diagnosed with cancer it meant they were dying. I knew that it would be a miracle if they survived. I grew up with fourteen family members of mine, including myself, who have gotten cancer. Cancer wasn't something in my life that was brand new when it hit me. I saw a lot that prepared me.

K.C. Armstrong: Fourteen family members?

Shannon: Yes, fourteen family members that had to deal with a diagnosis, including my twin sister.

K.C. Armstrong: And your sister had the same type, didn't she?

Shannon: She did. I believe it was emotionally connected. My twin sister was traumatized by my diagnosis because we are twins. She wasn't just afraid of losing her twin sister. She was afraid of getting cancer herself. There are scientific studies to support the connection between emotions and illness.

K.C. Armstrong: That is really interesting. You think you can sometimes trace serious illness back to an event or emotion? Please explain.

Shannon: Sure. My own emotional connection went back to the experience that I mentioned at the beginning: the violent stalker. I buried that, hid it, because I didn't want my family to find out something that horrific happened to me.

K.C. Armstrong: This had a direct effect on you with cancer, right?

Shannon: I truly think that it did. I think about how the body responds to the mind and vice versa. People can take placebo pills and get better. Well, your adrenals, your other body systems, can be overloaded when you're experiencing post-traumatic stress; when you are damaged. These emotion inciting events could be things like a pet dying, a divorce, a breakup—not necessarily horrible violence. Your mind, body, and emotions are all connected to your overall wellness.

K.C. Armstrong: You think that it's all related somehow.

Shannon: Yes. For instance, we know that when we are scared, it affects our stomach and we can lose our appetite. We know that when we have to run for our lives, we're not ready to have turkey and potatoes! When you're sick emotionally for a prolonged period of time, it can impact the physical. This phenomenon is written about in many books. Think of the word disease. Dis-ease. Dis-ease causes disease. Is that a coincidence?

K.C. Armstrong: When you were battling cancer, even though you had family and friends around, did you feel like you were alone?

Shannon: I felt like I was alone, especially because I had to hide my feelings. Mothers and fathers can understand this. When you have children that you love, you don't want them to see your fear. You need to act like nothing's scaring you. Hold your tears in.

K.C. Armstrong: After people told you, and I'm quoting, the "right thing" you're supposed to do when you have stage 3 and stage 4 cancer, and you decided to go a different way, how did you feel towards those people afterwards? Did you feel that you wanted to let them know that they were wrong, that maybe they didn't put enough time in, or put enough thought in? That you know your body better than anyone? How does one feel after someone tells you to get a certain treatment, and then you save your own life?

Shannon: When someone you love doesn't support your decision, you feel betrayal and abandonment. People will call me and say things like, "How do I do this? My mom doesn't want me to go there. She thinks I'm crazy."

When people aren't supportive, we don't know what they're feeling. We don't know their grief and their fear and what it's manifesting into, which can sometimes be anger and ugliness. So, I can look back and forgive because I know they went through something, too, and they were just scared. Fear manifests in many different ways, like anger. So, I don't have any ill feelings towards anyone, at all. I understand. No forgiveness necessary.

K.C. Armstrong: I got it.

Shannon: What's really cool about this, K.C., is when I walked into CMN, I felt peace. There was confirmation, like I did the right thing, like, "Good job!" And I even had to wait five months because we had to raise money to get me there. So, that's really having conviction over an intuitive feeling you have.

Our intuition! It's like a God-given trait, a gift. Look at how deer know not to eat from shrubs that are poisonous. They know to back away. We do, too. We know chemo has horrible side effects, and we know that radiation burns, but we do it anyway, like we're in a trance. "I've got to do this. If I don't do this, I could die." You know? I didn't want to do that.

K.C. Armstrong: This is kind of a loaded question: you must meet many people, because you're a celebrity and you're someone who has beaten the odds. People are gonna look up to you. Do you feel pressure because these people kind of idolize you?

Shannon: Yes, I used to feel more pressure in the first three years because I was not used to it, and I'm a very empathetic woman. When people contacted me, I could feel their pain. It's especially difficult because it is almost always the eleventh hour—when they've already tried chemo and it failed, and they tried surgery, radiation, and even trial drugs. Some may have even sought out alternative medicine locally in their hometowns. In the US, alternative medicine is limited because of FDA regulations. People reach out to me on many social platforms, Facebook Messenger, LinkedIn, and my website. Often times, it's a friend of a friend.

I used to be worried about whether people who reached out to me would respond as well as I did to alternative treatments. I went through this even with my twin sister when she got cancer. But we are not clones and are so unique in how we each became ill and how our bodies respond to treatment. Now, many years later, I don't feel like people's treatment outcomes are my responsibility just because they contacted me and chose the same hospital as I did. However, my twin sister did go to CMN Hospital, as well, and she beat breast cancer.

Everyone is on their own journey, and they need to trust their God-given intuition to guide them on where to go, what to do. I'm just a woman sharing my personal experience of treatments that saved my life and letting people who are terrified of chemo know that there are other options. If it doesn't work and they still want to do conventional treatments, at least they have a stronger immune system from all of these alternative healing treatments.

K.C. Armstrong: From my perspective, if I had gone through even half of what you have, I would've cursed God. I would've thrown in the towel, had a pity party. I don't know how I would've gotten through it. But, you're telling me and anybody who's going through this right now, "It's okay to feel these things," but, yet, you've gotta have the confidence in yourself that you will get through it?

Shannon: Yes, absolutely. I get these hard questions, K.C. The hardest question I get is when a mother calls me, "Why is this happening to my baby girl? She's twenty-six years old. I should be going before her." That's a very difficult question, and it took me a while to be able to answer it. I learned that perspective is our truth, and the perspective that I have now, that I delicately share, is that we're all going to die . . . and there's a time and a way to say that. I wouldn't just say that to a woman, a mother, who is scared for her daughter with stage 4 cancer. But I do teach it in advance, that we need to realize that we're here for a purpose.

We're here to learn how to love better. The sooner that we can realize that we're meant to have a purposeful life, and to leave a footprint for other generations, and that those who have faith like I do in God, that our perspective of death is different for each one of us. We're terrified of disappearing. We don't know what death is like, and it's terrifying for us to have to look at it. And that's what I'm faced with in most of these letters. Giving them peace.

K.C. Armstrong: Shannon, what do you say to the person who contacts you just after they get diagnosed with cancer?

Shannon: I tell them there is always hope. If they contacted me, then I know it's because they want to try alternative treatments other than chemo.

K.C. Armstrong: That's gotta be tough. "Hey, I'm just a tough girl and I happened to get through this, but you know, I can't say it's going to be easy." My question for you, Shannon, the biggest question I have is . . . is it easier to teach, or is it easier to learn? I'm not quite sure of the answer to that question.

Shannon: Good question. Well, it's kind of like this. We can't take someone anywhere that we haven't been already ourselves. So, it's about the teacher and what the teacher has gone through. And it's about the student, and what they're ready to learn, where they're at in life already.

K.C. Armstrong: Shannon, you're kind of a badass, and you're a real unique person. I don't see much scaring you, but looking back, you said it was the fight-or-flight-type thing, when you got this, and you just didn't have time to feel bad for yourself or anything like that. Looking back, was there a certain part of it that was the scariest? Was it the relationship with your kids, that they had to see you go through this? Was it the unknown?

Shannon: Being able to raise the money to get to Mexico was the scariest. Mexico does not accept American insurance so I was racing against the clock, trying to get the money, trying to keep peace in my marriage. That's why I needed God so much, to have someone to talk to, to pray to. I knew that I had to beat cancer and couldn't tell my kids what was going on because I wanted them to feel that Mom was okay, even though I was battling cancer.

I felt so alone, but my father helped me get through it. He is an artist, and he sent me an art therapy book and colored pencils when I had stage 3 breast cancer in 2006. I was bedridden; I had been through not only a bilateral mastectomy, which caused a staph infection; I went through my gallbladder being removed, both knees replaced, and I had a pin in my foot from a surgery as well. I needed help! When my father sent me those art supplies, that's when I learned about the therapy. I would get those pencils out, and I would draw fairies, and to me they symbolized freedom—their long, beautiful hair covered their chests, which helped me because I didn't have a chest for nine months. So, my father was an integral part in getting me through my battle with cancer, and I don't think he even realized what he did for me with the art supplies.

K.C. Armstrong: Your father sounds like an amazing guy and a great source of comfort. I'm sure he was a tremendous influence in the mental toughness you developed and demonstrated throughout all these challenges. Shannon, tell us now about the book, *Grateful Heart.*

Shannon: I always knew I was going to write books, and I wanted my first one to be a feel-good book. So, if someone is at stage 4 cancer and opens the book to any page, the content will lift them up. Each story gives an example of adversity and how I overcame it and how it shined a new light, a new perspective, on my situation to help me get through the most challenging, worst times in my life.

K.C. Armstrong: You're so busy, and you're helping so many people. Shannon, what do you do to make sure that you keep yourself healthy?

Shannon: One of the things I teach in the book is self-compassion. I have this picture of myself as a little girl, about five years old, next to a pony. It's my favorite picture. I make an effort to talk to myself the way that I would talk to her—with love, with understanding. When I find that I am being hard on myself, I pull out this photo and I practice. Suppose someone does chemotherapy and it doesn't work, and then they read this interview and say, "Shoot! I should've done what Shannon did." The very first thing I would say to them is, "No! Would you say that to your child? Would you say, 'How stupid of you to do that?'"

I practice self-compassion, and that's how I take care of myself. We have to pay attention to our self-talk. We have to realize that we are all still, in one way or another, children; that we haven't experienced everything and that we all make mistakes. Everyone can benefit from learning to be patient with themselves and giving themselves a break!

K.C. Armstrong: That's wonderful advice, Shannon. I think it's something we could all practice more. Thank you for taking the time to talk with me. I know readers will be blown away by your honesty and strength here and by your other inspirational stories in *Grateful Heart*.

Shannon: Thank you, K.C.! It's been my pleasure.

NOTE FROM THE AUTHOR

Thank you for spending time with us here at *World's Most Amazing People Radio!*

Please tune in to WMAP Radio (www.wmapradio.com) 24/7 for more interviews of amazing people all around the world who are living the best lives they can, even when faced with major setbacks. We can all dig deep, and the more we surround ourselves with people who demonstrate that, the more courage and belief we can sustain ourselves.

But before I go, I want to keep my promise and *literally* thank my fans. If your name doesn't appear below, my sincere apologies and gratitude for believing in me.—K.C.

Twitter:

Fran Banting, Tony Hanna, John Franklin, Felecia Nelson-Davis, Input Junkie Radio, Farlo Ben Truman, Mohammed Abdullai, AWEsome Women, Ramesh Katta, Joe Roberts, Jay Fly, Craig Alexander Bell, Tabetha Waite, Janelle Anderson, Karlyle Thomms, SternFan Mutt, Texlyn Reardon, Joe Lujan, Marc Salvato, Siobhan Clark, FTC Mass Comm, Toni Janotta, 7E Entertainment, Stacia Gates, Deplorable Becky, F.L. Ruby, Kerri Levine, Dr. Richard Tcherne, Caleb King, Barrington Mole, Mike Soke, Jordan Woodhouse, Charles Edgar, Scott

David Cassulis, Doug Boost, Adam Bernstien, Bethany Aroutunian, The Lo Fi Show, Aspen Brave, The Angelic Empryess, Mi Opa, A. Holland, Giuseppe Thomasone, Motosoene Thabethe, Anthony John Soprano, Mike Bova, Gabriella Van Rij, Sara Greenwell, Jason Greenwell, Dave Caines, PutYourHazardsOnPod, Divyanshu Mishra, Harry Richards, ThreeballPaul, Karly Kingsley, Angela Star, Sandra Struck, Foro Candanga, Dougie Almedia, Kiko Keal, Brijit Reed, Chop Dog Studios, Kathy Baker, Donna Hart, After Burn 739 Podcast, Act For Kids, Saurav Singh Gurjar, Kurt Robson, C. Beth Eichner, Heather Dunlap, Eagles Time, Mr. Nits, Ernesto Martinez, Scott Palmer, Scott S. Cooper, Adriana Mendez, Dirk Chud, Women Filmakers of Color, The Jason & Mindy Project, Tim Fargo, Barbra Farina, Khalid Butrus Marook, Andi Putra Cuy, Reverend Bob Levy, Patrick Chatman, Tito Martinez, David Harris, Andrea Nimchuck, Daisy Lou, Aragua Taman, Eric Sholmo, Gareth Thomas, Jacob F. R. Dr. Carache, John YBarra, Mel Lily Laura Primrose, Javier Mayorga, Nick Foleon, Tal Veneda, Rory Quinn, Dan Cox, Chris Solis, The Mike Jolitz Show, Oriana Fernendez, Jason Gutter, Micheal Blair, Greg Bone, Leslie Jenkenson, Tim Odoubles, Misty De Zutter, Tina Adver, Leo Dominiks, Paul Twig, Adam Malawista, Jack Hollis, Morgan Issaic, David Greco, Rosalinda Randell, Bill White, Robert Kramer, Cheryl B. Evans, Dr. Zybnek Kysela, Terezie Kyeslova, Claire Colbert, John Luke, Angela Murphy, Mitzi Szereto, J. M. Smig, Paul DeBlassie III, Mike J Mele, Laurene Hope, Born Mush

Instagram:

Christian Siani, Andrea Cladis, Suzanne D. Fisher, Whita Ape Films, Lisa, Jack Williams, Brian C. Reiter, Nick Longcore, Michael E. martin, Kevin Omell, Larry C. Wade, Aaron McClung, Jordan Tsunis, Cheryl Daniels, Felecia Nelson, Salvatore Governale, Nicole Valle, Jessica Citera, William Moen, Brandy Stewart, Tom Kelso, Jack Tezcan, David Winters, Paul Passi, Micael R., Kara Miller, Asha Prasad, Thomas Patrick, Adam Micael, Natalie McCook, Steve Lunny, Sonja Thompkins, Micki Lossen, Ray Osowski, Rich Rog, Jim Zimmerman, Karen Bate,

Jen Roberts, Brian Bryne, Ted Gustafson, Trent Collicott, Treacy Lambert, Christian Yalden McCauley, Emmett Lehman Geri Richards, Tim Penska, Robert W. Martin, Jason Clifton, Catlin McGowan, Audra Reed, Mike Kennedy, Joanne Mulcahy, John D'Astolf, Kris Rocchio, Chuck Leone, Justin Deremo, Matt Conneally, Al Romas, Justin Sobleman, Tim Hartz, Bill McHugh, jennifer Wade, Tim C., Stacy Cross, Kevin Marshall, Bill Delaney, Frank Iadonisi, Virginia Phillips, Dave Pamah, Michael Morrow, William O. Williams, Jen Zei, Nick Puccia, Micael Amorelli, Troy St Jacques, Matt Maxwell, Max Power, Sean Tremblay, Nathan Seward, Joe Pulcini, Fred M. Shannon, Ed Paciolla, Sean Lennon, Big Mike Mitchell, Derek Broszeit, Mark Yvervs, Ozzie Egas, Nicole Wacura, Adam Rodriguez, Jerime Francis, Issac Delgado, Dave Goldberg, Cory Draper, Ryan Bernholz, Danny Crawford, Chris Allen, Leigh Sinclair, Michael Goines, Hannah Ray, Bryan Falchuk, Shannon Seeberg, Kirsten Keffer, Corrado Salemi, Neal Deas, Kathleen Henderson. Migel Allen, Sean Smyth, Kristen Burns, Dana Cironi, Dilbert Grady, Brian Noble, Sara Dinielli, Litle Setan, Marc Zweben, Jenny Maher, David Norris, Nick W., Belen Nicole, Larry Parrot, Michael Calabro, Ryan Pirozzi, Phil Hughes, Debbie Vine, Colin Harrington, Scott Raynor, Terry Georgas, Warren Bauer, Jenna Breitstien, Tim Buxton, Brian Reed, Douglas Calderon, Dylan Lopez, Eric Koppelman, Andrew Milner, Shawn Prebil, Jason Wilkes, Joseph John, Thomas Stimmel, Shara May, ben Grance, Heather VanSickle, Dan Stuart White, Luciano DeSorboluciano, John Decker, Brittani Stansell, Alex MinnE, George Steiger, Jack Sullivan, Alex Yahn, J.M. Smig, Darren Solimeno, Shawn Wells, Trina Helmick, Tony Montana, Brad Collins, Erik Foerster, Glenn Risko, Abby Miller, Tih Moy, John Lupia, Barret Chaggin, Tanya Starkey, Rob Mcallister, Toby Hord, Micael Fattorsi, Steven Smith, Shannon Aston, Victor Joseph, Nancy Radcliffe, Timothy L'Abrigg, Marian Belyea, Noble A. Drakoln, Dave Forgoine, Howard Webb, Brijit Reed, Marjorie Rich, Christy Hennagan, Christian Losse, Chris Kisky, Alfonso Coreone, Carence Pruden, Deana DelMedico, Barry Lewis, Paul Fergeson, Scott Weiner, Gezima Azemi, Cindy Strobel, Joe Rivera, Greg VanOstrand. Ryan Galvin, James Vitale, james Csajaghy, Ivan Maffei, Lila Nicolas, Nadia Vanilla, Solo Nadir, Stuart MacKenzie, Bob Bundy, Tony Marcello, Katie Rekowski, Brian

Engle, James Melvin, Mike Mitchell, Ambre Dorsett, James Dicola, Dan Posner, Michael Gillingham, Rob Pagliuca, John White, Stephanie Johnson, Gelice Cohen Simon Eduardo, Khirey Carr, Peter Mtui, Dave Fahim, Rich Carucci, John Erlingheuser, Alfio Rossillo, Bobo Bowie, Ron Brigeford, Jenna Moylan, Seth Lapp, Gene Canfield, Shannon Land, Barby Himsel, Mark Stirett, John Levy, Johnathan Sherby, Courtney Riley, Kenny Casanova, Diane Harrington, Emma Elvins, Eric Paulen, Sandy Lunsford, Melody Farell, Sudesh Prasad, Everett Goodman, Thomas Biniakewitz, Chalres harris, Jeff Dietzel, Chris Symington, Kelley Draeger, Kelly Mills, Melissa Gatto, Jody Inman, John Henry Ngowi, Tom Tagliente, Roswell Stanley, Keith Mutch, Eric Powers, Marc Washburn, Brian Pearce, Caden Pick, Eddie Jarvis, Jeannette Nolan, Colin Harrington, Heather Williams, Diane Lang, Paul Winkler, Nancy Marks Sterner, Cary Psutton, Marco Renteria, Todd Gookins, Steve Scefers, Danielle Kelly, Ian Spanguolo, Daniel Duva, Howard Madover, lauren Ottewill, Thad Karbowsky, Frank Nowitzki, Chris Michaels, Danielle Kroener, Rober Sean Brubaker, Doe Jodd, Alex Hench, Rusty Shacklez, Jennifer Ratay, Owen Martin, Kerri Kelly, John Neal, Rob Rovenga, Gerry Heikkinen, Bob Wold, Gary Shoff, Danielle Cippitelli, Steve Mendelson, Peter Stancill, Dean Lealand, James Laffoon, Sean Faherty, Jon Steele, Josh Novak. Keith Kwazar, Barry Keith-Coe, Cpleen Pu, Sonya Farhat, Kris Durbin, Brian Kulbe, Dave Goodwin, Mickey Morelli, Devrah Howanaa, Andy Now, Micael Scott, John Rambo, Donald Dermers, Adam Harris, Elliot Shawrtz, Mery Hendrickson, Dani Johnson, RJ Lackey, Aviad S. Klayman, John Tole, Sculte Ray, Kevin D. Sargent, Mark Satter, Nick Herrera, Anne Mason, Andrea Swabb, Robert Brown, Ken Danieli, Lisa Politis Korpi, Marc Marsala, Dawn Cristine, Joe Smookler, Stacia Gates, Joe Rhino, Glenda Silva Ramos, Jared Bakin,l Brian Angell, Stephen Odett, Paul Tripodes. Tom Butts, Vladmir Noskov, Mike Sansenbach, Lou Smooker, Craig Levine, Nora E. Adams, Selcuk Arsan, Michawl Fonce, Frank DiDomeniko, Dan Jove, Danny McDermott, Shannon Eads Stockard, Chuck Keege, Rick Rome, David Still, Glen Braget, William Smith, Nikki Breslaw, Wendy Eden, Brian McAvan, Stefan Meir, Buddy Lee, Joe Cola, Joe Giannella, Ron Badgley, Jamie O'Brien, Scott Ivan, Chris French, Ginny Armstrong, Bonnie Parker, Michelle Miller, TIm Huwel,

Eddie Hosh, Pierre Sabourin, Ray Nedohon, Jimmy Settles, TJ Roche, Doug Brustman, Wade Watson, Alysia Berardi, Chris Dinielli, Evan Lavedar, John Pizzi, Eric Lemm, Bill Beck, Zack Regan, Paul Viggiano, Dee Burdett, Melissa Gray, Tara Sutton, Natalie Forest, Antonio Stevens, Al Hastings, Angela Rose Ellington, Barbra Mitchell, Bart Battieri, Ben Wilson, Bo Buckley, Bridget Morgan, Brian Hoeft, Bryan Pullman, Chris Caflom, Chris Henkel, Dan Morse, David Foreman, David S. Witek, Donatoe Cassle, Eddy Escrudo, Eric Williams, Evan Weiss, Frank Zimmel, Kimbo Alicata, Joe Savickas, John DeSanctis, Justin Deitrick, Kendra Bell, Marc Salvato, Matt Berger, Matthew Alan Shadwick, Michael Dove, Michael Rubino, Michael Schelke, Moe Kharrazi, Neil Garrio, Ray Bell, Robert T Hedden, Scott Elliot, Steve Infante, Steve Tepper, Von Rothinfink, Wayne Johnson, William Carboy,

Alignable:

Gary "Stephen Geez", Lyn Horner, Kevin Sisco, Michele Plunkett, Debra Morgan, Helen Cook, Kelsey Matheson, Cheril Goodrich, Barbara Dianis, Jennifer Lang, Steve Smith, Bobby Cherry, Laine Cunningham, Soren Petreck, RL Lane, Rena Sylvester, Gregory Poole, Andrea LaRosa, Allan Kiezel, Maria Wakefield, Melanie T. Collins, Johnny Bauman, Liz Sime, Joseph F. Marie, Lance Gibbs, John Fuller, Jennifer Guist, Jim Gramon, Ed Kiernan, Beverly James, Suzie Schuder, Tracy Harrington, Nafeesha Goldsmith, Timmothy King, Janelle Anderson, Caroline Clemmons, Jason Powers, Tonya Kelly, Marnie Tenden, Kathy Carlin, Kellie Fitzgerald, Gary Mayhew, Cliff Scniederman, Bredan Ford, Lillian Cauldwell, Jerry Giorlando Zev Halpern, Porsha Rufus, A.G. Moye, Virginia McGrath, Rob Mconnell, Jeffrey Ptak, Angela Monolo, Beth Hale, Lee Munch, Timothy Linomme, Duane Cohen, Cindy Sommer, Mellisa Hin, Paul Cataldo, Mike Gates, Debbie Anderson, Andrew Tetreault, Robert Blumberg, Jennifer Aderhold, Marilyn Grounds, Daniel Roy Baron, Victoria Espinosa, Harun Shah, Ewan Lillcii, Linda Eicholz, Cristina Lee Shmol, Tricia Campegna, Judy Lirman, Tim Baker, Ken Kroncke, Howard Kaufman, Brett Duggan,

Dennis Cardiff, Geri Monzillo, Doris Meridith, Bruce Cryer, Vinnie Mandese, Heidi Morell, Debbie Falkenham, Don Maclver, Karen Ungerer, David Fernendez, Jeff Stern, Kiran Wadhwa, Eric Twiggs, Alyare Morgan, Carol Roach, Lori Raynoha, Claudette Melanson, Pati Smith Okeem Palmer, Laura Mastriano, Berk Washburn, Lorraine Price, Mark Larson, George Ertle, Ron Pisiano, Christine Bartol, Nestor Eugez, Theresa Costa, Shierly Kenett, Bruno Ribeiro, Rhoda Koeing, Susan Donovan, Michael Amarosa, Bonnie Potthoff, Carol J. Amatto, Jeff Horton, Jeseca Lowell, Devi Kowlessar, Kim Robinson, Martin Aponte, Alberta Conter, Bella GG, Stephen Douglass, Virginia McCullough, Michael Bradford, Alan Silva, Elgon Williams, Kharisma Jeanette, Charles Rickard, Pastor Jenet Fears, Bejamin Hylden, Joshua Dyer, Alison Sutter, Jody Kaplan, Maria Kerr, Kharis Macey, John G. Schieman, Linda Klienshmitt, John Bucciarelli, Brad Raney, Marilyn Dalla Valle, Diane Harrington, Angel Santos, Dominique Ricks, Hope Hamilton Tate, Kishor Chaudbary, Eva Growney, Karen Cioffi-Ventrice, Mark Davis, Mira DeNatale, Serena Jade, Marlowe Witlowe, Oshana Himlot, Jae, Oh, Melanie Roberson-King, Al Lohn, Kevin Murray, Angela Rietini, Judeith Grant, Kevin Deblasi, Emmylou Davis, Jennifer Testa, Billy Desser, Sherry Sobel, Stephanie Mendelson, Sharon Infante, Daniel King, Douglas Firestone, Michael S Horney, Connie Tjaden, Joe Volpe, Bob Wolf, Deb Wertheim, Eduardo Planas, David Pollack, Douglas Spencer, Katherine Batal, Marcie, Marlene Weinstein, Brian Cohen, Daniel Dowling, Rob Leighton, Wendy, Richard Rotanz, Tina Marie Leard, David Montalvo, Phillip Sugarman, Bill DeLongis, Peter Walsh, Christian Puma, John Costanza, Christina Schmohl, Jannine Pergola, Jennifer Beckman, Marisa Chadbourne, Marty Mandelbaum, Richard Feldman, Joe Sciacca, Gary L. DiClementi, Anthony Rosalia, Ron Loveland, Joseph A. Darmiento, Kalli Suarez, Rena Ferguson, Donna Spadaro, Jim Chrystal, Robert Kratzke, Mark Kutch, Laura Cash, Sheila Skolnick, Kathleen Kuzmack, Kevin Koubek, Nicole Nenninger, Amanda Bisack, Brian LeDonne, Michael R. Bernstein, Julie Watterson, Panagiota B Tufariello, Richard Rosenka, Edwin Casanova, John Magnani, Gleb Tsipursky, Roger Singh, Lynette Reed, Christina Caravas, Marti Pagartanis, Laurie Burton, Gordon Hope, Lawrence Pagano, Leora Edut, Louie Frias, Samantha White, Mark Levine, Cat

Rosenboom, Veronica Mackey, Richard John Tscherne, Noble DraKoln, Rebecca Zylstra, Julie Escobar, Alan Allard, Laura Cochran, Cynthia Linder, Jaclyn Morena, Dr. Thomas Ianniello, Dawn Saliba Vasquez, Marianna Guenther, Melissa Hood, Sue Koch, Kenneth Nuss Jr., Marites Son, Frank McCoy, Alyse Parise, Sue Glenn, Dorcas Walker, Fritzi Gros-Daillon, John DeGarmo, Tanisha Shanee, Ruth King, Tim Jacquet, Joseph Labbadia DC, Mail Phonpadith, Kathy Pagartanis, Marlyn Milicia, Suzy Greenman, Stacy Gertz, Minnie Yancey, Art Donnelly, Andrea Feinberg, Allan Varela, Paul Ordonez, Sumner Davenport, Bonnie Taub, Kellen Kautzman, Douglas Baldwin, Emrick Garam, Dr. Joseph Papalia, Regine DeBerry, Helen Hipp, Dawn-Marie Mutell, Tom Katsaros, Phoebe Roome, Matthew Tuthill, Alex Fleming, Laura Bilotta, Maxwell Ivey, Amy Geils, Edward Dowling, Trey Olds, Spencer Hawkins, Nathaniel Borenstein, Casey DeSain, Barry Cohen, Luke Thomas, Adriana Laino, Danielle Lynn, Dr. John McGrail, Heather Havenwood, Troy Anderson, Marc Hoberman, Merrily Ottomanelli, Mark Cornelison, Julio Briones, Denise Dorman, Jacqlyn Charles, Bethanie Nonami, Carl David, Peggy Sealfon, Dr. Bob Weil, Lisa Lewtan, Mary Dravis-Parrish, Patricia Leonard, Steve DiGioia, Kay Sanders, Alfreda Love, Elisabeth & Sebastien Richard, Iris Barratt, Gwen Fedrich, Gayle Stock, Cindy Strobel

Facebook Friends:

Aaron Blackhawk Miller, Aaron Cooper, Aaron Dery, Aaron Ferguson, Aaron Gallagher, Aaron Golub, Aaron Harris, Aaron Ingersoll, Aaron Jonathan, Aaron Dahl, Aaron Lavin, Aaron McClung, Aaron Porter, Aaron Roberts, Aaron Rozenfeld, Aaron Schindler, Ab Thuthmose, Abbey Robertson, Abdul Farighi, Abe Kanan, Ablay Bal, Ace Guillen, Acee Wong, Adam Adler, Adam Akeley, Adam Al Daher, Adam Beizer, Adam Berlickij, Adam Biesecker, Adam Brown, Adam Byron, Adam Carney, Adam Dayton, Adam Di Dio, Adam Dolan, Adam Ferrannini, Adam Fractenberg, Adam Glasser, Adam Gordon, Adam Greenspan, Adam Guzman, Adam Harrington, Adam Hess, Adam Holm, Adam

Hunter, Adam J Knott, Adam Kulliver, Adam Lamb, Adam Meadows, Adam Michael Doran, Adam Mooney, Adam Pierce, Adam Prieto, Adam Rogers, Adam Ross, Adam Scardamaglia, Adam Starr, Adam Sulejmani, Adam Tinkler, Adam Twigge, Adam Villarreal, Adam Warmuth, Adam Willoughby, Adam Yarman, Addison LeMay, Adelle Villanueva Nabor, Adi Egar, Adi Raval, Adisa Rimaldi, Adolpho Dominguez, Adrian Fernandez, Adrian Greenberg, Adrian L. Caponera Peterson, Adrian Marcado, Adrian Villalba, Adrianna Marie, Adrienne Lapalucci, Adrienne Leigh, Agustin A. Iglesias, Ahron Rosenhamer, Ahmad Mohd, Aileen Kokell, Aimee Mitchell, Aimee S. Arnold, AJ Benza, AJ Cutler, AJ Sheridan, AJ Skelly, AJ Teets, Akhilesh Patel, Akira Prescott, Al Borelli, Al Cox, Al DeStefano, Al Guzzo, Al Martegna, Al Primario, Al Romas, Al Tellez, Alain Aleman, Alan Bagel, Alan Blair, Alan Del Duca, Alan Fern, Alan Gary, Alan Gilkeson, Alan Hastings, Alan Kennedy, Alan Ogletree, Alan Pleet, Alan Purdy, Alan Raffanello, Alan Seslowsky, Alan Singer, Alan Swartz, Alan Ulrich, Alana Metzger, Alayna Goldsmith, Alber Tito, Albert Miller, Aldo Gandia, Aldo Iannuzzi, Alec Turner, Aleco Yo, Alejandro Castellano, Alen Del Duca, Alesha McCoury Nesselrode, Alex Broches, Alex C Monn, Alex Davis-Floyd, Alex Dopp, Alex Duff, Alex Gasior, Alex Goldstone, Alex Hernandez, Alex Kuchik, Alex Louy, Alex Louy, Alex Marini, Alex Murden, Alex Muzyka, Alex Rivera, Alex Scott, Alex Smith, Alex Stein, Alex Theoret, Alex Tzavalas, Alex Vavas, Alex Vigneault, Alex Yahn, Alex Zamora, Alex Zoppa, Alex Condello, Alexander Casanova, Alexander Scarsella, Alexis Carter, Alexis Devan, Alexis Jackson, Alfio Rossillo, Alfred Koza, Alfred Mullendore Gumban, Alfreda Stukes, Alfredo Padilla, Algenis Valentine, Ali Hassan, Ali Hyler, Ali Kermani, Ali Long, Alicia Greenberg, Alicia McHugh, Alicia neth, Alicia Ozzy Johnson, Alison Bedell, Alison Brewer, Alison Vopni, Alissa Cohen Campo, Allan Albright, Allan D. Peters, Allan Dana, Allan Krayeski, Allen Grunas, Allen Law, Allen Meissner, Allen Pfaff, Allen Salamanca, Allen Thomas Rader, Allie Beatty, Allie Burr Hicks, Allie Tidwell, Allison Crawford, Allison Fuhrmann Frangis, Allison Glass, Allison Landers, Allison Pescatore, Allissa Monrone, Ally Armijo-Jackson, Ally Parker, Allyson Hubbard Morris, Allyson Seeger, Alo-Jarmo Küppas, Alonzo Sosa, Alpesh C. Joshi, Alyse Dwyer Masserano, Alysia Berardi, Alyssa Wolff,

Amal Manal, Amanda Corvelle, Amanda Crossley Schneider, Amanda Hagan Hammond, Amanda Karstedt, Amanda Miller Broughton, Amanda Simpson, Amarachukwu Diamond Ozoani, Amaya Sr Paul, Amber Clark, Amber Kramer, Amber Simons Klimek, Amber Simpson Ambre Dorsett, Amer Bokhari, Amplifier Kim, Amy Bailey, Amy Bartsch Kish, Amy Beaver, Amy Carter, Amy Compton, Amy Dangerously, Amy Elizabeth Ward-Robertson, Amy Fonseca, Amy Gumbus, Amy Kaye, Amy Khokar, Amy LB, Amy Lutz, Amy Maret Specht, Amy Raitt Besuden, Amy Risley Schuster, Amy Rosen, Amy Valade, Amy Vitale, Amy Waite, Ana Carolina, Ana Weiss, Anderson Lawfer, Andre Courtemanche, Andre Crowe, André Gardner, André Nunes, Andre Turning-Araujo, Andrea Andrea, Andrea Brooke Ownbey, Andrea Burdett Kennedy, Andrea Calvano, Andrea Dinger Morgan, Andrea Forrest, Andrea Gibson Shaner, Andrea Jarrette, Andrea Jo Fowler, Andrea Jung, Andrea Lieberman, Andrea Merlonghi, Andrea Puskar Metcalf, Andrea Ridlon, Andrea Swabb, Andres Barbosa, Andrew Allen, Andrew Anderson, Andrew Bernstein, Andrew C Houston, Andrew Camara, Andrew Chappell, Andrew Clark, Andrew Cosci, Andrew Deacon, Andrew Duso, Andrew Edge, Andrew Ferreri, Andrew G-Dot, Andrew Gilbert, Andrew Grett, Andrew Gurevich, Andrew Howe, Andrew Karluk, Andrew Klingelhofer, Andrew Lepkowski, Andrew MacKenzie, Andrew Michael Parodi, Andrew Milner, Andrew Misha, Andrew Morse, Andrew Nagel, Andrew P Ruiz, Andrew P. Sterner, Andrew Pucella, Andrew S Green, Andrew S. Adams, Andrew Sigman, Andrew Smith, Andrew Snell, Andrew St Pierre, Andrew Stern, Andrew Stobbe, Andrew Tanner, Andrew Theodorakis, Andrew Valenti, Andrew William Wright, Andrew Young, Andromedha Deewa, Andy Baird, Andy Baker, Andy Barovsky, Andy Bone, Andy Boswell, Andy Brand, Andy Childs, Andy Dick, Andy Droffilc Clifford, Andy Fox, Andy Jones, Andy Kalce, Andy Keppler, Andy Kozel, Andy Noe, Andy Ottaka, Andy Richmond, Andy Roberts, Andy Ross, Andy Simone, Andy Skidd, Andy Steinle, Andy Thom, Andy Thompson, Andy Toth, Andy Williams, Anela Sejdin, Anfisa Zelenia Yusupova, Angel Berlanga, Angel Bundalan, Angel Cassidy, Angel Ihrig, Angel Lynn DiGiacomo, Angel Lynne, Angel Ramirez. Angela Changizi, Angela Cobb, Angela Fratto Fisher, Angela Hall Pease, Angela Lansbury, Angela Mirando,

Angela Nash, Angela Rossi, Angela Siconolfi Terrano, Angelo Palozzi, Angie Kourounis, Anita Hennessey, Anita Infantolino, Anita Jacob Gilbert, Anita Pologa, Ann Lakeview, Ann Marie E. Merz, Ann Marie Folan, Ann Piazza Beall, Ann Savina, Anne Cooper, Anne Godsil-Friesz, Anne Marie Zappitielli Beno, Annette Achzet-Ltaif, Annette Wozniak, Annmarie Guarino, AnnMarie Hernley, Anselmo Martinez, Anthea Nicole, Anthony Agate, Anthony Aguilar, Anthony Andalft, Anthony Barbato, Anthony Bellucci, Anthony Brooks, Anthony Brunetti, Anthony Buonafede, Anthony Cacioppo, Anthony Castagnoli, Anthony Castellane, Anthony Chirico, Anthony Corsino, Anthony DeCicco, Anthony DiDomenico, Anthony Eastman, Anthony Filippi, Anthony Florio, Anthony Galmarini, Anthony Haralabatos, Anthony Hernandez, Anthony Hutton, Anthony J DeCaro, Anthony Johnson, Anthony Lanaire Martin, Anthony M. Amore, Anthony M. Drago, Anthony Mando, Anthony Mangrum, Anthony Marino, Anthony Matassa, Anthony Mendola, Anthony Mignone, Anthony Mongeluzo, Anthony Montez, Anthony Moreno, Anthony Napalitano Jr., Anthony Nardone, Anthony Perna, Anthony R Maniscalco Jr., Anthony R Marraffino, Anthony Sanburn, Anthony Savarese, Anthony Scalise, Anthony Sean Valdivia, Anthony Studioso, Anthony Trivolette, Anthony Vertucci, Anthony Viera, Anthony Waltz, Anton Eggendorfer, Äntöniä Pextön, Antonio Beltre Jr., Antonio Hasty, Antonio Marino, Antonio Stevens, Antonios Hatzis, Antonne Burgess, Antwan Floyd, Apollo Sa'Deek The'Apollonian, Apple Stern, April Carletto Perez, April Feliciano, April Howland-Artist, April L McCart-schultz, April Macie, April Marie Bucci, April Rose Gedney Ramirez, Aquatic Concepts, Araknid Moore, Aramis Hernandez, Arashi Il Campione, Arben Borincaj, Archibald Lowe, Ari M. Eden, Arianna Higgins, AriAnne Prashad-Cerdas, Ariel Kashanchi, Arlene Kiste, Armand Sylvie, Arnold Sullivan, Art Ackerman, Art Clow, Art X Karenluneau, Arthur Ekram, Arthur Goldman, Arthur Lang, Artie Fletcher, Artie Lange, Arwen Moore, Ashlee Blansett, Ashlee Romero, Ashley Anderson, Ashley Barlowe, Ashley Blackstone, Ashley Clark, Ashley Craib, Ashley Gamba, Ashley Gillick, Ashley Greco, Ashley Hoover Baker, Ashley Iocco, Ashley Jacobs, Ashley Koch, Ashley Matthau, Ashley Scott, Ashley Tinius, Ashley Warrington, Ashlyn Brooke, Ashwin Kochiyil Philips, Aster Phoenix, Atticus Ingram Rowe,

Aubrie Ernst, Audra Katz Greenspan, Audra Reed, Audrey Barba, Augie Carmelo, Aurelia Simeon, Austin Gabbard, Austin Scher, Austin Shafer, Autumn Santomauro, Axle Lewandowski, Ayodeji Adediran, B St Roeder, Babba Booey, Bacwa Dan, Bake McBride, Balki Sirius, Bandi Caro, Bảo An, Barb Moore, Barbara Hynek Faeustle, Barbara Keefe Grego, Barbara Larimer, Barbara Sobel, Barbara Tuzzolino, Barbara Verruto, Barbie Mitchell, Barbie Sanford, Barby Mitchell Himsel, Barrett Ludwiczak, Barrett Tamaren-Leddy, Barry Bena, Barry Buckelew, Barry C Kappes, Barry Franklin, Barry Godin, Barry Grossman, Barry L Clement, Barry Lewis, Barry Mezey, Barry Mort, Barry Orlow, Barry Shapiro, Barry Wilson, Barry X. Kuhle, Bart Ducharme, Bart Vattieri, Bay Ragni, Baziota Reagan Baziota Dj-virus, Becca Swanson, Becky Adkins Strum, Becky Barlow Moore, Becky P, Becky Stefonich-Brady, Becky Wagner, Belle Gunz, Ben Benedict, Ben Blenke, Ben Boulay, Ben Brookover, Ben Coombs, Ben Galvin, Ben Gonzalez, Ben Goodyear, Ben Grance, Ben Hadd, Ben Hokanson, Ben J. Szczepkowski, Ben Ja Min, Ben Jones, Ben Lilly, Ben Luxford, Ben Roth, Ben Saltzburg, Ben Saltzberg, Ben Sherman, Ben Sparks, Ben Vineman, Ben Wilson, Benito Codella Jr, Benjamin Armiger, Benjamin Bronk, Benjamin Ginter, Benjamin Perlmutter, Benn Stimmel, Berhane Shawn Tewelde, Bernard Oakley, Bernard Reynolds, Bernie Frank, Bernie Kolman, Bernie Mulvaney, Bert Dandy, Berty Hildreth, Beth Friedman, Beth McAvey Graziani, Beth McDevitt Bufala, Beth Mills Tessandori, Beth Mordaunt, Beth Tishkoff Pampush, Betsey Johnson, Betsy Evans, Bettina Louise, Bettina Salazar, Betty Cantley, Beverly Hills Angels, Bhausaheb Aher, Bhengz Golucino, Bhengz Golucino, Bhengz Golucino, Bike Murns, Bilal Esq, Bile Stew, Bill Adkins, Bill Bailey, Bill Baker, Bill Battle, Bill Beauvais, Bill Beck, Bill Borgeson, Bill C Mcpherson, Bill Campbell, Bill Castellini, Bill Collins, Bill Cyr, Bill DeGrasse, Bill Delaney, Bill E Rogers, Bill Edwards, Bill Entenman, Bill Fairbanks, Bill Fletcher, Bill Fried, Bill Hanson, Bill Heinrichs, Bill Henderson, Bill Johnson, Bill Kelly, Bill Kohne, Bill Kramer, Bill Kress, Bill Lee, Bill Lohnes, Bill Mulhearn, Bill Mulhearn, Bill Mulligan, Bill Murray, Bill Neshan, Bill Reames, Bill Rodger, Bill Shank, Bill Soto, Bill Stif, Bill Thompson, Bill Unruh, Bill Veverka, Billy Bingoo Denis, Billy Bonn, Billy Bradley Wise, Billy Chase, Billy Ciaramitaro Jr., Billy Cooper, Billy Cronin, Billy

Fogz, Billy Fradys, Billy Kelly, Billy L Crawford, Billy Lawson, Billy Mira, Billy Moran, Billy Nizolek, Billy Novitsky, Billy Paniaha, Billy Van Iderstine, Billy Vector, Billy West, BJ Byrne, Bjørn Erik Hundland, Blain Smith, Blaine Dannheisser, Blaine DeLorenzo, Blair Robert, Blake Belding, Blake Berger, Blake Camden, Blake Fayling, Blake McCrossin, Blake Young, Blasian Saddles, Blenda Indigo Danielsson, Bo Allen, Bo Buckley, Bob Abbott, Bob Ando, Bob Arnoldy, Bob Barnett, Bob Bdf, Bob Belt, Bob Blickwede, Bob Butterworth, Bob Cambra, Bob Cook, Bob Couture, Bob Curtin, Bob Ducca, Bob DuPuis, Bob Estelle, Bob Farrell, Bob Forster, Bob Freeman, Bob Gero, Bob Glovik, Bob Goldberg, Bob Golub, Bob Harvey, Bob Hittelman, Bob Iswalt, Bob Kirchhan, Bob Leach, Bob Levy, Bob Martin, Bob McFarlane, Bob Misuro, Bob Paton, Bob Piacine, Bob Rizzo, Bob S Page, Bob Spero, Bob Summers, Bob Wolf, Bobbie Aday, Bobby Carroll, Bobby Castro, Bobby Cazaurang, Bobby CG, Bobby Chorizo Guy, Bobby Kirby, Bobby Kramer, Bobby Lonis, Bobby Mason, Bobby Moore, Bobby Petrosky, Bobby Stines, Bobby Warshowsky, Bobby Zuckerman, Bonnie Crockett Sellner, Bonnie J. Irby, Bonnie Parker, Boo Scooter, Booey Dosanjh, Boris Basiouk, Bounty Hunter Pictures, Brad Collins, Brad Crompton, Brad Cunningham, Brad Daugherty, Brad Fultz, Brad Gilbert, Brad Hynze, Brad Jorgenson, Brad Kruty, Brad McNary, Brad Miller, Bray Moyer, Brad O'Kurily, Brad Sawyer, Brad Six, Braden Chapman, Bradley Holsten, Bradley May, Bradley Peters, Bradley Wilson, Brandee Edwards, Branden Sellons, Branden Westrich, Brandi Ambrose, Brandi Dennis, Brandi Mossor Fenske, Brandon Barnes, Brandon Blake, Brandon Boyd, Brandon Bulb Lacewell, Brandon Church, Brandon Curtis Seevers, Brandon Deeb, Brandon Ferrazzi, Brandon Ficara, Brandon Gould, Brandon Hayes, Brandon Johnson, Brandon L. Solomon, Brandon Martin, Brandon McFall, Brandon Mikolaski, Brandon Null, Brandon Phillips, Brandon S Bassett, Brandon Sandri, Brandon Sheer, Brandon W. Crosby, Brandon Warpath Psaila, Brandy Stewart, Brantley Pendleton, Breet Xu, Bren Ben, Bren Hallihan, Brenda Gissell, Brendan Lynch, Brendan Shanahan, Brendan Smith, Brenden Kelly, Brendhan Gambino, Brendon Lachance, Brent Bester, Brent Hammonds, Brent Hartman, Brent MacGirr, Brent Munger, Brent Musser, Brent Shepherd, Brent Stone, Bret Oltjen, Brett Bolton, Brett Goldstein, Brett Holcomb,

Brett Michaels, Brett Newman, Brett Purdy, Brett Stone, Brett Vickers, Brett Wax, Brett Weir Jr., Brian Alemany, Brian Alex, Brian Anderson, Brian Angell, Brian Barrio, Brian Benson, Brian Berryman, Brian Betz, Brian Beukelaer, Brian Bluefield, Brian Boyd, Brian Boylan, Brian Brookshire, Brian C. Reiter, Brian C. Stevens, Brian Cabrera, Brian Cardonick, Brian Celecia, Brian Chowdah Freedman, Brian Clark, Brian Cline, Brian Costello, Brian Dahlquist, Brian Davis, Brian Defusco, Brian Devlin, Brian Diemar, Brian DiPiazza, Brian Dodd, Brian Donnelly, Brian Dunn, Brian Dussault, Brian Edwards, Brian Engle, Brian Fellers, Brian Finn, Brian Floren, Brian Frederickson, Brian Fye, Brian Garland, Brian Gonzalez, Brian Grisham, Brian Healy, Brian Heyman, Brian Hoeft, Brian Hornidge, Brian Hulett, Brian Hunt, Brian Jacob Kooy, Brian Jeffrey-Zone, Brian Karcher, Brian Kenny, Brian Kerman, Brian Kramer, Brian Kulbe, Brian Lawson, Brian Lengyel, Brian Lowe, Brian Lynch, Brian Lyons, Brian M. Fischer, Brian Mac, Brian McAvan, Brian Mcguire, Brian McMahon, Brian McRory, Brian Millinger, Brian Monarch, Brian Morton, Brian Mund, Brian Nestor, Brian Nicolini, Brian Noble, Brian Notarianni, Brian P Kelly, Brian Patti, Brian Penot, Brian Perone, Brian Pilson, Brian Pitts, Brian Popp, Brian Redman, Brian Reed, Brian resnick, Brian Riback, Brian Richard, Brian Rouillard, Brian Rowlands, Brian Rudd, Brian Russell, Brian S. Young, Brian Schwinge, Brian Scott Gross, Brian Sennett, Brian Serne, Briane Shanks Jr., Brian Sharby.com, Brian Slagel, Brian Smith, Brian Sowerby, Brian Spence, Brian Stevens, Brian Strobel, Brian T. Staley, Brian Talamo, Brian Terry, Brian Tomarchio, Brian Trujillo, Brian Warner, Brian Welch, Brian Winters, Bridges Mobley, Bridget Daur Richards Lmt, Bridget Miller, Bridget Morgan, Bridget Uddo, Bridgette Schooley, Brie Anne Bentley, Britanie Michae-Leigh Warner, Brittany Lotshaw, Brittney Michelle Trujillo, Brody Brodo, Bronson Cigancik, Brooke Ashley Warner, Brooke Curren Kelly, Brooke Haselton, Brooke Lima, Brooke Llyod, Brooke Scherr, Brooks Rice, Bru Nyc, Bruce Bobzien, Bruce Boyd, Bruce Hutchinson, Bruce Macgurn, Bruce Martinez, Bruce Miller, Bruce Thomson, Brückl Mandy, Bruno Gomes, Bryan Anthony, Bryan Cronin, Bryan Daniel, Bryan Flynn, Bryan Foulke, Bryan J Berner, Bryan Kaschak, Bryan Kennedy, Bryan Nantz, Bryan P Stevens, Bryan Pullman, Bryan Quenelle, Bryan Rogers, Bryan

Rose, Bryan Scott, Bryan Tietjen, Bryan Tillett, Bryan Zampino, Bryant Hannie, Brynne Mckeone, Bryson Warner, Bub Daddio, Bubba Hamdinkler, Bubba Nangle, Bud Hanke, Buddy Lee, Buddy Mione, Burton Mione, Burton Martin, Buster Brown, Buster Little, Butchie L Dine, Buz Terry, Byron Melvin, Caela miller, Caitlin McGowan-Northrop, Cal J Vi, Calla Lilly, Calvin Clark, Cam Andrews, Camecia Talbott, Cameron Taylor, Cameron Vozzella, Cameron Wilson, Camile Lee, Camille Belt, Candice Chloe Watson, Candice Saccone Stefanelli, Candy Caraftis, Candy Friedman, Candy Guerrero, Candy Shaw, Canice Neary, Canyon Miwa-Vogan, Cara DeBerardinis Pivovarnik, Caraftis Fishing Station, Carey Bacon, Carey Jones, Carl Bowden, Carl J Drumgoole, Carl Joseph, Carl Miller, Carl Nebhut, Carl O NJ, Carl Talamantes, Carla Meadows, Carlene Marin, Carlis Phillips Jr., Carlito Cross, Carlo Ocando, Carlo Castillo, Carlos Charlie Lovestruk Sainz, Carlos Hernandez, Carlos Lorenzo, Carlos Pinto, Carlos Quarles, Carlos Vargas, Carlos Whitesel, Carma Frutiger Smith, Caro Nelson, Carol A. Cannata, Carol Chloe, Carol J Gardner, Carol Lislevatn, Caroline Blackman Coakley, Carolyn Thomas, Carrie Ann Schwarz, Carrie Biser Sampson, Carrie Chapman, Carrie Cryer Morgan, Carrie Jill, Carrie MacFadden, Carrie Rotfeld, Cary Psutton, Case Johnson, Casey Ann, Casey Brunt, Casey Crum, Casey Donohue, Casey Felago Guglielmo, Casey Fu, Casey Hages, Casey Loddigs Veit, Casey Moore, Casey Patridge, Cassandra Laine McGlaughlin, Cassidy Marcus, Cassie Sstrwbrry, Cassius Morris, Catherine Ortiz, Catherine Stearn, Catherine Wood, Cathie Morrissey, Cathy Corley, Cathy Cull Lanter, Cathy Farmer, Cathy Ryan, Cathy Sama Ingargiola, Cathy Spear, Cathy Tobin, Cecilia Parra, Celina Marie Ceo, Cesar E Reyes, Cesar Romero-Savage, Cezar Zota, Cha Cha Pendlebury, ChaCha Fiorillo, Chad Ayres, Chad Browder, Chad Burns, Chad Calderone, Chad Cleary, Chad Cramer, Chad Dahc, Chad Dibo, Chad Fisher, Chad Frangipane, Chad Fraser, Chad Gadomski, Chad H Johnson, Chad Lucas, Chad Mead, Chad Russell, Chad Spittle, Chad Zawisza, Chadwick Barnes, Chalaire Miller, Chance Whidden, Chanonita Flo, Charlene Yorhey-Reinert, Charles Anthony Nichols, Charles Barbato, Charles Chalik, Charles Cosci, Charles Fleischer, Charles Fuentes, Charles Grove, Charles Hickle, Charles L Hidalgo Jr, Charles Lyon, Charles Parslow, Charles Rocamboli,

Charles Thomas, Charles Wyvill, Charlette Whitley, Charley Thompson, Charlie Bell, Charlie Costello, Charlie Kaoud, Charlie Lanter, Charlie Robbins, Charlie Stream, Charlotte AnneNv, Charlotte Davis Bischoff, Charlotte Forrester, Charlotte Miriam, Charlotte Oldbury, Chase Lively, Chase Wilson, Chaunce Hayden, Ched Vivas, Chef Franco Lania, Chelsea Hood, Chelsea Parson, Cheri Bishop, Cheryl Daniel, Cheryl Fender Wagner, Cheryl Ling, Cheryl Romeo, Cheryl Uribe, Cheryl Wright, Chet Langridge, Chett Abramson, Chivis Gilbert, Chola Grande, Chris Allen, Chris Anderson, Chris Armstrong, Chris Babb, Chris Bailey, Chris Balmanno, Chris Behm, Chris Bernard, Chris Berthelot, Chris Biadasz, Chris Booker, Chris Brightwell, Chris Brown, Chris Bruno, Chris Bucolo, Chris Buda Budenbender, Chris Bunion, Chris Bygonaise, Chris Camplese, Chris Capo, Chris Carmon, Chris Carpenter, Chris Cassler, Chris Chapin, Chris Chiarmonte, Chris Ciolino, Chris Ciulla, Chris Clark, Chris Colgan, Chris Colombo, Chris Conrad, Chris Conrad, Chris Cummings, Chris D Foley, Chris Davis, Chris De Meo, Chris Dennis, Chris Diot, Chris DiPesa, Chris Duncan, Chris Ebbott, Chris Ellington Long, Chris Eppolito, Chris Forrest, Chris Frederickson, Chris French, Chris Gaeta, Chris Geoghegan, Chris Glass, Chris Graves, Chris Greene, Chris hale, Chris Hancock, Chris harris, Chris Harwood, Chris Havens, Chris Hefner, Chris Heinig, Chris Henkel, Chris Hogan, Chris Hopkins, Chris Horton, Chris Howell, Chris Humphries, Chris Hunt, Chris Johnston, Chris Kanto, Chris Kazakos, Chris L Caldwell, Chris Landry, Chris LePoer, Chris Lundgren, Chris Maguire, Chris Marzola, Chris Mason, Chris Mayo, Chris Meyer, Chris Milano, Chris Miles, Chris Mintz, Chris Mintz, Chris Monk, Chris Morosoff, Chris Mudd, Chris Mullins, Chris Noth, Chris Nurczyk, Chris Olivia, Chris Power, Chris Procopio, Chris Prunk, Chris Randazzo, Chris Rauch, Chris Redondo, Chris Riggins, Chris Robbins Okrasinkski, Chris Roberts, Chris Robinson, Chris Roman, Chris Royal, Chris Ryan, Chris Saganich, Chris Sannella, Chris Sape, Chris Sara Dinielli, Chris Schneider, Chris Schommer, Chris Shea, Chris Sheehan, Chris Sie, Chris Sixsixeight, Chris Sky, Chris Speidell, Chris Symington, Chris Takach, Chris Tawney, Chris Taylor, Chris Thomas, Chris Topher, Chris Torrey, Chris Totillo, Chris Unger, Chris Van Son, Chris Vandee, Chris VanZandt, Chris Von Nieda, Chris Wahl,

Chris Watson, Chris Whaley, Chris White, Chris Williams, Chris Williamson, Chris Wilson, Chris Windle, Chris Woolie, Chris Zadie, Chrissy Bogue, Chrissy Ellinas, Chrissy Franz Trimbur, Chrissy Morrow Ackerman, Christa Mooney, Christen Smith, Christian Alshire, Christian Andersen, Christian Binder, Christian Clothier, Christian Kludjian, Christian Nicklaus, Christian Santos, Christian Siani, Christiansoldier Matthew, Christie Kane, Christie Kirk, Christie Turocy Pratt, Christin Annette, Christina Chen, Christina Gilam, Christina Hayes, Christina Louise Smith, Christina Smith, Christina Zipley, Christine Bartol, Christine Distor, Christine Governale, Christine Khoshabeh, Christine Kramperl, Christine LaLonde Cooper, Christina M. Chapis Loader, Christine Montanti, Christine Neely, Christine Shomo, Christine Terry Bonura, Christine-Chrissie Barrett, Christoffer Speck, Christopher Acosta, Christopher Alan, Christopher Annino, Christopher Baran, Christopher Blake, Christopher Breen, Christopher Burk, Christopher Cabral, Christopher Caverly Buffalo Schommer, Christopher Church, Christopher Cunningham, Christopher Davis, Christopher Fort McMurray Aitchison, Christopher Francis, Christopher Grako, Christopher Harte, Christopher Higgins, Christopher Joseph, Christopher Juhl, Christopher Laudando, Christopher Maier, Christopher Mansfield, Christopher McMahon, Christopher Miller, Christopher Nottleman, Christopher Palesado, Christopher Peters, Christopher Picone, Christopher Pietrzyk, Christopher Ramsey, Christopher Reynolds, Christopher Ritter, Christopher Rizzo, Christopher Scheurich, Christopher Schwenk, Christopher Scum, Christopher Shotmeyer, Christopher Stank Coté, Christopher Sweet, Christopher Taylor, Christopher Thompson, Christopher Tovar Curry, Christopher Wujek, Christopher Zuccaro, Christy Madrid, Christy Paciolla Hennagan, Chrysti Sparkle Warner, Chuck Becker, Chuck Conway, Chuck Dickinson, Chuck Donohue, Chuck DuBois, Chuck Eaton, Chuck Ehret, Chuck Finley, Chuck Gawne, Chuck Ghoulie, Chuck Griffin, Chuck Haber, Chuck Helveston, Chuck Henson, Chuck Hoover, Chuck Jones, Chuck Kosola, Chuck Leone, Chuck Maley, Chuck Saragossi, Chuck Simcox, Chuck Stipak, Chuck Wingate, Chucko Fett, Cinco Sanderss, Cindy Baysarowich-Pennett, Cindy Burns, Cindy Faust, Cindy Gold, Cindy Lancaster Brown, Cindy Waugh

Zaby, Cisco Rodriguez, CJ Hernandezz, Claire Power Murphy, Clarence Pruden, Clark Elms, Claudia Stavola, Claudine L Morgan, Claus Holm, Clay Benedict, Clay Butler, Clayton Biggsby, Cleedon Johnson, Cliff Martin, Cliff Perciavalle, Cliff Zimowski, Clifton Wayne Holloway, Clint Fayling, Clint Popp, Clint Richardson, Clint Savarese, Clinton Bistodeau, Clinton Newkirk, Clive McKay, Coach-Andy Mcleod, Cody Barra, Cody Douglas, Cody Smit, Colby Christofferson, Cole Joseph, Coles Williams, Colin Gallagher, Colin Harrington, Colin MacDonald, Colleen Lord, Colleen Martin, Collin Cq Quinn, Colton Fisher, Coma Jim, Connie Anderko, Connie Baublis, Connie Henriquez, Conor Durcan, Conor Luskin, Conrad Perry, Conrad Rios, Cookie Carosella, Coop N CHeryl Hack, Cooper Kael McShane, Corey Aiello, Corey Byrd, Corey Chapman, Corey Gugisberg, Corey Hobbs, Corey Lobb, Corey Stremcha, Cori Elizabeth Barton, Cori Lahners, Cory Murphy, Corinna Luise Mendis, Corrada Salemi, Corry Dissinger, Cort McCown, Cortney Massey, Cory Bass, Cory Calhoun, Cory Chad, Cory Draper, Cory Fernandez, Cory Himsel, Cory Jones, Cory Jurentkuff, Cory Laehn, Cory McAvoy, Cory Rockwood, Cosmo A Tropiano, Coty Jorgensen Tyacke, Courtney Bella, Courtney Ca, Courtney Sheehan, Courtney Stone, Craig Alan Smithline, Craig Anderson, Craig Balzano, Craig Beight, Craig Blaha, Craig Blevins, Craig Chernoff, Craig Cypress, Craig Donaldson, Craig Ell, Craig Gass, Craig Goldberg, Craig Greer, Craig Levine, Craig Liguori, Craig Lisogorsky, Craig Loydgren, Craig MacLeod, Craig Macnaughton, Craig Mauro, Craig Mele, Craig Nichols, Craig Rolsin, Craig Scandone, Craig Schorr, Craig Schwartz, Craig Siegelbaum, Craig Sirois, Craig Smith, Craig Walters, Cris Italia, Crishana Leigh, Cristina Fersedi, Crysha Shaw, Crystal Alosa Reynolds, Crystal Burnham, Crystal Lynn, Crystal Needham, Crystal Vahzz, Crystal Vieyra, Cuervo CN Jose, Curt Warfield, Curtis Larkins, Curtis Larkins, Cuyler Edwards, Cyndee Somers, Cynthia Davis, Cynthia Dickerson, Cynthia Gutierrez, Cynthia John, Cynthia Kilonsky, Cynthia Riegler, Cynthia Tolbert, Cyrus Johnson, D.c. Hoffman, Dagny Bolen, Daisy Everson, Daivd Tooth Vogel, Dale Armstrong, Dale Barnes, Dale Ellison, Dale La Rocque, Dale Lee, Dale Riv, Dale Rutan Jr., Dalelynn Johnston, Dallas McCue, Dallis Clint Graham, Damien Infantino, Damien K Ramirez, Damien Lee, Damion Lupo, Damon Feldman,

Damon LaFlamme, Damon Leach, Damon Meros, Dan Anastasia, Dan Ariel, Dan Babeu, Dan Baesler, Dan Beard, Dan Berkowitz, Dan Blatt DBlizzat, Dan Boxer, Dan Calma, Dan Carter, Dan Cessna, Dan Clancy, Dan Cohn, Dan Colbert, Dan Cooper, Dan Crespo, Dan Daly, Dan Dauley, Dan Davis, Dan DeLiberty, Dan Fingers, Dan Greenberger, Dan Hermanns, Dan Hunt, Dan Joseph, Dan Jove, Dan Justis, Dan Kay, Dan Krueger, Dan Laird, Dan Lewis, Dan Lunde, Dan Martin, Dan McCabe, Dan McGrath, Dan Mclaughlin, Dan Mezzalingua, Dan Moffitt, Dan Morrison, Dan Morse, Dan Nulton, Dan Ny, Dan Olson, Dan Patch, Dan Pavelis, Dan Pike, Dan Posner, Dan Prato, Dan Reheuser, Dan Richards, Dan Riley, Dan Rosenberg, Dan Rowland, Dan Rutledge, Dan Ryan, Dan S. White, Dan Scolnick, Dan Shiff, Dan Shuster, Dan Sonn, Dan Spm Cooper, Dan Stange, Dan Storey, Dan Suh, Dan Whittaker, Dan Winograd, Dan Wiznewski, Dan Wolfgang, Dan Wroblewski, Dan Zachary, Dana Cassidy, Dana Centolella, Dana Cironi, Dana Copley, Dana Gottlieb-Gabay, Dana Graziano, Dana Zak, Dandy Lion, Dani Cabral, Dani Losangeles, Daniel Baldwin, Daniel Bogdanoff, Daniel Boone Simmons, Daniel Brown, Daniel Brownell, Daniel Cox, Daniel Dudek, Daniel Duva, Daniel Florentine, Daniel Goldman, Daniel Gorwitz, Daniel Greene, Daniel Kevin Ball, Daniel Kotok, Daniel Kurzban, Daniel L Saunders, Daniel Lock, Daniel Mcnaught, Daniel Nasi, Daniel Padgett, Daniel Perez, Daniel Robillard, Daniel Rufo, Daniel Staffey, Daniel Tuttle, Daniel Vaught, Daniel Watterson, Daniel Watterson, Daniel Weston Hurst, Daniel Wexler, Daniel Wylie, Daniela Vidal, Daniella M. Cippitelli, Daniella Mendez, Danielle Amus Stone, Danielle Car, Danielle Chase, Danielle Cosgrove, Danielle Held, Danielle Koljer, Danielle Kroener, Danielle Marblestone, Danielle Marlowe Young, Danielle Nickole, Dannah Smith, Danni Krash, Danny Bradley, Danny Carpentieri, Danny Cohen, Danny Crawford Dwoskin, Danny Delmore, Danny Fineman, Danny Ganz, Danny Hizami, Danny Lebovitz, Danny Maldonado, Danny McDermott, Danny McMullen, Danny Mizrahi, Danny Turner, Danny Valencia Lima, Dano Withers, Daphanie Lawler, Daralyn Kelleher, Darcy Burkholder, Darcy Dibble, Daren J. Fleming, Darlene Mercado, Darlene Westgor, Darrell Bennett, Darrell Drayton, Darren C Goldstein, Darren Hanna, Darren Leider, Darren Mohr, Darren Solimeno, Darren

Templeton, Darrin Chapman, Darrin E. Connell, Darrin L. Haug, Darryl Cassell, Darryl Richmond, Darryl Scott, Daryl Colden, Daryl K Houston, Daryl Rene, Dasha Slepuhova, Daug Cat, Dave Anne, Dave Baigis, Dave Baldwin, Dave Bartl, Dave Bernal, Dave Berns, Dave Boulden, Dave Cassiere, Dave Caswell, Dave Clausen, Dave Cox, Dave Daniello, Dave DC, Dave DeGeare, Dave DeLuca, Dave Ercolini, Dave Fahim, Dave Fantigrossi, Dave Forgione, Dave Frank Macias, Dave Gain, Dave Godwin, Dave Goldberg, Dave Gould, Dave Granata, Dave Green, Dave Grenley, Dave Haddleton, Dave Harris, Dave Hassan, Dave Hibbs, Dave Hogarth, Dave Hoj Hojnowski, Dave Josuttes, Dave Keene, Dave Klawansky, Dave Krueger, Dave Lerman, Dave Macdonald, Dave Manns Jr., Dave Marvin, Dave Melkonian, Dave Nickerson, Dave Orque, Dave Ouellette, Dave Pham, Dave Redlin, Dave Rowles, Dave Salkin, Dave Scherer, Dave Sherman, Dave Soriero, Dave Stewart, Dave Stotts, Dave Tina, Dave W Downing, Dave Walter, Dave Wilson, Dave's Other Page, Davey Galvan, Davey Pendergrass, David Allyn, David Alvarez, David Aronowitz, David Aurelius Holtzman, David Bartol, David Bermender, David Bonza, David Breda, David Brink, David Brooks, David Bussotti, David Calone, David Campbell, David Carter, David Christian Beard, David Cichetti, David Coelho, David Combs, David Czuprynski, David DePue, David Diaz, David DiCarlo, David DiVenti, David Divjak, David Donaldson, David Dubay, David DuBow, David Dunaway, David Elson, David Fagin, David Feigeles, David Feldman, David Forman, David Forth, David Foster, David Ganhao, David Gatehouse, David Gauci Jr., David Greenman Haroon, David Gulley, David Hanania, David Hauser, David Hernandez, David Hoptman, David Hurley, David Ira, David Johnson, David Kaplan, David Karson, David Kennedy, David Korman, David L. Weiner, David Lippman, David Lloyd, David Lorrain, David M. Gears, David Mann Jr., David Marcus, David Marshall, David Martin, David Mathews, David Michael Perkins, David Miles, David Moises Hulse, David Mongelli, David Moody, David Morell, David Narciso, David Nicols, David Nosala, David Nuzzy Nussbaum, David Ostrovsky, David Overbaugh, David Pakman, David Pan, David Pearson, David Peters, David Pingree Jr, David Plastik, David Przybylinski, David Robinson, David Rocamboli, David Rodriguez, David Roland, David Romo,

David Ross, David Rothenberg, David S Silberg, David S. Witek, David Sandoval, David Scalisi, David Schleyhahn, David Schmidt, David Secemski, David Shapiro, David Shem, David Sigman, David Simpson, David Stein, David Still, David Stitch Patrick, David Sundbom, David Swift, David Sypniewski, David T Wozniak, David T. Lenzi, David Taylor, David Thompson, David Torres, David Tully, David Tuminello, David Uline, David Waghorn, David Walmer, David Wasniski II, David Weightman, David William Farmer, David Williams, David Wolff, Davie Dukes, Davina Lawler, Davio Socci, Davo Baboorian, Dawn Christine, Dawn Dalzell Nix, Dawn DeLeonardis Moody, Dawn Faith Williams, Dawn Macut, Dawn Marshall, Dawn Olsen, Dawn Simmons, Dawn Stauss, Dawn Swetnicki Stanzione, Dayna Anne, Dayna Cirrotta Grella, Dayna Levy, DB Frick, De Henri, Dean Brunt Jr., Dean DeMilio, Dean Manzerolle, Dean Papazidis, Dean Parker, Deana DelMedico, Deanna Jones Falchook, Dearrion G. Snead, Deathor Glory, Deb Canter, Debbie Castello, Debbie Di Orio, Debbie Ferrari, Debbie Lynn, Debbie Sue Goodman, Debbie Sullivan, Debbie Tonyes, Debbie Tuz, Debbie Vine, Debora Oswandel, Deborah Brooks, Deborah Charney, Deborah Tomaro, Debra Jfsc, DEbra Palladino Mancuso, Debra Pearce Vonwinckler, Debsue Hayden, Dedhead Ken, Dee Burdett, Dee DMawl Muldrow, Dee Hill, Dee Snutz, Deena Lurman, Deirdre Coen Filippi, Deirdre Marie Capone, Deke Dasilva, Delia Lina Huss Delvin Walton, Demetrios Rallatos, Dena Zee, Denis Berthiaume, Denise Boland, Denise Casella Weakland, Denise Davis Berna, Denise Elaine, Denise Jennings, Denise Petrosini-Blandi, Denise Sharron Johnson, Denise White Smith, Dennis Amodio, Dennis Batelli, Dennis Coburn, Dennis Gramolini, Dennis J. Riveron Jr., Dennis Jacob, Dennis Johnson, Dennis Leon, Dennis Mazza, Dennis McCarthy, Dennis Nourry, Dennis Trentler, Dennis Twombley, Denny Brooks, Denny Meinert, Deon Grobler, Deon Harton, Derek Broszeit, Derek Carrafa, Derek Carrafa, Derek Cohen, Derek Fleece, Derek Kelly, Derek Movalli, Derek Peter, Derek R Hall, Derek S Cilibrasi, Derek Seale, Derek Skovron, Derek Sullivan, Derick Wheeler, Derrick Fiori, Derrick Hart, Desirae Dixon Kehn, Detkata Ustov, Devin Ensign, Devin Kramer, Devon McGinnis, Dián Wilson, Diana Fitzgerald, Diana Lynn Nelson, Diana Mayson, Diandra DiClaudio Reinfeld, Diane Bartol Harrington, Diane Diot,

Diane Grisham, Diane Jefferis, Diane McAuley-Wacker, Diane Nicholson Cathcart, Diane Uzwack, Dick Buttons, Diedrich Jones, Diego Serrano, Dina Reed, Dinah Leffert, Dino Bonilla, Dion Drama, Dirk Miller, DM Tyler, Döc Ivan, Dodger Dave, Dom Levy, Dom Marino, Domanick Ferry, Domenick D'Angelica, Dominic Chianese, Dominic Dias, Dominic Geraci, Dominick DiMichele, Dominick Irish Puerto Rican, Don Barris, Don Bates, Don Botkin, Don Cerbone, Don Cheech, Don Edwards, Don Ferris, Don FP, Don Herring, Don Jamieson, Don Knowles, Don Laning, Don Lipton, Don Mahon, Don Maloney, Don Michell, Don Pomrielo Hoof, Don Roberts, Don Shumway, Don Sill, Don Sniffen, Don Sowell, Don Stracaluzi, Don Thorvund, Don Pomrielo Hoof, Don Roberts, Don Shumway, Don Sill, Don Sniffen, Don Sowell, Don Stracaluzi, Don Thorvund, Dona McCall, Donald Church, Donald Hill, Donald Keohane, Donald Stanley, Donald Vane, Donato Casale, Dong Hoang, Doni Schiltz, Donna Alley Seaton, Donna Cooper, Donna Cubbage, Donna Fasulo, Donna Florio Spector, Donna Manzella, Donna Rose Thompson, Donna Wright Hignutt, Donny Garzino, Donovan Spearman, Donte' Pimpleton, Dora Martinez, Dora Stavrolakes, Doran Bradford, Doreen Petrillo, Doreen Simone Napolitano, Doren L Andersen, Dorie Dowling Rickard, Doug Albertson, Doug Anacreonte, Doug Austin, Doug Berry, Doug Biddle, Doug Brewster, Doug Brustman, Doug Christenson, Doug Dawson, Doug Ferguson, Doug Filardo, Doug Gossard, Doug Limpwerst, Doug Lotten, Doug Marsyla, Doug Martin, Doug Miller, Doug Mullen, Doug Rapko, Doug Shippy, Doug Wəåtherholtż, Doug Z. Goodstein, Douglas Calderon, Douglas Frank, Douglas Quealy, Douglas Scott Ocheltree, Douglas von Oiste, Douglas Weiss, Douglas Wood, Drew Batman McInnes, Drew Cosentino, Drew DaPuzzo, Drew Freudenberger, Drew Gould, Drew H. Fash, Drew James, Drew Shapiro, Drew Stewart, Dr Matt Lipschitz, Dr Suzie Schuder, Duane Amado, Dug Lloyd, Duke Fightmaster, Durwin Diaz, Dustin Glodney, Dustin Liggit, Dusty Bartlett Menser, Dusty Sargent, Dwaine E Peacock, Dwayne Johnson, Dwayne Miller, Dwight C. Holder, Dwight Coblazo, Dwight Crawford, Dwight Ellis, Dwight Rattet, Dylan A Hamblin, Dylan Gadino, Dylan Gray, Dylan Smith, Dylan Vanasse, Ed Ayala, Ed Brown, Ed Campo, Ed Carr, Ed Claypoole, Ed Cunning, Ed Fontanese,

Ed Golden, Ed Leduke, Ed McGonigal, Ed McKernan, Ed McKirdy, Ed O'Hanlon Jr., Ed O'Nell, Ed Paciolla, Ed Radin, Ed Reagan, Ed Ritchotte Jr., Ed Romero, Ed Simon, Ed Stymerski, Ed Torian, Ed Witchey, Ed Zakhary, Eddie Annunziata, Eddie Barnwell, Eddie Barojas, Eddie Dunne, Eddie Earl, Eddie Finocchiaro, EdDie Garcia, Eddie Godoy, Eddie Hosh, Eddie Inman, Eddie Jarvis, Eddie Kabana, Eddie Madrigal, Eddie Matranga, Eddie Santiago, Eddie Spry, Eddie Thompson, Eddy Blasco, Eden Jacobowitz, Edgar Sanchez, Edmond Durana, Edward Brett, Edward Burger, Edward Cruz, Edward Fernandez, Edward Fidler, Edward Harrmann IV, Edward Joey Escott, Edward Joseph, Edward Kosenski, Edward Leheny Jr., Edward Stern, Eeser Smith, Efrain Escobar, Egereonu Kelechi, Ehab Elhag, Eileen Grace Delosreyes, Eileen Mertes-Dolansky, Eileen Walsh, Eissa Alb, EJ Scott, El Ninio, El Tarasco, Elaine Barnes-Bailey, Elaine Der Boghosian, Elaine Martin, Elaine Richie, Elaine Simon, Elbow's Bell, Eleanor Westaby, Elena Ballesteros, Elfrieda Colangelo, Elie Abrahamovitz, Elina Nulman, Eliot Offen, Elis Diaz, Elisa A Schwartz, Elise Palazzo Crapser, Eliz Sho, Elizabeth Cronin, Elizabeth Dubin, Elizabeth Geary, Elizabeth Luna, Elizabeth Sutton, Elizabeth Wert, Ella Mejia Saldivar, Elle Latsch, Elliot Elrod Schwartz, Elliott Baxter, Elroybob Johnson, Elton Garcia, Elva Barr, Elvin Cutler, Elyse Demayo Glover, Emely Newman, Emeraldflo D Kaczmarek, Emiliano Ferazzini, Emilio Cianfarano, Emilio De Soto, Emily Cihos, Emily Grace Di'Tomo, Emily Kornbluth Aronson, Emily Megan Hearne, Emily Rachael, Emily Sloan, Emma Jean, Emma Jean McClellan, Emmett Lehman, Emotional Friend, Enis Dingby, Enrique Eduardo Guerrero Garcia, Eri Fern, Eric Adam Conner, Eric Adams, Eric Amicone, Eric Anno, Eric Brackett, Eric Bronson, Eric Butz, Eric C. Jaye, Eric Carter, Eric Caswell, Eric Chapman Jr., Eric Cheng, Eric Chepanonis, Eric Deery, Eric Dwyer, Eric Flores, Eric Ford, Eric Freeman, Eric Gibbs, Eric Giuliano, Eric Greenberg, Eric Grey, Eric Jason DeBono, Eric Javor, Eric Jones, Eric Kemp, Eric Korenman, Eric Lancy, Eric Larsen, Eric Lemm, Eric Logan, Eric Long, Eric Lynch, Eric Mace, Eric Manchester, Eric Markham, Eric Martinez, Eric Mayoral, Eric McWhorter, Eric Medeiros-Rice, Eric Mendez, Eric Molbegat, Eric Ochoa, Eric Orta, Eric Paulen, Eric Pearlstein, Eric Potts, Eric R. Mintz, Eric Reetz, Eric Rhein, Eric Rienzie,

Eric Roberts, Eric S. Lynch, Eric Seal, Eric Shannon, Eric Shantz, Eric Silva, Eric Strohl, Eric Swarr, Eric Thomas, Eric Van Sleet, Eric Wagner, Eric Walden, Eric Williams, Eric Zimmerling, Erica America, Erica Kiertz Bartol, Erica Waters-Felice, Erich Steinberg, Ericson Rivera, Erik Bleaman, Erik Chopin, Erik Delvecchio, Erik Dentry, Erik Foerster, Erik Gallardo, Erik Hann, Erik Hernandez, Erik Kucich, Erik Landreth, Erik Lievano, Erik Schoenwetter, Erik Selisker, Erik Westberg, Erika DeWald Toman, Erika Jones, Erika Marie, Erika Witherspoon, Erin Brown, Erin Colleen, Erin Hart, Erin Rnville, Erin Stevens Beshear, Erin Varvaro, Erin Zumbo, Ernest Lupinacci, Ernie Botze, Erron Palmatory, Esteban Fudge, Etsy Nounette, Etan G TheJewishRapper, Ethan Cohen, Ethan Dreyfuss, Ethan McEthan, Ethan O'Daniel, Ethan Schreiber, Ethan Ullman, Euclides Leonidas Villagomez, Eugene Driscoll, Eugene Kramer, Eugene Ostermiller, Eugene Zimmer, Eva Frausto Emler, Eva Magdalenski, Evan Deli, Evan Echenthal, Evan Evan, Evan Lambert, Evan Marz, Evan Ravkin, Evan Weiss, Eve Eriksson, Eve Lenkowsky Zilm, Eve Sangenito, Evelyn Reynoso, Everett Goodman, Everett McMullen, Fabian Magallanes, Fabian N Peluso, Fabio Dacre, Fabrizio Rotondi, Falxifer Occisör, Fayez Al-mhjoub, Feilong Zhang, Felice Cohen, Felice Leecy T Triolo, Felicia Hernandez, Felipe Quintanilla, Feliu Oriols Codina, Feo Delto, Fern Marie Burke, Fernando Batista, Fernando Jackson Dacruz, Fil Triolo, Flint Adkins, Flip Tha Script, Flynn McCaffrey, Folly Paro—Posenauer, Forrest Garth, Forrest Miller, Fran Coleman, Fran Gelman Levine, Fran Quinn, Fran Tague, Franca Elisa Minasi, Francesc Gutierrez Agüí, Francesca Fradella, Francesco Cutugno, Francisco Bermejo, Frank Albanese, Frank Celauro, Frank Cerra, Frank D'Addario, Frank DeMarco, Frank D'Errico, Frank DiDomenico, Frank Dolce, Frank Franceschini, Frank Giuseppe, Frank Houston, Frank Iadonisi, Frank J Gallo, Frank J. Clark Jr. Frank Kolcaj, Frank L. Atkinson, Frank Lestarchick, Frank Leyenaar, Frank MacKay, Frank Murray, Frank Musante, Frank Perrone, Frank Plantamura, Frank Raso, Frank Rivera, Frank Rizzo, Frank Rodman, Frank Sebastiano, Frank Skolonis, Frank Sledjeski, Frank Spoto, Frank Thomas Demmerle Jr, Frank Urso, Frank Van Alstine, Frank Wang, Frank Wechter, Frank West, Frank Zavadil, Frank Zimmel, Frankford Frank, Frankie Scalize Jr., Frankie Seance, Frank Joseph Bilello, Franky's

Silverlake, Frazer Smith, Fred Forgione, Fred Grenzebach, Fred Krause, Fred Nolan,Fred Norris, Fred Noschese, Fred Rubble, Fred Segal, Fred Wilson, Freddie Bott, Freddy Bottone, Freddy Contreras, Freddy Lewis, Frederick A. Hartman, Fredo Martinez, Freeman Vashier, Fu Tao, Funnyvideos Kh, Fuquan Johnson, G Jerome DeCarlo, Gabe Solo, Gabriel Bencomo, Gabriel DeHerrera, Gabriel Killian, Gail Ann Messina, Gail Gramlich, Gail Hendricks, Gail Weintraub Galazan, Galileo Vitruvius, Gamaliel Alex Aguilar, Gao Wei Martinetti, Gared Alan Roessel, Garret T. Sato, Garrett Collins, Garrett Hagler, Gary Blach, Gary Cannon, Gary Cohen Wood, Gary DeLuca, Gary Dennis, Gary G Umstetter, Gary Garver, Gary Gastmeyer, Gary Gentile, Gary Goodrich, Gary Gorman, Gary Hornstein, Gary L Smiley, Gary LeVan, Gary Malone, Gary McConihay, Gary Michaels, Gary moore, Gary O'Connor, Gary Peterson, Gary Sanders, Gary Wolf, Gary Zamek, Gavin Freitas, Gavin Scalissi, Gavin Shuck, Gayle Kahkonen, Gena Marie Gegich, Gene Canfield, Gene Lopez, Gene Rozell, Gene Schwartz, Gene Sherry, Geno Bisconte, Geno Carter, Geno Harambe Garcia, Geoff Shipp, Geoff Wargo Jr., Geoffrey A. Stamets, Geoffrey Curry, Geoffrey Gottlieb, Geoffrey Robe, George Ananyan, George Bacon, George Baker, George Burkoski Jr, George Cash, George Fairey, George Gallo, George Gamache, George Gibson III, George Guzman, George Kalty, George Kessler, George Moore, George Nagy, George Nov, George Perez, George Rizsanyi, George Seviour, George Solowan, George Steiger, George Vonelm, Georgie Grillo, Georgine Madigan Stoner, Geova Gomez, Gerald Cece, Gerald Zecker, Gérard Cohen, Gerard Hoekzema, Gerard Ryan, Gerard Siani, Gerardo Ahumada, Gerardo Ahumada, Gerardo Rodriguez, Gerd E Poppinga, German Deer, Gerry Libertelli, Gerry Lonn Florence, Gerry NewLamb, Getty Cavitt, Gezima Azemi, Giacomo Del, Giacomo Jack Grosso, Gibbs Paulina, Giga Granada Hills, Gli Sanchez, Gilbert Gottfried, Gilberto Plaza, Gill Valerio Sr., Gilles Galoustian, Gina Amaro-Sutterfield, Gina Ferraro-Lochren, Gina Marie, Gina Naccarato Clark, Gina Savoca Myers, Gina Serafine Boren, Gina Simone, Gina Von Lach, Ginny Freese Barbara, Gino Disisto, Giovanni Aurilia, Glen Braget, Glen Miller S., Glen Turpening Jr., Glenn A. Czik, Glenn Cooper, Glenn Derle, Glenn Douglas Gould, Glenn Grilley, Glenn Hoffert, Glenn M. Risko, Glenn

Reeder, Glenn Remler, Glenn Sandberg, Glenn Tesmacher, Gman Atman, Goin Gine, Gold N Bachelor, Gonzo Wakamoto, Good Hctim, Gordon Rutledge, Govan Anthony Martin, Grace Dizon, Grace-Anne Waters, Graham Molzahn, Graham Young, Grahmn Morgan, Gramma Jan, Granger RL, Grant Craig, Grant Landers, Grant Looney, Grant Moninger, Gray Marv, Grayson Bithell, Greg A Smith, Greg Alprin, Greg Boasberg, Greg Bonilla, Greg Bowser, Greg Brosseau, Greg Burroughs, Greg Burton, Greg Busch, Greg Cates, Greg Charles, Greg Combs, Greg Czerwinski, Greg Daniels, Greg Dean, Greg Dickson, Greg Fritzler, Greg Goehle, Greg Goldman, Greg Hall, Greg Hardie, Greg Hillebrand, Greg Ilukowicz, Greg Keesee, Greg Lawrence, Greg Loeser, Greg Mamula, Greg Mandile, Greg Nercessian, Greg Preece, Greg Purri, Greg Reifsteck, Greg Renna, Greg Smith, Greg Stocker, Greg Tiderington, Greg Vaccariello, Greg VanOstrand, Greg Virtue Tufaro, Greg W. Huebner, Greg Wadden, Greg Ward, Gregg Boron, Gregg Katz, Gregg Laframboise, Gregg Rempkowski, Gregg Singer, Gregorio Adam Davila, Gregory Bowser, Gregory Cortese, Gregory Edward, Gregory K. Haralabatos, Gregory Ramkhelawan, Gregory Snutch Knowles, Gregory Soeder, Gretchen Gibson, Grisel Diaz Meir, Guy Opochinski, Guy Santostefano, Gwenne Luvs Greg, Haikel Maikel, Håkon Øiestad, Hal Jordan, Hal Norris, Halo Ices, Hampton Yount, Hank Thedwarf, Hanna Mant, Hannah Bartol, Hannah Espudo, Hannah Friedman, Hannah Ray, Hans Hahn, Hans Von, Haole Harry, Hardin Hester, Harlan Friedman, Harley Clark, Harmony Reed, Harold R Zimmerman, Harrison Scott, Harry Hall, Harry Levin, Harry Ralph Libbert, Harry Windsor, Harvey McCarter, Havard Moltu, Hayden Pickles Klassen, Heather Abbott, Heather AC, Heather Anderson, Heather Ann Abuel, Heather Ann Larder, Heather Armstrong Williams, Heather Cavitt, Heather Henderson, Heather Holman Benson, Heather J. McAdams, Heather Krug, Heather L. Arnold, Heather Larsen, Heather Lynn, Heather Reining Kaiser-Tyler, Heather Rusaw-Fazio, Heather Turman, Heather VanSickle, Hector Mercado, Hector ThetalentedMr Arocho, Hefen Howser, Heidi Cortez, Helder Ferreira, Helen Nu-Metal Maiden, Helen Vaughan, Hellion Ruiz, Henrik Frost, Henry Hill, Henry Juliano, Henry Muhlenberg, Henry Ramirez, Henry Thomas Rogacki, Hernan Pabon, Herrera Alvarez Sergio, Herschel

Dixon, Hil Moyers, Hildebrando Barrera Rojas, Holly Dusoe, Holly Hanley, Holly Kenyon, Holly Medrano, Holly Morphew, Hombreblanko Mann, Hortencia Cabral, Hoss Ridgeway, Howard Dubansky, Howard Feinberg, Howard Gering, Howard Gross, Howard Handler, Howard Jones, Howard Lesnik, Howard Liebeskind, Howard Madover, Howard Webb, Howie Amrani, Howie Goldberg, Howie Jastrow, Howie Petracca, Howie Zwang, Hugh Janis, Hugh Patrick Jr., Hugo Morales, Humberto Misteroni, Hunter Ahrens, Hunter Cray, Hunter Snow, Ian Adkins, Ian Bookman, Ian D Scottish, Ian Gresh, Ian Johnson, Ian Karr, Ian Michael Spagnuolo, Ian Papkov, Ian Sangenito, Ian Steven Hill, Ike Banoun, Ilana Possner Buxbaum, Ilene Bader, Ilene Yulick, Imran Hanzi Khan, Ira J Katz, Irene Corcoran, Irfan Sheikh, Iris Donitz, Iris Zimberg Filippi, Irish John Mulhere, Iron Grip Dave, Iron Sheik, Irwin R Fletcher, Isaac Abadi, Isaac Taylor, Isaac Webster, Isabella A. Lagdameo, Isabella Nichole, Isak Samuel Edvardsson, Ishai Lingan, Ishmaël Ortega Garcia, Israel Horowitz, Issy Horowitz, Itsall A Sham, Ivan Hidalgo, Ivy Silberstein, Izzy Casaletto, J Arsenio D'Amato, J Brian Koonce, J David Znacko, J Ryan Wilton, J Scott Reeve, J.C. Cole, J.d. Avarmy, J.d. Bowers, J.M. Smig, J.R. Preston, Jack Assadourian, Jack Barlow, Jack Cutler Sr, Jack Devaney, Jack Edmunds, Jack Eskew, Jack Feeney, Jack Godwin, Jack Greenberg, Jack Herold, Jack Johnson, Jack Mieoff, Jack P Fogel, Jack Shlapak, Jack Sullivan, Jack Wilson, Jack Wu, Jackie Clark, Jackie DeMott Janovec, Jackie Knoph, Jackie Martino Roff, Jackie Martling, Jackie McGurn, Jackie Rascon, Jackie Rubino, Jackie Tetreault, Jaclyn Zepernick, Jacob Ashton, Jacob Gunter, Jacob Hamburger, Jacob Hodge, Jacob Johnson, Jacob Newton, Jacob Trabert, Jacqueline Bolier, Jacqueline Hall, Jacqueline Patricia, Jade Gummer, Jaeci King, Jaime Alberto Flores, Jaime Damico, Jaime Flores, Jaime Ledoux, JaimeLynn Amato, Jaimie Anzelone Mauro, Jake Bierganns, Jake Caldiero, Jake Heaton, Jake Lee Bowden, Jake Martin, Jake Miller, Jake Moore, Jake Seed, Jakof Yussef, James A. Brannan, James Adams, James Barreto, James Black, James Borocz, James Brisciana, James Byrum, James Calderon, James Case, James Caverly, James Cordova, James Costa, James Creaney, James Creelman, James Dascole, James Davidson, James De Nitto, James DeBenedetto, James Dyer, James Elder, James Forero, James G Britt Jr., James G Amodei, James Genoe, James Harvey Heard

Kenyon, James Howes, James Hughes, James L. Jones, James L. Warren, James la Gala, James Lampe, James Lazarin, James Lederer, James Lester, James Lightbody, James Lonano, James M. Leahy, James MacKenzie, James Makarius, James Mathias, James McCann, James McIntosh, James McLaren, James Melvin, James Michael Roselli, James Mitro, James Moran, James Murphy, James Noblett, James Oden, James Parker, James Power, James Ramsey, James Riddle, James Rotta, James Ryan, James Ryczkowski, James Santiago, James Stan Kola, James Stimola, James Taylor, James Tortorice, James Vincent, James W. Brinkerhoff, James Walker, James Warden, James Wright, Jami Linnea Forseth, Jamie Colburn, Jamie Harmeyer, Jamie Jasta, Jamie Kramer, Jamie Kunkle, Jamie Leigh Fischer, Jamie Mack, Jamie N Danielle Triail, Jamie Norsigian, Jamie O'Brien, Jamie Sans, Jamie StJohn, Jamie Sue Lightning, Jammy Johnson, Jan Doe, Jan Hein, Jane Campbell, Jane Vassas, Janet Baker McCauley, Janette Richardson, Janice Rantz, Janie Cullen, Janie Meadows, Janna Phillips, Jared Baer, Jared Bakin, Jared Hogeg, Jared Marnin, Jared Neumann, Jared Phillips, Jarrod Blanc, Jarrod Minger, Jason Andrew, Jason Atkins, Jason Becerra, Jason Becker, Jason Belfer, Jason Boyd, Jason Brenner, Jason Calhoun, Jason Chui, Jason Clifton, Jason Collins, Jason Cook, Jason Cooper, Jason Cox, Jason D'Agostino, Jason David, Jason Deeh Pitre, Jason Douglas, Jason Dyke, Jason E Ridgeway, Jason Evelyn, Jason Forlano, Jason Franks, Jason Gallant, Jason Glover, Jason Goldfarb, Jason Gross, Jason Halegoua, Jason Hernandez, Jason Hoffman, Jason Irwin, Jason Jacobs, Jason Jamison, Jason Johnson, Jason Jurado, Jason Katz, Jason Knutti, Jason Kraft, Jason Kull, Jason LaHue, Jason LaPorte, Jason Lash, Jason Laviana, Jason Lazarus, Jason Long, Jason Lovestar, Jason Luff, Jason M Svec, Jason M. Gudzik, Jason Mandle, Jason Mazzio kiiiii, Jason Miller, Jason Mizrahi, Jason Moore, Jason Murphy, Jason Nowlin, Jason Peña Mata, Jason Polkes, Jason Potere, Jason Proskurin, Jason R. Donnelly, Jason Rakes, Jason Roberts, Jason Rute Roudebush, Jason S Bray, Jason Scott, Jason Seaver, Jason Short, Jason Shreve, Jason Sidelman, Jason Sirotin, Jason Sìxx, Jason Smith, Jason Spires, Jason Stm, Jason Valasek, Jason van Teylingen, Jason Vitale, Jason Wachowski, Jason Weaver, Jason Whitsell, Jason Wilhite, Jason Wilkes, Jason Wood, Jasper Flax, Jav Morales, Javier DaSilva, Javier Delgado, Javier Palenzuela, Javier

Parrales, Jay Anderson, Jay Ann B. Silvestre, Jay Barnett, Jay Beasley, Jay Cee, Jay Gilbert, Jay Holbrook, Jay Houghton, Jay I. Erickson, Jay Jerdee, Jay LeClaire, Jay Livingston, Jay Low, Jay Moore, Jay N Jess, Jay Negus, Jay O'Brien, Jay Ozzy Hernandez, Jay Passerino, Jay Picolo, Jay Plamjack, Jay Richard, Jay Sellers, Jay Sosnicki, Jay Stone, Jay Such, Jay Warsinske, Jaymie Lisa Horowitz, Jayne Caswell, Jayne McKillop-Verdon, Jayson Lotano, Jayson Stewart, Jayson Zammerilli, Jazzmyn Banks, Jb Trebilcock, Jc Hernandez, JD Good, Jean Browder, Jean Gathercole, Jeanette C. Rumsey, Jeanette Tupper Shearer, Jeanne Bligh Marinello, Jeanne Kiebler Loftis, Jeannette Tatum Wright, Jeannine Ehrlein Sparhuber, Jean-Pierre Padilla, Jebadiah Daniel Harris, Jed Given, Jeff A. Bossi, Jeff Amsden, Jeff Ash, Jeff Atkins, Jeff Bartoli, Jeff Beaver, Jeff Beerbaur, Jeff Binczyk, Jeff Bonilla, Jeff Brennan, Jeff Brett, Jeff Brooks, Jeff Bruno, Jeff Buckley, Jeff Clayton, Jeff Culver, Jeff Curro, Jeff Dell'Acqua, Jeff Dietzel, Jeff Essex, Jeff Field, Jeff Fife, Jeff Folger, Jeff Francis, Jeff Fugitt, Jeff Gans, Jeff Garcia, Jeff Gardner, Jeff George, Jeff Ginnis, Jeff Giosi, Jeff Gotelaer, Jeff Grant, Jeff Harding, Jeff Hart, Jeff Hollon, Jeff Jameson, Jeff Jones, Jeff Keeton, Jeff King, Jeff Klein, Jeff Koffler, Jeff Krapf, Jeff Kunze, Jeff Lau, Jeff Lawrence, Jeff Lazar, Jeff Levy, Jeff Liss, Jeff Lockey, Jeff Mirman, Jeff Montagna, Jeff Myerow, Jeff Newhook, Jeff Nolan, Jeff Oakley, Jeff Orr, Jeff Poisel, Jeff Quinn, Jeff Raffensberger, Jeff Reagan, Jeff Reed, Jeff Renick, Jeff Reynolds, Jeff Rosa, Jeff Schimmel, Jeff Schnarr, Jeff Schottmuller, Jeff Shaw, Jeff Sheehan, Jeff Shepard, Jeff Sheridan, Jeff Singer, Jeff Smith, Jeff Snyder, Jeff Socalington, Jeff Speidel, Jeff Steiner, Jeff Sylvia, Jeff Thigpen, Jeff Twiller, Jeff Wagner, Jeff Warren, Jeff Wick, Jeff Wingfield, Jeff Zipp, Jeffery Walsh, Jeffrey Axelrod, Jeffrey Burton, Jeffrey Butterworth, Jeffrey C Swartz, Jeffrey Crockett, Jeffrey Dean Gray, Jeffrey Gibson, Jeffrey Goldin, Jeffrey Gross, Jeffrey Pines, Jeffrey Ross, Jeffrey Silverman, Jeffrey Soto, Jeffrey Thomas, Jeffrey Totillo, Jen Creedon, Jen Dub Carter, Jen Gemmy Bolier, Jen Graff, Jen Kuchmy, Jen Miller, Jen Moore, Jenevieve Amaris Strine, Jenifer Huerto, Jenifer Tracy-Pellegrino, Jenn Jacobs, Jenna Levinson Breitstein, Jenna Newsome, Jennifer Ancelo, Jennifer Anderson, Jennifer Andrea, Jennifer Avery, Jennifer Blick, Jennifer De Alba, Jennifer Eder, Jennifer Eiden, Jennifer Emil, Jennifer Fincannon, Jennifer Fountain Papa, Jennifer Gonzales, Jennifer Hicks,

Jennifer Horvath, Jennifer Jco Coburn, Jennifer Joyce, Jennifer Keitel Klein, Jennifer Leedom Snyder, Jennifer Leonard, Jennifer Lombardino, Jennifer Lynn Murphy, Jennifer Lynne, Jennifer Marie, Jennifer Marie Heatherton, Jennifer Massalon Stimpson, Jennifer Mercer, Jennifer Moellering-Caros, Jennifer Nelson Rocca, Jennifer Petrucciani, Jennifer Pilkin Nelson, Jennifer Ricca-Chiapperino, Jennifer Salzman, Jennifer Schmied-Zyontz, Jennifer Seidell, Jennifer Sherry, Jennifer Sims, Jennifer Staas, Jennifer Sweeny, Jennifer Tombs, Jennifer Vollaro, Jennifer Wade, Jennifer Wellesley Ornstein, Jennifer White Corcoran, Jennifer Williams DeLuise, Jenny Farrell, Jenny Joy Filicky, Jenny Keifer, Jenny Meade, Jenny Oliveto Ayoub, Jenny Pizzathong, Jenny Quam Buchhagen, Jeramie Luing, Jereme Muller, Jeremiah Keevy, Jeremiah Marshall, Jeremy Baumhower, Jeremy Blaber, Jeremy Crosby, Jeremy Fabrizio, Jeremy Fritz, Jeremy Hanson, Jeremy Horn, Jeremy Levine, Jeremy Marcus, Jeremy McIsaac, Jeremy Murley, Jeremy Nixon, Jeremy Rice, Jeremy Robinson, Jeremy Ross, Jeremy Salzman, Jeremy Silverthorn, Jeremy Tominberg, Jeriann Credidio, Jerime Francis, Jerome Cleary, Jerramy Rockman, Jerry Adamo, Jerry Blatt, Jerry Capito, Jerry Chase, Jerry Conway, Jerry Del Valle, Jerry Foster, Jerry Henderson, Jerry Kilgo, Jerry Lee Peters, Jerry Maiforth, Jerry Perisho, Jerry R Guevara, Jerry Rous Plumbing, Jerry Rowan, Jerry Vaughan, Jess Lynn, Jesse Banks, Jesse Barton, Jesse Calderon, Jesse Colon, Jesse Grider, Jesse Hayes, Jesse Switzer, Jesse Tucker, Jessica Abolafia, Jessica Bowes Dillon, Jessica Ceraso, Jessica Dwyer, Jessica Earl, Jessica Ferreira, Jessica G Gerrish, Jessica Hilton, Jessica Lauren, Jessica LeeAnne, Jessica Loyal, Jessica Martin, Jessica McDonald, Jessica Price, Jessica Richardson Hague, Jessica Vardeman, Jessie Della Femina, Jessie Powell, Jessie Sanchez, Jessyca Rayanne Phichit, Jeton Ademaj, Jewels McCullough, JG Faherty, Jill Heinlein McGhee, Jill Huey, Jill Landrigan, Jill Mosby, Jill Sharp, Jillian Ann Sniffen, Jillian Chiappones, Jillian Weston, Jim Angehr, Jim Baker Rvmc, Jim Bartko, Jim Bell, Jim Bigham, Jim Bonomo, Jim Carey, Jim Carson, Jim Charters, Jim Chern, Jim Ciesinski, Jim Creighton, Jim Curtis, Jim Custer, Jim Del, Jim Desandro, Jim Dimitri, Jim Faulknor, Jim Florentine, Jim Genda, Jim Gourd, Jim Greenleaf, Jim Horne, Jim Johnson, Jim Joyce, Jim Kenniff, Jim Lafferty, Jim Maher, Jim Maroney, Jim McBride, Jim McLaughlin, Jim Meaney, Jim Oney, Jim Polizzi, Jim

Poorman Trenton, Jim Powell, Jim Rotoli, Jim Schnyder, Jim Seese, Jim Shannon, Jim Sharky, Jim Shea, Jim Slade, Jim Steal, Jim Stewart, Jim Sweet, Jim Thompson, Jim Tidwell, Jim Tohill, Jim Trocchio, Jim Wilson, Jim Zimmerman, Jimbo Schaffer, Jimmie Sanders, Jimmy Alicata, Jimmy Anderson, Jimmy Costa, Jimmy Cox, Jimmy D'Angelo, Jimmy Earll, Jimmy Gleacher, Jimmy Graham, Jimmy James, Jimmy Locker, Jimmy Mounts, Jimmy Paulsen, Jimmy Petonito, Jimmy Reilly Gallagher, Jimmy Ryan, Jimmy Saffelle, Jimmy Saunders, Jimmy Settles, Jimmy Sholes, Jimmy Torcaso, Jimmy Vee, Jimmy Ward, Jimmy Wheelcock, JJ Aragon, JJ Aurigemma, JJ Bruno, JJ O'Brand, JJ Vail, Jm Goretechs, JM Martinez, JM Palmer, Jo Ann Maher, Jo Antinozzi, Jo Colapietro, Jo Islands, Joan Muir Lobosco, Joan Quinn, Joanie Elizabeth, Joanie Sexton-Johanson, Joann Bellenkes, Joanna Cosci Balchi, Joanna Vulakh, Joaquin Garcia, Jode Sanchez, Jodi Bustillo, Jodi Dame-Potter, Jodi DeStefano, Jodi Lipton, Jodi Morelli, Jodie Swayze, Jody Castillo, Jody Goldwasser, Jody Inman, Jody Pflipsen, Jody Southworth Morgan, Joe Alber, Joe Anelli, Joe Angelino, Joe Barone, Joe Bienz, Joe Blowinski, Joe Bongarzone, Joe Carroll, Joe Casteleneto, Joe Cieslak, Joe Colling, Joe Conner, Joe Costello, Joe Daniele, Joe Davis, Joe DeMaria, Joe DiCarlo, Joe Difano, Joe Dinki, Joe D'Urso Jr., Joe Duva, Joe El-Deiry, Joe Fair, Joe Farley, Joe Festa, Joe Flood, Joe Florio, Joe Giannella, Joe Gonzalez, Joe Grugan, Joe Gushen, Joe Guzman, Joe Hamilton, Joe Henderson, Joe Henley, Joe Hoeler, Joe Hora Jr., Joe Howard, Joe Iavaroni, Joe Jen Gaglione Semancik, Joe Kearney, Joe Kerr, Joe Kirwan, Joe Kotarski, Joe Kuczma, Joe Kuefner, Joe Leighthardt, Joe Loughran, Joe Lucchesi, Joe Maleitzke, Joe Manfredi, Joe Marett, Joe Martin, Joe Martino, Joe Micatrotto, Joe Mineo, Joe Miraglia, Joe Morgan, Joe Morganella, Joe Mormino, Joe Naccarato, Joe Nazaro, Joe Nocella, Joe Nolan, Joe Onufer, Joe Ortiz, Joe Pardo, Joe Peters, Joe Picolli, Joe Puglisi, Joe Pulcini, Joe Purton, Joe Reid, Joe Rhino, Joe Rodriguez, Joe Rom, Joe Rosario, Joe Rovinsky, Joe Ryan, Joe Salvato, Joe Savickas, Joe Seph, Joe Silvia, Joe Simplot, Joe Smookler, Joe Stevenson, Joe Stockton, Joe Taggart, Joe Ternes, Joe Vause, Joe Vennari, Joe Wehinger, Joe Welsh, Joe Wood, Joe Zane, Joe Zatarga, Joe Zelasko, Joedee Hulgan, Joel Johnson, Joel Meltzer, Joel Plotkin, Joel Quiñones, Joel Sawyer Small, Joel St Germain, Joel Stamnes, Joey B Johnson, Joey Boots, Joey

Chianese, Joey Clevenger, Joey Crail, Joey Denoyer, Joey Gallinal, Joey Gay, Joey Kelly, Joey King, Joey Kola, Joey Litterello, Joey Reynolds, Joey Roberts, Joey Sigona, Joey Smith, Joey Strader, Joey White, Johan Varde, John Adams, John Alice, John Ankelman, John Anthony, John Arm Bogdan, John Bababooey, John Babecki, John Bachelor, John Balch, John Barkbiter, John Barlow LaChapelle, John Beyer, John Biondo, John Blaze, John Bligh, John Borle, John Boulton, John Brady, John Butera, John Canttellme, John Capuano, John Carbone, John Carson, John Cavanagh, John Charles Hunt, John Chartier, John Chiarenza, John Christopher O'Leary, John Cicero, John Ciurciu, John Conroy, John Costello, John Cullen, John Cunningham, John Dalby, John DaSilva, John D'Astolfo, John David, John Decker, John DeGennaro, John Deno, John DePalma, John Dexter, John DiClementi, John DiSanto, John Doherty, John Doran, John Doxsey, John Dro, John Duke, John E Wade, John E. Hofmann, John Erlingheuser, John Evans, John Fay, John Ferretti, John Filippone, John Fitzgibbon, John Fitzsimmons, John Fleming, John G Jacubovics, John Geluardi, John Gennawey, John Gensert, John Geraghty, John Gilbert, John Graden, John Gravereaux, John Gullbonny, John Hardin, John Haro, John Hildebrandt, John Hoff, John Hvidsten, John J McKnight, John Jennings, John Jigitz, John Jude Cook, John Kane, John Kensil, John King, John Kleppe, John Kobus, John Kraft, John Krempa, John Kwilman, John Langan, John Leider Alvarez, John Lepine, John Levy, John Luca, John Lupia, John Lupo, John Magliocco, John Matthews, John Mazzullo, John Mccurry, John McDowell, John Mchugh, John McNamara, John Melendez, John Meyers, John Michael Josephs Jr., John Michelle Parks, John Migliore, John Mitchell, John Molnar, John Monteforte, John Montone, John Motell, John Murphy, John Myers, John Nelson, John Nolan, John O. Santiago, John Oakley, John Oatmeal Hartzog, John O'Sullivan, John Otto, John P Parker, John P Staltaro, John Patrick, John Patrick Barry, John Patrick Kopp, John Paul, John Paul Mckenna, John Paul Velasquez, John Phillip, John Pizzi, John Poje, John Poling, John Rambo, John Ramsey, John Rebello, John Reilly, John Re-Surch McGhee, John Richard Morris, John Rinaudo, John Rini, John Robinson, John Scarangello, John Scheuerman, John Scouler, John Sell, John Sheppard, John Sigler, John Simmons, John Snider, John

Spina, John Stone, John Szefcyk, John Tole, John Troglin, John Trotsky, John Tucker, John Tully, John Valdastri, John Viducich, John Voigt, John Wedemeyer, John Weill, John White, John Wickum, John Willis, John Wilson, John Wolcson, John Zafaranloo, John Ziegler, Johnnie Allen Phillips Jr., Johnnie Jackson, Johnny Barre-Haesn, Johnny Cardinale, Johnny K. Telos, Johnny Koho, Johnny Lew Fratto, Johnny Mattei, Johnny McCarthy, Johnny R. Fratto, Johnny Russo, Johnny Sportez, Johnny Summers, JoJo Carey Shane Ernst, Jolene Youngster Weaver, Jon Barry, Jon Bondroff, Jon Cohen, Jon Conover, Jon Dancik, Jon Davenport, Jon Day, Jon Farrugia, Jon Harris, Jon Heaberlin, Jon Jonelis, Jon Koga, Jon Leiberman, Jon Lotano, Jon Marchese, Jon Mathis, Jon Neipris, Jon Ridenour, Jon Scratches, Jon Smith, Jon Stewart, Jon Thompson, Jon Tisko, Jon Waitneight, Jon Zepnick, Jona Brun, Jonas Garvin, Jonathan Ayes, Jonathan Berman, Jonathan Briggs, Jonathan Buncke, Jonathan Conrad, Jonathan D Jewell, Jonathan DeSanctis, Jonathan Fowler, Jonathan Graham, Jonathan Harris, Jonathan Hersholt, Jonathan Jorgenson, Jonathan Kralic, Jonathan Mason, Jonathan Osborne Cote, Jonathan Paul Selman, Jonathan Pumphrey, Jonathan W Steele, Jonathan Walmsley, Jonell Lennon, Joni Alsfasser, Jonny Loquasto, Jordan David, Jordan Flitter, Jordan Garnett, Jordan Kantrowitz, Jordan Kurtzman, Jordan McAllister, Jordan Mitchell James-Kattan, Jordan Nuston, Jordan Silver, Jordan Simon, Jordan Verbin, Jordan Wiles, Jorge Delcarpio Dr., Jose Cervantes, Jose Manuel, Jose Vega, Joseph A. Giannino, Joseph Banasiak, Joseph Brusznicki, Joseph Bunnicelli, Joseph Carfino, Joseph Ciarleglio, Joseph DeLuca, Joseph Fetcher, Joseph Gallo, Joseph Herrera, Joseph James Castaldo, Joseph Jiron, Joseph Lewis Turner, Joseph LiCausi, Joseph Limandri, Joseph Loughren, Joseph Magliacane, Joseph Mancuso, Joseph Mazzoni, Joseph Michael, Joseph Mooski, Joseph Morris, Joseph Myers, Joseph O'Neill, Joseph Ortega, Joseph Politi, Joseph Reding, Joseph S Lukaszewski, Joseph Scarlata, Joseph White, Joseph Woodby, Joseph Zunic, Josephine Arroyo, Josh Banks, Josh Barthel, Josh Cohen, Josh Forgione, Josh Fourrier, Josh Garcia, Josh Hartman, Josh Hauser, Josh Joyner, Josh Klynn, Josh Lozano, Josh Nazar, Josh Parriott, Josh Pearman, Josh Pech, Josh Pearlman, Josh Ranes, Josh Raposo, Josh Sheffield, Josh Steevenz, Josh Steinberg, Josh Stokes, Joshua Cox, Joshua

Finkelstein, Joshua Forbes, Joshua Goodman, Joshua Kammerman, Joshua Kelly-Morgan, Joshua Mack, Joshua Magid, Joshua Moyer, Joshua Murray, Joshua Oren, Joshua Sam, Joshua Stratton, Joshua West, Joshua Wright, Josse L Garcia-Alonso, Jowanka Fratto, Joy Dier Elkins, Joy Saunders, JR Bilney, Jr Vaca, Jt Churpakovich, Juan Carlos Beltra, Juan Gallinal, Juan Grand, Juan Manuel Olivetto, Juan Martinez, Juan Rivera, Juan Vides, Juanathan Cuthberto, Juancito Gonzalez, Jude Poggiali, Judith Regan, Judy Picazo, Juergen Hess, Juice Jones, Jules Abadi, Jules Mares, Julia Brown, Julia Gulia, Julia Schwartz Martin, Julian Chaidez, Julian Picucci Schuett, Julie Ann Dunlavy, Julie Beers, Julie Cantor, Julie Dolan Frombach, Julie Garner, Julie Holmes, Julie Hunt, Julie Kathryn, Julie Kottakis, Julie Kuhn, Julie Marsolais, Julie Paulus Shoemaker, Julie Sammon Gheitantschi, Julie Wellman Huber, Julie Wolf, Juliebeth Scholl, Julien Sokol, Juliette Sanders, Julius James, Jumrocski Oner, June Wagner, Junior's Spycoast, Just Supersitemaker, Justa Djfreak, Justin Barrett, Justin Bielecki, Justin Bishop, Justin Compo, Justin Deitrick, Justin Dellinger, Justin Deremo, Justin Dupchak, Justin Hawkins, Justin Hill, Justin Jennetto, Justin Johnson, Justin Katschke, Justin Klementowicz, Justin Kuhns, Justin Kuperberg, Justin Mallow, Justin McCord, Justin Merchant, Justin Perry, Justin Ruggieri, Justin Scheman, Justin Smith, Justin Stavracos, Justin Sweeney, Justin Thind, Justin Thomas, Justin Thompson, Justin Weston, Justin Williams, Justin Yadon, Justin Zoras, Kacy Knight, Kaia McColl, Kaleena Massaker, Kalman France, Kalorin Wijaya Kalorin, Kamil Azcona, Kanysha Janet Moore, Kara Rose, Kareen Belin, Karel Sabanate, Karen Andrews, Karen Antonucci Curley, Karen Belinda, Karen Caputo Ellis, Karen Correia, Karen Donovan, Karen Gannon, Karen Hall-Inglese, Karen Hicks, Karen Hoddle, Karen Kalmar, Karen Louise, Karen Mattis Mier, Karen Mistretta Kennedy, Karen O'Marra-Alexander, Karen Pierce Gonzalez, Karen Rizzo, Karen Shields, Karen Sorice, Karen Stevens, Karen Tucci, Karian Michelle, Karl Messemer, Karl Niemoller, Karma L. Schopp, Karol Young Bureau, Karon Viggiano, Karyn Frasca Kulliver, Kat O'Sullivan, Kat Soul, Katalyna Anne, Kat Washnis, Kate Williams, Katerina Egorshina, Kateřina Erlebachová, Katharine Wien, Kathi Szukala Black, Kathleen Bodnar-Vertucci, Kathleen Stapleton Schultz, Kathryn Fulk Steward, Kathy Bay, Kathy

Kane, Kathy Karp Cohen, Kathy Srokowska, Katie Elsner Bodenhamer, Katie Lafferty, Katie Pachuta, Katie Stonacher, Katy Jurgens, Kaya Suleyman, Kayla Christine Arellano, Kayla Mirandy, KC Vance, Keira Citera, Keith Beizer, Keith Corbin, Keith D. Thomas, Keith Edinger, Keith Farrell, Keith Flournoy, Keith Friedman, Keith Hickox, Keith Jenkins, Keith Juceam, Keith Kwazar, Keith McEachern, Keith Michael, Keith Roland, Keith Rosebrock, Keith Russo, Keith Sellons, Keith Tomasek, Keith VanDeusen, Keith Westphal, Kell Lynn, Kelley Wood, Kellie Cano, Kellie D Watson-Woodside, Kellie Leigh Heather Koch, Kelly Archambeault, Kelly Bock Yeckley, Kelly Connolly, Kelly Elaine Anker, Kelly Fair, Kelly Jean, Kelly Kay, Kelly Kraft, Kelly Logan Gould, Kelly McGrath, Kelly Michael Glynn, Kelly Mills, Kelly Needham, Kelly Papsodero, Kelly Radiovik, Kelly Schlieve, Kelly Summey, Kelly Vallely, Kelly W. Patterson, Kelly Wannagot, Kelsie Marie, Kelvin Gutierrez, Kelvin Harper, Ken Brancheau, Ken Broome, Ken Cammarata, Ken Daly, Ken Danieli, Ken Davis, Ken Dunkin, Ken Fraser, Ken Hames, Ken Jones, Ken Kaye, Ken Mark, Ken Pachucki, Ken Pettigrew, Ken Truffen, Ken Vice, Ken Wilson, Ken Zito, KenandKel Hurst, Kendell Briggs, Kendra Ball, Kendra Payne Mitchell, Kendra Rossi, Kenn Griswold, Kenneth Keith Kallenbach, Kenneth Perry, Kenneth Sager, Kenneth Sohn, Kenneth Van Dyke, Kenny Ball, Kenny Casanova, Kenny Cherrin, Kenny Fink, Kenny Gallo, Kenji Kenny H Hendrix, Kenny Hakimian, Kenny Kent, Kenny Lee, Kenny S. Hiott, Kenny Scheivert Jr., Kenny Stowell, Kenny Strode, Kenny Wendel, Kent Aaron Dauderman II, Kent Sansone, Kenya Johnson, Keri Kissane-Hagadorn, Kerin Agnew Quick, Kerin Stover, Kermit Blaney, Kerri Edelman, Kerri Holmes, Kerry Kelly, Kerri Matuszak, Kerri Petersen, Kerrie Anne, Kerrie Coughlin, Kerrie Favalaro, Kerry A. Welland, Kerry Bassett, Kerry Berthen Brodman, Kerry Carty Fleckenstein, Kerry MaliKerry Needle, Kevin Binder, Kevin Bobertz, Kevin C. Watson, Kevin Callirgos, Kevin Carbone, Kevin Carlin, Kevin Binder, Kevin Bobertz, Kevin C. Watson, Kevin Callirgos, Kevin Carbone, Kevin Carlin, Kevin Casey, Kevin Christman, Kevin Claffey, Kevin Corbett, Kevin D Rea, Kevin DiPlacido, Kevin Duke, Kevin Eaton, Kevin Ellis, Kevin F. Brignole, Kevin Farrell, Kevin Field, Kevin Forster, Kevin Francis, Kevin Frank, Kevin Gokey, Kevin Gorman, Kevin Hamburg,

Kevin Hansen, Kevin J. Lennon, Kevin Kaplan, Kevin Keowitz, Kevin Kinney, Kevin Kling, Kevin Lahaie, Kevin Laurence Hirshorn, Kevin Lawlor, Kevin Lecce, Kevin MacKenzie, Kevin Marshall, Kevin Mccambley, Kevin Mcdonald, Kevin McGarry, Kevin McKee, Kevin Moriarty, Kevin Murray, Kevin Noble, Kevin Noonan, Kevin O'Brien, Kevin Olthaus, Kevin Omell, Kevin Pakkala, Kevin Patrick Toomey, Kevin Plantz, Kevin Reiten, Kevin Roberson, Kevin Rooney, Kevin Scalese, Kevin Seck, Kevin Seybert, Kevin Shea, Kevin Shields, Kevin Smith, Kevin Snyder, Kevin Sullivan, Kevin Train Moxley, Kevin Tryon, Kevin White, Kevin William Hand, Kevin Wolff, Kevin Wood, Kevin Woodring, Kevin Wright, Kevin X. Hooey, Key Fitz, Keyon Malone, Khristian Singson, Kieran Bathory, Kiley Vaught, Kim Briese, Kim Clarke McBride, Kim Gronquist Dennison, Kim Hanstein Roberts, Kim James Mason, Kim M. Clark, Kim Miele-Krott, Kim Petro, Kim Raiani, Kim Siegel, Kim Smith, Kimber VanSant, Kimberly A Chase, Kimberly Buck, Kimberly Cubelo, Kimberly Goldklang Thaw, Kimberly Kokta Ficek, Kimberly Loper Castellana, Kimberly Osborne Bland, Kimberly Salter, Kimberly Spizewski, Kimberly Thomas, Kimmi Gregory, Kimora Cosar, King Brett Miller, King Kane, Kinga Suto, Kira Carino, Kirche Obetkovski, Kirk Gillman, Kirk Kitsch, Kirk Thompson, Kirsten Anderson, Kirsten Johnston, Kirsten Kappenberg, Kirsten Keffer, Kiyemba Vicent, Kj Smith, Klutch Hendrix, Knox Lee, Korey A Shienfield, Korey Kleovoulou, Korn Laosri, Kris Durbin, Kris Kershaw, Kris Medler Rone, Kris Pinola, Kris Primlani Koopmans, Kris Robbie Malin, Kris Rocchio, Kris Primlani Koopmans, Kris Robbie Malin, Kris Rocchio, Kris Tapia, Krissy Freeman Cilluffo, Krista DeMaria Conte, Kristen Conover Reilly, Kristen Elyse, Kristen Habig, Kristen Lee Coale Marcus, Kristen Spence Foy, Kristi Nelson Corbett, Kristi Riley Parker, Kristi Waters LoRusso, Kristi Wells Doran, Kristin Carroll Downes, Kristin Christy, Kristin Dicey, Kristin D'Orso Burns, Kristin Goutzos, Kristin Jezuit, Kristin Poth, Kristin Swanberg, Kristina Hooks, Kristina Maria Pedersen, Kristine Bennett, Kristine Finizio, Kristy Arnett, Kristy M Tantillo, Kristy Ranta, Krystal Roberts, Kulan Barney, Kurt Belbin, Kurt Ditzler, Kurt Knutson, Kurt Kretzschmar, Kurt Lavertue, Kurt M Burkhart, Kurt N Smith, Kurt Ritterpusch, Kurt Wagner, Kurtis Bell, Kurtis Wagner, Kyle Baird, Kyle Bell, Kyle Eddy, Kyle Goebl, Kyle

Hershorn, Kyle Heyen, Kyle Jefferson, Kyle Kenyon, Kyle Knowlton, Kyle Kramer, Kyle Mathias Keller, Kyle McConnell, Kyle Mendelsohn, Kyle Riddle, Kyle Smith, Kyle Wagner, Kymberli Hemberger, La Dawn Whitman, La Nad, Laci Mae, Lacie Molnar, Ladd M. Lanz, Lady Pesqueira, Lame Flame, Lance Freeman, Lance Hess, Lance Jacuzzi, Lance Juke, Lance Mo, Lance Durante, Lane Just Lane, Lane Steele, Lang Parker, Lanni Billian McCall, Laquetta Taylor, Lara Hunter, Lara Neal, Lara Perkins, Larios Bizarro, Larry Attard, Larry Caruso, Larry Ciarlo, Larry Evans, Larry Ferguson, Larry Ferrari, Larry James, Larry Klesser, Larry Lawrence, Larry Lee Moniz, Larry Parrott, Larry Racevice, Larry Ratso Sloman, Larry Sadofsky, Larry Sass, Larry Singer, Larry Steinberg, Larry Welnowski, Larry Willis, Larry Wise Jr., Larrysdirty Draws, Lars Högblom, Latravis Powell, Laura Austria, Laura beth, Laura Claudia Huacac Barazorda, Laura Eskenazi Mulhare, Laura Hayden, Laura Hunt, Laura Johnson, Laura Lathan Steward, Laura Lee Clinton, Laura Lieberman, Laura Lynn Solomon, Laura McFadden Murray, Laura McMullen, Laura Pasquale, Laura Pierson, Laura Rebecca, Laura Sorrano, Laura Spaeth, Laura Valdivia, Lauren Bernhardt-Rhone, Lauren DeLong, Lauren Mazur, Lauren Ottewill, Lauren Starrantino-Mitchell, Lauren Stefanie, Laurence H. Proscia, Laurence H. Proscia, Laurence R. Rifkin, Laurence Victor Greenblatt, Laurie GiGi Fielder-Moore, Laurie Janelle, Laurie Tuttle, Laurie Winston, Law D Michael, Lawrence A Moochie Turner, Lawrence Bedrosian, Lawrence Clark, Lawrence Coward, Layne Magnuson, Laysi S. Wälte, LE Garage, Lea Sabato, Leah Billingsley Nelson, Leah Eve Isabelle, Lee Cabbie Siegfried, Lee Conte Pettirossi, Lee DiNapoli, Lee Drake, Lee Emil Hernandez, Lee Mayne, Lee Panas, Lee Richard Navarrette, Lee Roden, Lee Schloss, Lee Siegfried, LEe WaYne JoHn, Lee White, LeeAnn Lynn, Lego-headed Gent, Leigh Horan, Leigh McKenna Adler, Leigh Sinclair, Leighanne Smith, Leighanne Vorel, Leland Avants II, Leland Grossman, Len Mazur, Lenny Di Sisto, Lenny Ligotti, Lenny Reid, Lenny Shelton, Leo Butera, Leo Delgado, Leo Ramirez, Leonard Goltz, Leonard Williams, Leonel Collazo III, Leroy O. Jackson, Les Palmer, Les Walgreen, Les Young, Lesley Anne Tata, Leslie Barbara, Leslie Klaidman, Lester Green, Leticia Cline, Lew Pisani, Lex Morales, Lexi Gray, Lexy Estoqie, Leyla Leigh, Liam Baxter, Liam Klein, Liezel Oliva Rezano, Lillha Ray

Somerhalder, Lillian Curet, Lillian Jonas Wain, Lilly Smith, Lina Hanna, Lina Quintero, Linda Jonach Kirkman, Linda Mackey Williams, Linda Marie Maldero, Lin, Linda Schorn Torino, Linda Thomas-Bradley, Lindley Wert, Lindsay Knaub, Lindsay Schneider, Link Leftwich, Linus Bäckström, Lisa Allen, Lisa Blake, Lisa Chadwick Mongiardo, Lisa DiFlorio Brigandi, Lisa Faria, Lisa Fazzino, Lisa Firth, Lisa Franey, Lisa G Smith, Lisa Giano, Lisa Holub Cross, Lisa Jezernik, Lisa Johnson, Lisa Kalmanson, Lisa Kurdyla, Lisa L. Leandro, Lisa Legacy, Lisa Lewtan, Lisa LiCausi Okonsky, Lisa M. Elias, Lisa Marie, Lisa Max, Lisa Mazzotta Morris, Lisa Pawigon, Lisa Petrano, Lisa Politis Korpi, Lisa Ratto, Lisa Renee Fowler, Lisa Ricco, Lisa Rodriguez, Lisa Rondinelli, Lisa Ryan Usher, Lisa Schinelli Caserta, Lisa Schwartz, Lisa Waters, Lisa Wolfinger, Lisl Brink, Lito Mason, Liz Ayers Bukowski, Liz Belmont, Liz Beth, Liz Goltra, Liz Russo, Liza Manuel, Lj Carpenter, Lois Burak, Lois Cornell Resnick, Lois Spieler Lee, Lola Marie Messina, Lola Zen, LoLo Burak, Long Dong Wang, Lonnie Cooper, Lopez Barbie, Lora Lucas, Loran Storts, Loren Meadows, Loren Zo, Lorena Bobbit, Lorenzo Vasquez, Loretta Gilmore, Lori A Brown, Lori C. Dodd, Lori Hackney, Lori Jackson Sanders, Lori Levine, Lori Palminteri, Lori Sharp Ellis, Lori Stryker, Lori Watson Messmer, Lori Williams, Lorrie Salem-Guevara, Lote Valencia, Lou Adams Jr., Lou Bottino, Lou Casbarro, Lou Corsaro, Lou Cypher, Lou DeRosa, Lou Pickney, Lou Smookler, Louie Calderon, Louie Iorio, Louis Bednar, Louis Cacciatore Jr, Louis Fr. Lotito, Louis Heimerl Jr, Louis Napolitano, Louis Salera, Louis Stepp, Louise Callahan-Fleig, Lovelyrose Patricialyn, Loveth Onuobia, Loyal Ploof, Lu Lu, Lucas Youngberg, Luciano DeSorbo, Lucy Fuher, Luger Patrick, Luigi A. Gallace, Luis Araten-Castillo, Luis Carlos Rodriguez, Luis Collazo, Luis De Mello, Luis Guillen, Luis Montiel, Lukas Rossi, Luke Brainard, Luke Gillespie, Luke Hadley, Luke Kjersten, Luke Ruggieri, Lydiane Interdonato, Lyle Martin, Lynette Alves, Lynjho Francisco Padernilla, Lynlee Still, Lynn Thomas, Lynn-Ann Belluso, Lynne Cuva, Lynne Koplitz, Lyssa Hadley, M Christopher Tevis, M.C. Spode, M.g. Dockery, Ma Katrina Vargas, Mable Wilson, Mac Dorfner, Maciej Koziol, Madelene Cheney, Maja Ignjic, Make Gange Malena Pranzo, Mambawear Mike, Mandee Bagalacsa, Mandy Rubinoff, Mang Rang, Manny Chuck Vazquez, Manny Dela Rosa, Manuel Oretga, Mara

Shapshay, Marc A. Danin, Marc Brierley, Marc Briner, Marc Carbone, Marc Fine, Marc Goldberg, Marc Lalonde, Marc Levine, Marc Linder, Marc Lord M Andris, Marc Marsala, Marc Nussbaum, Marc Rosete, Marc Salvato, Marc Schwartz, Marc Tamburri, Marc Townsend, Marc Warner, Marc Washburn, Marc Weiss, Marc Wiweke, Marc Zweben, Marcel Sorgi, Marci Mertz Malak, Marcie Berger, Marco A Garcia, Marco Carulli, Marco Jesus, Marco Renteria, Marconi Bologna, Marcos Martinez, Marcos Quinones, Marcos Villalobos, Marcus Deacon Swartz, Marcus Mayer, Marcus Ochoa, Marcus Young, Marcy Morse, Margaret Bee, Margaret Peggy Durand, Margarita Chavez, Margie Gratten Kirkpatrick, Mari DeSalvo, Maria Christiansen, Maria Frances Guy, Maria Zukin Shkolnik, Maria Elaina Silaco-Landolfi, Mariah Bailey, Mariann Brooklyn, Mariann Hughes Casali, Marianne Garvey, Marianne Terry, Marie A Brocato, Marie Faustin, Marie Gerke, Marie Immediato, Marie Reilly, Marie Simon, Marilyn Bosley Utter, Marilyn Payne Bergjans, Marilynn Ulrich, Marina Kaljaj, Marina Larsi, Mario Corona, Mario Georgatos, Mario Guerra, Mario Nargi, Mario Reyes, Mario Ruales, Mario Saenz, Marisa Cohen, Maritees Maas, Marites Son, Marivic Agustin, Marixxa Kushner, Marjorie Levine, Marjorie Oakley Rich, Mark Alan Six, Mark Aller, Mark Baranowski, Mark Blake, Mark Bova, Mark Bzdyk, Mark C. Romofsky, Mark C. Bortolin, Mark Camp, Mark Carangelo, Mark Cassel, Mark Cassino, Mark Cianciosi, Mark Closson, Mark Crabtree, Mark Cretella, Mark D Antonio, Mark D'Amico, Mark Davis, Mark DiLodovico, Mark Dolan, Mark Erskine, Mark Essner, Mark Fagin, Mark Faria, Mark Farrell, Mark Fiorentino, Mark Fornaro, Mark Goertzen, Mark Gregerson, Mark Griffin, Mark Hall, Mark Hammer, Mark Heathen, Mark Herzog, Mark Hoadley, Mark Hunter, Mark Jason Wallace, Mark Jeacoma, Mark Kalinski, Mark Kittmer, Mark Kitzmiller, Mark Kocienski, Mark Kosakura, Mark Laganella, Mark Lampman, Mark LeGault, Mark Maners, Mark Maningo, Mark Mathew, Mark McCollum, Mark McElwee, Mark McGrath, Mark McLain, Mark Mercer, Mark Miller, Mark Minahan, Mark Mitchell, Mark N. El-Deiry, Mark Nather, Mark Nather, Mark Newcomb, Mark O'Brien, Mark Pelrine, Mark Pollard, Mark Potash, Mark Powell, Mark Puttock, Mark Quisenberry, Mark Rallas, Mark Razz, Mark Robbins, Mark Robert Smith, Mark Rosenberry, Mark

Rosenthal, Mark Sagerstrom, Mark Sara Davis, Mark Shaw, Mark Snyder, Mark Speck, Mark Spooner Jr, Mark Stirrett, Mark Stone, Mark Suh, Mark Taunton, Mark Verville, Mark Vesci, Mark Walters, Mark Wardzinski, Mark Warner, Mark White, Mark Wolfe, Mark Young, Markanthony Henry, Marki McRae, Marko St-Koulev, Marlene Silva, Marlin Price, Marni Rosenthal-Chaikin, Marnie Farnam, Marnie Grundman, Marnie Jardine, Marq Piocos, Marsha Cailin Cobb, Marshall Kanfer, Marshall Ulrich, Marta Yalitza Declet, Martijn Tenniglo, Martin Cohen, Martin F Bowden III, Martin Golizio, Martin Mangan, Martin Piecuch, Martin Richardson, Martin Schombs, Marton Varo, Marty Abrahams Marty Byk, Marty Hayes, Marty Rozzy, Marty Sklar, Marty Tankleff, Marty Thomsen, Marty Weitzman, Mary Burns, Mary Caraftis-Schook, Mary Elizabeth Klimas, Mary Frances Wilkens, Mary Frezza Nouman, Mary Jo Plews, Mary Lang, Mary M Farrell McCrossen, Mary M Mathewes, Mary Miller, Mary N Frembgen, Mary Noonan Vigano, Mary Pelloni, Mary Shea, Maryam Laypan, Maryann Benett, Maryann Little Cadella Dodge, Maryann Veith, Maryellen Minnichbach Corbett, Marylynn Fratesi Cassone, Mascheria Perdue Nabbs, Mason Landis, Mason Sal, Mat Karess Kandell, Mateo Bernabé Fierros, Matheus Castro, Mathew Campbell, Matin Sabz, Matt Allen, Matt Amoroso, Matt Armstrong, Matt Bardram, Matt Benson, Matt Berger, Matt Bernal, Matt Bliss, Matt Bowman, Matt Buchhagen, Matt Campbell, Matt Clark, Matt Claybrooks, Matt Coleman, Matt Crayton, Matt David, Matt Eidschun, Matt Errington, Matt Ferrara, Matt Garry-Holzer, Matt Gentry, Matt Granozio, Matt Grossman, Matt Gunnels, Matt Hall, Matt Heron, Matt Hiott, Matt Hodges, Matt Hoover, Matt Innis, Matt Irwin, Matt Jacobs, Matt Jenco, Matt Keleshian, Matt LaFrankie, Matt Leighton, Matt Lowe, Matt Markland, Matt Milius, Matt Miller, Matt Mooney, Matt Morgan, Matt Munro, Matt Nelson, Matt Nunan, Matt Oneill, Matt Pepitone, Matt Piccione, Matt Pranzo, Matt Redding, Matt Rohlfing, Matt Ross, Matt Sager, Matt Sagona, Matt Schweikert, Matt Sheldon, Matt Sleeper, Matt Snyder, Matt Spinelli, Matt Touchette, Matt Walker, Matt Weiner, Matt Weston, Matt Whitman, Matt Wilson, Matt Wohlfarth, Matt Wolin, Matt Yarmosh, Matthew Abrams, Matthew Adelman, Matthew Aiello, Matthew Alan Shadwick, Matthew Anello, Matthew Ballantyne,

Matthew Butash, Matthew C White, Matthew Craig, Matthew D. Farber, Matthew Gefter, Matthew Goodman, Matthew Hajko, Matthew Harbin, Matthew Huckabey, Matthew Hummel, Matthew Impellizeri, Matthew Katakis, Matthew Lillian, Matthew Mahgerfteh, Matthew McFadden, Matthew McGurn, Matthew Mendillo, Matthew Mentecky, Matthew Nemes, Matthew Newman, Matthew Oppedisano, Matthew Patrick Reilly, Matthew Rahaley, Matthew Randazzo V, Matthew Reynolds, Matthew Savage, Matthew Scerpella, Matthew Segreto, Matthew Siani, Matthew Sica, Matthew Smith, Matthew Smookler, Matthew Stevens, Matthew Verruto, Matthew Wright, Matty Denz, Matty Denz, Matty Mak, Matty Odell, Maureen Hedderman Taylor, Maureen Innamorato, Maureen Sullivan, Maureen Zurlo, Maurice Grooms, Maurice King, Max Feldman, Max Jon Perez, Max MuscleTustin, Max Power, Max Ruttenberg, Maximo Vazquez, Maxwell J. Brown, Mayo Makinde, Mayzja Love, Meagan Robinson Haley, Medi Bendanna, Meg Moore Travers, Megan Brooks, Megan Donovan, Megan Knight, Megan Powell Turnas, Megan Shea, Megan Shersty Cummings, Meghann Mustico, Meika Lee, Mel Johnson, Mel Quinn, Mel Rappleyea, Melani A Benedetto, Melanie Harmon Dillon, Melanie Tilchen Alexander, Melanie Trulby, Melanie Walker, Melbi Styles, Melinda Otero, Melissa Baiocchi, Melissa Cornelius, Melissa Crow, Melissa Engdahl, Melissa Franko, Melissa Gates, Melissa Gatto, Melissa Gray, Melissa Greyhill, Melissa Haynes Lilly, Melissa Hewitt, Melissa Kellermann, Melissa Lane, Melissa Leeper, Melissa Marvin Melzer, Melissa McGinnis, Melissa Picuillo, Melissa Rice, Melissa Sara Matthews, Melissa Vecchio, Melody Smerk, Mely Bungato Ocampo, Melyssa Cornell, Memet Walker, MemoryOf Salvatore Leoni, Meredith Lyn, Meredith Skye, Meredith Snook, Meri Zawolik-Blandi, Meridith Berger Jaffe, Merissa MacEwen, Merissa Mackin, Meristel Shaw, Merrie Pendlebury, Merrill Davis, Merrily Ottomanelli, Meta Stopa, Mevy Valentino, Mia Johnson, Mich Yonkoski, Michael A. Michail, Michael Achille, Michael Acosta, Michael Allroy, Michael Amorelli, Michael Amorgianos, Michael Anthony Garcia, Michael Arter, Michael Attanasio, Michael Augustine Reed, Michael Baranowski, Michael Barry, Michael Blasi, Michael Blatchford, Michael Bradley, Michael Brand, Michael Bregy, Michael Brightman, Michael Brouthers, Michael

Brown, Michael Budnick, Michael Calleo, Michael Cantor, Michael
Carrieri, Michael Casey, Michael Cerulo, Michael Christy, Michael
Cicchetti, Michael Clancy, Michael Clarity, Michael Comforti, Michael
Comon Jr., Michael Connor, Michael Copeland, Michael Crisp, Michael
Cummings, Michael D Preston, Michael Danishevsky, Michael Dean
Dedonado, Michael DeGeorge, Michael Deignan, Michael DelCampo,
Michael DeLoach, Michael Dennis France Jr., Michael Devine, Michael
Devlin, Michael Diaz, Michael Dolan, Michael Domal, Michael Dorety,
Michael dove, Michael Dowdell, Michael Duretz, Michael Edwards,
Michael Epsenhart, Michael Eric, Michal Fabrizio, Michael Falkenstern,
Michael Fattorosi, Michael Feagans, Michael Felci, Michael Ferraro,
Michael Ferrazzano, Michael Fields, Michael Finkelman, Michael Fire,
Michael Fleig, Michael Fonce, Michael Forde, Michael Frank, Michael
Franzone, Michael Gallant, Michael Gallo, Michael Gil, Michael
Goines, Michael Goudreau, Michael Gould, Michael Habicht, Michael
Haft, Michael Hahn, Michael Harper, Michael Hart, Micheal Hawes,
Michael Heller, Michael Herbertson, Michael Hilburn, Michael Hill,
Michael Hodgdon, Michael Hogue, Michael Horkan, Michael
Huddleston, Michael Huse, Michael J. Cordeiro, Michael J. Burke,
Michael Jason Carbajal, Michael John, Michael John Scuderi, Michael
Jones, Michael Kadmiri, Michael Kammers, Michael Kolody Jr, Michael
Kruzewski, Michael Lasley, Michael LeDuc, Michael Lohan, Michael
M Diamond, Michael M. Bartell, Michael Madison, Michael Malone,
Michael Mangone, Michael Maroney, Michael Martin, Michael Marvin,
Michael Mastro, Michael Maxon, Michael May, Michael McDonald,
Michael McFadden, Michael Mcguire, Michael McNeff II, Michael
Melton, Michael Metzger, Michael Mike Rodriguez, Michael
Mikolajczyk, Michael Miller, Michael Morales, Michael Morochnick,
Michael Morrow, Michael N Grace Parker, Michael Newman, Michael
O'Leary, Michael Olson, Michael O'Marra, Michael Ortiz, Michael
Patrick Hennessy, Michael Patrick Tuite, Michael Phillips, Michael
Poirier, Michael Quartararo, Michael Quu, Michael R Gowcharan,
Michael Race, Michael Ranfone, Michael Reynolds, Michael Robinson,
Michael Rockower, Michael Roohan, Michael Ross, Michael Rubino,
Michael Rubinstein, Michael Running, Michael Russell, Michael Russo,
Michael S. Kelly, Michael Saucedo, Michael Savino, Michael Schneider,

Michael Scholl, Michael Schuelke, Michael Scott, Michael Seitz, Michael Shorty Hopkins, Michael Sigsworth, Michael Slater, Michael Sofra, Michael Stone, Michael Tacker, Michael Taliercio, Michael Tierney, Michael Vander Kley, Michael Vessa, Michael Volkman, Michael Wargo, Michael Weinberg, Michael Welby, Michael White, Michael Williams, Michael Winton, Michael Wittenberg, Michael Yoder, Michael Young, Michael Zarella, Michael Zielanski, Michael Zuckerman, Michael-Patrick Harrington, Miche Cojt, Michele Cojt, Michele Danielle Kahnis, Michele Robinson, Michelle Cavanaugh Giorgianni, Michelle Crimmins Bernstein, Michelle Czik Spitz, Michelle Ellul, Michelle Gailey, Michelle Hamblin-Schulman, Michelle Jude, Michelle Jutras, Michelle Karl, Michelle Katz, Michelle Krow, Michelle Kwiecinski, Michelle Mare, Michelle Maxin, Michelle Miller, Michelle Norman, Michelle Rose, Michelle Smith, Michelle Sweatt, Michelle T-Rex Fuchs, Michelle Webb, Michelle Wendell, Mick Stern, Miguel Angel, Mick Stern, Miguel Angel Martinez, Mihailo Danilovic, Mike Adams, Mike Aiello, Mike Alex, Mike Allen, Mike Anderson, Mike Annunziata, Mike Beck, Mike Beidler, Mike Beliles, Mike Bell, Mike Betcher, Mike Bewley, Mike Bosmay, Mike Bradley, Mike Brangaccio, Mike Bulbeck, Mike Burke, Mike C Rogers, Mike Campbell, Mike Carey, Mike Caringella, Mike Carrion, Mike Ciurzynski, Mike Clay, Mike Coca, Mike Culler, Mike Curly Howard, Mike Dagney, Mike Dammann, Mike Davis, Mike Davitt Jr, Mike DeFuria, Mike DelFavero, Mike Delin, Mike DeNight, Mike Di Paöla, Mike Dooley, Mike Dougherty, Mike Ehlers, Mike Flood, Mike Fox, Mike Frizol, Mike Gange, Mike Garone, Mike Garvey, Mike Gillingham, Mike Goodrich, Mike Goodwin, Mike Gruber, Mike Harbison, Mike Hartman, Mike Henrico, Mike Hoffpauir, Mike Horgan, Mike Iatauro, Mike Ice, Mike Imburgia, Mike Incantalupo, Mike Jeffrey, Mike John, Mike Jung, Mike Keegan, Mike Kennedy, Mike King, Mike Kirschner, Mike Kuzma, Mike La Vita, Mike Lackner, Mike Leen, Mike Lewis, Mike Lightbody, Mike Loeb, Mike Luna, Mike Lupo, Mike Machover, Mike Macri, Mike Mahoney, Mike Mancuso, Mike Mangone, Mike Manzelli, Mike Marino, Mike Marsala, Mike Maurra, Mike McAvoy, Mike McCarthy, Mike McGee, Mike McMahon, Mike Meadows, Mike Meir, Mike Merschbach, Mike Michels, Mike Migliore, Mike Mills, Mike Misulonas, Mike Mitchell, Mike Moreau,

Mike Morelli, Mike Morgan, Mike Morse, Mike Muratore, Mike Naddeo, Mike Naftaly, Mike Nilsson, Mike Novak, Mike Palm, Mike Palmese, Mike Poirier, Mike Punk, Mike Rampolla, Mike Rehbein, Mike Rich, Mike Robbins, Mike Roman, Mike Rose, Mike Runyan, Mike Rutigliano, Mike Sansenbach, Mike Santoro, Mike Schimmel, Mike Sehl, Mike Senerchia, Mike Shomaker, Mike Simmons, Mike Sneller, Mike Soke, Mike Soper Barrett, Mike Spe, Mike St. Hilaire, Mike Stacchi, Mike Sullivan, Mike Tartaglia, Mike Teller, Mike Thomas, Mike Thompson, Mike Tong, Mike Trzeciakiewicz, Mike Velazquez, Mike Werman, Mike Wiggins, Mike Wilmoth, Mike Winkleman, Mike Winkenhofer, Mike Woods, Mike Yaple, Mike Zyjeski, Mike's Vegas, Mikey Gatten, Mikey Roohan, Mikey Valentine, Mikhail Satansson, Miles Maxx, Milo Milouk, Milo Speranzo, Milton Koropshinsky, Mily Haskiell Ball, Minaa Qarabaghi, Mindi Smith, Mindy Glenn, Mindy Tucker, Minna Greenland, Missy Barr, MisterMo Pfanner, Misty Greer, Misty Rock, Mitch Cohen, Mitch Djkaz Howard, Mitch J Kneute, Mitch Smith, Mitchel Stockton, Mitchell Hoch, Mitchell Kobold, Mitchell Leiman, Mitchell Reisbord, Mitchell Thomas, Miture Ben Ezderte, Mo Dane, Mo Martinez, Mo Morrissey, Moataz Brokless, Moby Waller, Moe Kharrazi, Molly Ort, Monica Cekovsky, Monica Dewey-Hemingway, Monica Meehan, Monica Serva, Monica Shepherd, Monica Weisman, Monika Golon, Montgomery Morais, Moon Trent, Morgan Cj Brown, Moriah Ray Britt, Morna Sullivan-Hermann, Morris Lighthouse, Moxie Tara Gallaway, MrFrame Omar, Munsey Ricci, Murray Betesh, Murray Brannen, Mycah Williams, Mylene Doublet, Nancy Baek, Nancy Marks Sterner, Nancy Niles, Nancy Radcliffe, Nancy Ravick Horwitz, Nancy Swanson, Nando Gutierrez, Nash DoubleMint Dean, Nastassia Vulaj, Nataleigh Gulley, Natalie Aley, Natalie Ashby Bain, Natalie Caudill, Natalie Cervini Kuhn, Natalie Gray, Natalie Love, Natalie Madrigal-Lee, Natalie Scavuzzo Gill, Natalise Kalea, NaTasha Ahlin, Natasha Gunaratne, Nate Baker, Nate Bottone, Nate Gerards, Nate VanPoelvoorde, Nate Weiner, Nate Zamora, Nathan Adler, Nathan Klepeckas, Nathan Miller, Nathan Millspaugh, Nathan Pinnegar, Nathan Rex, Nathan Segal, Nathan White, Neal Berger, Neal Deas, Neal Siegel, Neena Richie, Neil Berliner, Neil Garrio, Neil Henning, Neil Jay, Neil Klein, Neil Markham, Neil

Masters, Neil Prendergast, Neil Strauss, Neil Wagman, Neil McDonald, Nena Lourdes, Nerry Vargas Cuazon, New Lenox Rosati's, Nguyễn Quang, Nicholas Allen Lutz, Nicholas Davis, Nicholas Di Paolo, Nicholas Doliveira, Nicholas Gamble, Nicholas Kaminsky, Nicholas Michael, Nicholas Neece, Nicholas Skarvan, Nicholle Hempel, Nick Baker, Nick Barsocchini, Nick Berger, Nick Brand, Nick Bruno, Nick Cuellar, Nick D'Amore, Nick Del Guercio, Nick Evans, Nick Farrer, Nick GarSuperstar, Nick Graham, Nick Green, Nick Herrera, Nick Hofmann, Nick Humphrey, Nick Korunovski, Nick Milinkovich, Nick Muglia, Nick Novellino, Nick Panteles, Nick Puccia, Nick Serafin, Nick Shaffer, Nick Tursi, Nicky Smith, Nico Romano, Nicol Paone, Nicola Cecchino, Nicole Bass, Nicole Bernard, Nicole Cardillo Barisic, Nicole Conradt, Nicole D'Angelo, Nicole Johan Rand, Nicole Marie, Nicole Neff, Nicole Palazzo, Nicole Pierce-Jansen, Nicole Richards Onesti, Nicole Rox, Nicole Wacura, Nigel Allen, Nikea Jackson, Niki Abrew, Niki Hinds, Nikki Breslaw, Nikki Jae, Nikki Love, Nikki Nearing, Nikki Silva, Nikka Withrow, Nikky DiMeo Wright, Nikolas A Saia, Nimos Rellak, Nina Gi Arrusso, Nina Masterjohn, Nina Zeigerman Youncofski, Noah Apodaca, Noah Berlow, Noah Fentz, Noah Gyles, Noble DraKoln, Noe Ayala, Noe Beatle, Noe Mendoza, Noel N Ashman, Noor Aburaneh, Nora E. Adams, Norman Gray, Norman Green, Norman W. Gray III, Nove Moyes, Nu Doubt, Nuno Leal, Nykki Hu, O.J. Stephens, Olabisi Janey Bisqueen, Oliver Axelrod, Oliver C. Seneca, Oliver Haughton, Olivia Amato, Olivia Whelan, Olympia Arizeliz, Omar Dangerfield, Omar Schamout, Oren Bornstein, Orghipchick Livermore, Oriyan Gitig Schwartz, Orlando Bishop, Orlando Jerome Vera, Oscar Angelo, Otto Petersen, Owen Murphy, Ozzie Egas, P.J. Lang, Pablo C. Vergara, Pablo Ponce, Paige Medina, Paige Reilly Hutchinson, Paige Westfall Stein, Pam Kennedy, Pam Russo DiAntonio, Pamela Paige, Pamela Perso, Pamela Price, Parker Bent, Parvin M Greene, Pascal Payant, Pastor Joe Staffa, Pat Brennan, Pat Carmody, Pat Craney, Pat Dowd Grant, Pat Dowdell, Pat Duane, Pat Fitzgerald, Pat Godwin, Pat Hughes, Pat Pogue, Patricia Davila, Patricia Di Giovanni Sabella, Patricia Graham, Patricia Kline, Patricia Redmond, Patricia Reisin, Patricio Ordega, Patrick B Croteau, Patrick Barnett, Patrick Barry, Patrick Benson, Patrick Budani, Patrick Cogley, Patrick Condron,

Patrick Connolly, Patrick Denig, Patrick Dion, Patrick Francomacaro, Patrick Geen, Patrick Haggerty, Patrick Hayden, Patrick J Guice, Patrick James Ganley, Patrick Kolb, Patrick Laugherty, Patrick Leborio, Patrick Lennon, Patrick Leon, Patrick Malarkey, Patrick McCarthy, Patrick Mick Gilleece, Patrick Mitchell, Patrick Moran, Patrick Morse, Patrick Nickel, Patrick Odonnell, Patrick Poston, Patrick Seholm, Patrick Tierney, Patrick Tobin, Patrick Tucci, Patrick Veasey, Patrick Walsh, Patrick Wiegand, Patrizia Iuliucci, Patti Pappalardo, Pattie A. Hassan, Pattie Kuhn, Patty Caneda, Patty Masters, Paul Anthony Encinias, Paul Blume, Paul Borzell, Paul Cameron, Paul Caridi, Paul Cauchi, Paul Cha, Paul Clark, Paul Contos, Paul Covfefe Salerno, Paul Cratty, Paul Davis, Paul Deese, Paul Dell'Angelo, Paul Duhaime, Paul Ferguson, Paul Fishbein, Paul Grant, Paul Gray, Paul Hartmann, Paul Hudson, Paul Just, Paul Kaplan, Paul King, Paul Kiselewsky, Paul Knot, Paul Kraz, Paul Ladd, Pual Langlois, Paul Lohman, Paul M. Field, Paul M Perrott, Paul M. Lisun, Paul Mcfall, Paul McKinnon, Paul Minor, Paul N Dapontes, Paul O'Callaghan, Paul O'Reilly Baldwin, Paul Papazian, Paul Passi, Paul Phillips, Paul Russell Wagner, Paul Sacco, Paul Saxton, Paul Scudds, Paul Shahood, Paul Silva, Paul Smith, Paul Thomas, Paul Turner, Paul Ulino, Paul Valenzano, Paul Viggiano, Paul Vincent Saurini, Paul Ward, Paul Winkler, Paul Wontorek, Paul Wroblewski, Paul Wylde, Paul Yaretz, Paul Godles Maynard, Paul Judy, Paul Thacker, Pauline Breitenbach James, PeaJr Mi, Pedro Encarnacion, Pedro J Rodriguez, Peg Davidson McCaskey, Peggy Jensen, Pegi Van Buskirk, Pepe Equizi, Pepe Silvia, Perry Cuni, Perry Dix, Perry Noid, Pete Barbara, Pete Bongiovi, Pete Borowicz II, Pete Carney, Pete Crawford, Pete Dennean, Pete Digger, Pete Dominick, Pete Fanell, Pete Ferraina, Pete Gilbert, Pete Hrycak, Pete Manfredo, Pete Mann, Pete Nugent, Pete Piasecki, Pete Pisacano, Pete Sasanecki, Pete Schoen, Pete Silverman, Pete Sloane, Petr Banko, Peter Brown, Peter Cascio, Peter D. Reed, Peter DeSimone, Peter E Pellegrino, Peter F Procopio IV, Peter Fredotovich, Peter Garrido, Peter Helicopter, Peter Hoffman, Peter Jorge Dampor, Peter Joseph Petrino Jr, Peter Lee, Peter Loukopoulos, Peter Mac, Peter Maggio, Peter Mayer, Peter Mcheffey, Peter Mennona, Peter Mulhern, Peter Nicholas Lizarzaburu, Peter Prins, Peter Roessler, Peter T Pavlou, Peter Theobald, Peter Woods, Peter Woodward, Petey Pabs, Petra

Verkaik, Phaedra Deland-Ippolito, Phil Blackmon, Phil Ferrante, Phil Hanes, Phil Hodgson, Phil Leotardo, Phil McCrackin, Phil McKracken, Phil Naumann, Phil Stellar, Phil Titolo, Philip Beattie, Philip Berkery, Philip Chilly Cross, Philip Meoli, Philip Otto, Philip Smyth, Philip Freeman, Philip Rife, Philip Seamon, Philthy McGirt, Phon-Del Myands, Pia Broderick, Pierre Sabs Sabourin, Pietro Franco Antonelli, Pink Lisa, Pink Cerro, Piper Oakland, Piroska Farkas, Pito Perez, PJ Landers, Polo Rodriguez, Povilas Bacevicius, Power Morales, Pranav Bhopale, Preston Tucci, Prince Menon, Princess Marris, Qi Lee, Quinn Leavey, Quintin Allen, Ra Zito, Rachael Worby, Rachel Butera, Rachel Castillo, Rachel Dares, Rachel Karolyi, Rachel La Monica Petersen, Rachel Lauren, Rachel Reigottie, Rachel Solomon, Rachelle Parmegiani McDonough, Radziewicz David, Reagan Cowger, Rafael Morales, Raina Fleegle, Rainier Wortelboer, Ralph Casale, Ralph Cindrich, Ralph D'Amato Jr, Ralph Goodwin, Ralph Marra, Ralph Sparaney, Ralph Vincent DiTucci, Ramon Mojica-river, Randi Lusak DeWitt, Rando B Hossler, Randy Brenham, Randy Fabian, Randy Herschelman, Randy James, Randy LaRosa, Randy Merritt, Randy Moser, Randy Quinn, Randy Ryno, Randy Vogt, Randy Weaver, Randy Young, Raul Aguilar, Raul Victores, Raul Weeks, Ray Beaudoin, Ray Bell, Ray Culver, Ray Falk, Ray Lee, Ray Marshall, Ray Melendez, Ray Nedohon, Ray Petty, Ray Privett, Ray Raymond, Ray Rideout, Ray Spoolstra, Ray Vandiver, Rayen Arbi, Raymond Benson, Raymond Bryant, Raymond Camm, Raymond De Filippis, Raymond Sabbatini, RC Zimmerling, Reagen Unrau, Reanna Smith, Rebecca Gaby Halioua, Rebecca Hortensia, Rebecca Johnson, Rebecca Kingsley, Rebecca Leib, Randy Moser, Randy Quinn, Randy Ryno, Randy Vogt, Randy Weaver, Randy Young, Raul Aguilar, Raul Victores, Raul Weeks, Ray Beaudoin, Ray Bell, Ray Culver, Ray Falk, Ray Lee, Ray Marshall, Ray Melendez, Ray Nedohon, Ray Petty, Ray Privett, Ray Raymond, Ray Rideout, Ray Spoolstra, Ray Vandiver, Rayen Arbi, Raymond Benson, Raymond Bryant, Raymond Camm, Raymond De Filippis, Raymond Sabbatini, RC Zimmerling, Reagen Unrau, Reanna Smith, Rebecca Gaby Halioua, Rebecca Hortensia, Rebecca Johnston, Rebecca Kingsley, Rebecca Leib, Rich Gustafson, Rich Hahn, Rich Jennings, Rich Kleinman, Rich Lyerla, Rich Maddox, Rich Rennie, Rich Rochlin, Rich Rog, Rich Russell, Rich

Sorviggio, Rich Stanzione, Rich Tunnicliffe, Rich Urban, Rich Walker, Rich Wiley, Richard Welcher, Richard Bright, Richard Buckout, Richard Carrell, Richard Conley, Richard D Olivas, Richard Danglin, Richard Dawson, Richard Dempsey, Richard DiMatteo, Richard E. Wolfe, Richard Faughnan, Richard Ferrante, Richard Gier, Richard Hacker, Richard Hartmann, Richard Hawkins, Richard Hurley, Richard James Finkel, Richard Llyod, Richard Marino, Richard Medina, Richard O'Brien, Richard P. Klein, Richard Parks, Richard Quell, Richard Raskin, Richard Regan, Richard Rodriguez, Richard S. Bronstein, Richard Shikora, Richard Skora, Richard Slater, Richard Smith, Richard Spencer, Richard Taylor, Richard Virgilio, Richard W. Nelson, Richard Withers, Richard Woods, Richie Woods, Richie Carden, Richie Imrit, Richie Legouri, Richie Miller, Richie Realms, Richie Rosati, Richie Stratton, Rick A. Oberle, Rick Allen, Rick Backer, Rick Bissonnette, Rick Black, Rick Broscoe, Rick Cahall, Rick Campbell, Rick Corbett, Rick Fishman, Rick Foley, Rick Garvey, Rick Green, Rick Groper, Rick Habeeb, Rick Heath, Rick Hitchcock, Rick Huss, Rick Jobin, Rick Kelly, Rick Kowalski, Rick Kutler, Rick Lasher, Rick Marotta Jr., Rick Medina, Rick Piontek, Rick Rome, Rickard Östlund. Ricky Baarck II, Ricky Nicholopoulos, Ricky Pushkin, Ricky Ramirez, Ricky Theberge, Rico Sumarna, Riley Park, Rina Gregory, Rj Davis, Rk Levine, Ro DelleGrazie, Ro Hurley, Rob Abbatiello, Rob Anthony Kopec, Rob Baer, Rob Bergeron, Rob Berry, Rob Bingham, Rob BoRo Rovegna, Rob Cooper, Rob Coughlin, Rob de Beer, Rob DeSaro, Rob DeVol, Rob Drapeau, Rob Duga, Rob Eldredge, Rob George, Rob Greenberg, Rob Hegarty, Rob Hennessy, Rob Hirschbuhl, Rob Hoerning, Rob Hughes, Rob Jeanes, Rob Kreuger, Rob Kudyba, Rob Majka, Rob Martino, Rob Mcallister, Rob McGuire, Rob Miller, Rob Morosca, Rob Miller, Rob Morosca, Rob Nelson, Rob Pagliuca, Rob Penco, Rob Pompi, Rob Schuller, Rob Scott, Rob Slipshod, Rob Smith, Rob Spencer, Rob Sprance, Rob Stephen, Rob Stone, Rob Tarulli, Rob Teitelbaum, Rob Thomas, Rob Udovich, Rob Wetzel, Rob Wilson, Rob Zahner, Robb Mathis, Robbie Nickell, Robbie Rob, Robbit Keating, Robby Abraham, Robby Rodriguez, Robby Skidmore, Robby Williams, Robert A Booey, Robert Abernathy, Robert Abuie, Robert Altman, Robert Anthony Peralta, Robert Blade Lewin, Robert Bonsignore, Robert Brokine,

Robert Brown, Robert Buturla, Robert Carvounas, Robert Chalker, Robert Cianfarano, Robert Chalker, Robert Cuillo, Robert Cusato, Robert D'Allesandro, Robert DAmato Sr, Robert Dargan, Robert Dean Klein, Robert DeAngelis, Robert Dervin, Robert DjMagic Marquez, Robert Garippa, Robert Giovanni, Robert Goldman, Robert Heaps, Robert Jackson, Robert Jacobs, Robert Jacobson, Robert Kehlenbeck, Robert Kramer, Robert Lackner, Robert Lariviere, Roberto Leo, Robert Levine, Robert Luehring, Robert M Zito Sr, Robert M. Narvaez, Robert Markell Rice, Robert Martin, Robert Martinez, Robert Meyer, Robert Minnich III, Robert Moore, Robert Moran, Robert Muench, Robert Piskothy, Robert Quayle, Robert Ramon Zimmerman, Robert Reaper, Robert Renna, Robert Sidney, Robert Slavinski, Robert Stark, Robert T. Hedden, Robert T. Homlar, Robert T. Rosenblatt, Robert Tanner, Robert Toomey, Robert Vosganian, Robert Vozzi, Robert W. Martin, Robert Weems, Robert Wetmore, Robert Yalden, Roberta Parmegiani Hennelly, Roberta Viscuso, Robêrtœ Kêńńéth, Robin A. Morgan, Robin King, Robin Quivers, Robin Radzinski Wong, Robin's Wrong, Robyn Bryant Weindel, Robyn Buehler Thurber, Robyn Feudo, Robyn Kaufhold, Robyn Mayer, Robynn Smith, Rocco DiBenedetto, Rocco Joel, Rochelle Ponsky, Rocky Azzara, Rocky Dennis, Rocky Dennis Jr., Rocky McCracken, Rod Bickford, Rod Black, Rod Holcomb, Rod Smart, Rod Trotter, Rodney Allen Gill, Rodney Simas, Rodrigo Arcuri, Roger Birdman Mattingly, Roger Black, Roger Brosky, Roger Doneff, Roger Lay Jr, Roger Nicholson, Roger Puffinberger, Roger Rojas, Roger Sadlo, Roger Shaw, Roger Yucko Black, Rogney Rodriguez, Rohit Jain, Roland Justice, Roland Radcliffe, Roland Todacheenie, Rolls Andre, Roman Joseph, Roman M. Karpa, Romy Ní Haligneán, Ron Badgley, Ron Cote, Ron Dove, Ron Edwards, Ron Figg, Ron Hed, Ron Kelly, Ron Mills, Ron Norell, Ron Pack, Ron Parmegiani, Ron Patterson, Ron Pustizzi, Ron Renn, Ron Riot, Ron Romans, Ron Sandler, Ron Shope, Ron Sklar, Ron Spriggs, Ron Sullivan, Ron Wilson, Ronald Cohen, Ronald Jones, Ronan Conlon, Ronda Long, Ronda Phils Cebu, Roni O'Connor, Ronnie Gee, Ronnie Sapp, Ronny Schnell, Rory Hope, Rosa Kennedy, Rosalinda Oropeza Randall, Rosaline Marisa, Rosanna Lisa Arquette, Rosanna Richichi Williamson, Rosario Sferrazza, Rose Le Blanc Laino, Rose Wood, Rose Yeevee, Rosella Vadala Claxon, RoseMarie

Saccio, Rosemary Seaver, Rosie Papageorge, Rosita Marroquin, Ross Baird, Ross Bergman, Ross Burns, Ross Donnelly, Ross Fishberger, Ross Garber, Ross Hoppers, Ross Mallor, Ross Mark, Ross Mcclinton, Rosstipher Labossiere, Rosy Morales, Rosyline Crist, Roxana Molinari, Roxanne Akard Chapman, Roy Brunston, Roy Panes, Roy Ramos, Ruben Mosqueda, Ruchelle Harston, Rudy Brady, Rudy Romano, Rudy Romo, Rudy Varga, Rula Hanania, Russ Abitz, Russ Booth, Russ Hensley, Russ Meneve, Russ Smith, Russell Ells, Russell Lusak, Russell Schutte, Russell Siminoff, Rustie Davies, Rusty Inohio, Ruth Surrey, Ry Chance, Ryan Bentley, Ryan Bernholz, Ryan Bessinger, Ryan Biddulph, Ryan Bigos, Ryan Biren, Ryan Boehmer, Ryan Cns, Ryan Crist, Ryan Dalton, Ryan Davidson, Ryan Dennis, Ryan Dinehart, Ryan Dobbins, Ryan Duffin, Ryan Esposito, Ryan Galvin, Ryan Hamelin, Ryan Hamm, Ryan Henkel, Ryan Hilton, Ryan Hoppe, Ryan Horner, Ryan James Davis, Ryan James Secret, Ryan Jerome, Ryan Johnson, Ryan Justason, Ryan Kitta, Ryan Koch, Ryan Kyler Bailey, Ryan Laveder, Ryan Maher, Ryan Mangano, Ryan McCormick, Ryan McDermott, Ryan McEwing, Ryan McGrath, Ryan Meara, Ryan Mooney, Ryan Peachy, Ryan Pirozzi, Ryan Politi, Ryan Pope, Ryan Reiss, Ryan Russotti, Ryan Spinner, Ryan Steel, Ryan Striano, Ryan Tindale, Ryan Tracy, Ryan Wenkus, Ryan Wilson, Ryan Winn, Ryan Worrell, Ryan Wymer, Ryk Allyn, Rylee ANoel, Ryo Matsuyama, S.G. Darling, Sabiha Khan, Sabrina O'Brien, Sahar Shishabi, Sal Catalfumo, Sal Governale, Sal Pena, Sally Brunski, Salvaje Corona, Salvatore Governale, Salvatore James Rizzo Junior, Sam Barney Gibbs, Sam Campbell, Sam Fanelli, Sam Hagler, Sam McKinney, Sam Nail, Sam Rizzo, Sam Robilotta, Sam Rostow, Sam Salkin, Sam Storey, Sam Williams, Sam Younkin, Samantha Mastellos Pinter, Samantha Muhlrad Karp, Samantha Noelle Baker, Samantha Oths Rauber, Samantha Ross, Samantha Turcotte, Sami Karzazi, Samir Maher, Sammy Herremans, Sammy Romano, Samuel Capaldi, Samuel Jay Robertson, Samuel Kaufman, Samuel Lolla, Samuel Parisi, Samy Dimermanas, San Dra, Sandi Patterson, Sandie Tucker Reames, Sandra Estrada, Sandra Goering Waghorn, Sandra Hartig, Sandra Hutchins Dixon, Sandra Marie Rose Osipavicius, Sandra Watters, Sandro Iocolano, Sandy Beaches, Sandy Muhlenberg, Sandy Munti, Sara Berelsman, Sara Cannon, Sara Carter, Sara O'Neill Faranda, Sara Ray

Rider, Sarah Cortazzo, Sarah Cosolo, Sarah Jones, Sarah LeClaire, Sarah Maria Paul, Sarah Newell, Sarah Newman, Sarah Newman, Sarah Ogden, Sarah Reyna, Sasha Babic, Sasha Petryna, Scot Porter, Scott Albrecht, Scott Anderson, Scott Arvoy, Scott B Lees, Scott Barglof, Scott Brody, Scott Bronson, Scott Brooks, Scott Buono, Scott C. Gresens, Scott Cronick, Scott Davis, Scott Demo, Scott DePace, Scott Dumont, Scott Dunkers, Scott E. Stoffel, Scott Einziger, Scott Engel, Scott Evans, Scott Focht, Scott Ford, Scott Garger, Scott Ian VonFrankenstein, Scott Israel, Scott J. Kalinowski, Scott J. Parisi, Scott Johnson, Scott Jones, Scott Kantor, Scott Kearns, Scott Kevin, Scott Kleeger, Scott Lacey, Scott Lennon, Scott Lichterman, Scott Livingston, Scott Mandel, Scott Marks, Scott Mathews, Scott Middlemiss, Scott N. Elliot, Scott Nicholas, Scott Pennington, Scott Pierce, Scott Platt, Scott Porter, Scott R. Cichetti, Scott Rayow, Scott Richardson, Scott Rosenthal, Scott Rubin, Scott S. Strawsburg, Scott Salem, Scott Schroeder, Scott Schwartz, Scott Shubert, Scott Smith, Scott Spiegel, Scott Staples, Scott Tingen, Scott Weiner, Scott Wenner, Scott Wolkoff, Scott Zamek, Scott Zwick, Scotty Free, Scotty Goldberg, Scout Hoyden, Sean Blickem, Sean Brubaker, Sean Burke, Sean DeCiancio, Sean Dougherty, Sean F Milke, Sean Flaherty, Sean Gavigan, Sean Gencsy, Sean Geraty, Sean Glaze, Sean Green, Sean Haines, Sean Harrington, Sean Holland, Sean Kelly, Sean Landry, Sean Lennon, Sean Lewis, Sean Magill, Sean Mannion, Sean McDermott, Sean McFarlane, Sean Miller, Sean Morrissey, Sean Morton, Sean Murphy, Sean Neil Meehan, Sean Nugent, Sean Pon, Sean 'Rail' Conway, Sean Riney, Sean Ritchie, Sean Rivers, Sean Rohwedder, Sean Ryan, Sean Ryder, Sean Sexton, Sean Smyth, Sean South, Sean Stack, Sean Stewart, Sean Tremblay, Sean Vickery, Sean Warren, Sean Whelan Dempsey, Sean You, Sean-Michael Longstreth, Sebastian Blicharz, Sebastian Lawrence, Selcuk Arsan, Sendil Krishnan, Serafina Fiore, Seth Bass, Seth Cummings, Seth Kaufman, Seth Lapp, Seth Matthews, Seth Shapiro, Sev Moro, Seven Istheman, Shaadi Shoubaki, Shad Brown, Shad Hernandez, Shad Schoen, Shamus Peck, Shana Elizabeth, Shana Sterling, Shane Barnes, Shane Bittner, Shane Carter, Shane Corey, Shane F Delaney, Shane Gabbard, Shane L Lynn, Shane Leipold, Shane Ogden, Shane Ricketts, Shang Forbes, Shannon Algieri Seeberg, Shannon Cheveldayoff, Shannon Davis Franz, Shannon

Donovan, Shannon Eads Stockard, Shannon Fochtman, Shannon Freeman, Shannon Land, Shannon McCoy, Shannon Pham Fornelli, Shannon Rease, Shannon Reed, Shannon Tarsha, Shannon Wright, Shantelle Nichole Schmalz, Sharesz T. Wilkinson, Shari Gold, Shari Meehan, Shari Silver W, Sharon Coburn, Sharon Post Baranowski, Shaun Alimbini, Shaun Arsenault, Shaun Conolly, Shaun Eaves, Shaun Lauren Parker, Shaun Lewin, Shaun McKinley, Shaun Robens, Shauna O'Donnell, Shauno McCullagh, Shawn Alexander, Shawn Bethke, Shawn Charles, Shawn Decker, Shawn Galbreath Mccann, Shawn Gallahue, Shawn Geltman, Shawn Harris, Shawn Hecker, Shawn Keith, Shawn Mac, Shawn McCarthy, Shawn McDowell, Shawn McHenry, Shawn Morris, Shawn Murphy, Shawn Peachers, Shawn Prebil, Shawn Rafuse, Shawn Shapiro, Shawn Shirey, Shawn Swahilli, Shawn Tarango, Shawn Taylor, Shawn Wells, Shawna Casey, Shay Imerys, Shay McFalls, Shay Peyote, Shay Siobhan Ax, Shay Smores, Shayna Singh, Shayne Donsky, Shayne Montpetit, Sheila Marikar, Shelby Berry, Sheldon Benoit, Sheldon Cameron, Shelia Harvey, Shelly Collins, Shep Ashton, Sheri Harris-Utz, Sherrene Ryan Wells, Sherri Harper, Sherry Clancy, Sherry Dunham Sullivan, Sherry Keeley, Sherry Kinison, Sherry Rahm, Sherry Smith Payne, Shira T. Weiss, Showin Galleries, Shuli Egar, Shweta M Sah, Shy Shyy, Sid Rosenberg, Sidney Gonzalez, Sidra Saucedo, Sigfredo Velez, Siggy Bski, Silas Pollitt, Silvana Nicosia, Sim Tweed, Simha Meyer Trollman, Simon Alvelos, Simon Partridge, Simon Smith, Simon Suh, Simran Kapoor, Sinah Hoffman, Sinatra Mandracina, Sindee Kritzberg, Sindy Thomas, Sinead McNamara, Siobhan Meow, Sirius Stern, Sith Mall, Sixto Delgado, Skip Brady, Skip Matthews, Slack Magick, Smacky Jr. lee, Snir Ochakovsky, So Kim, SoCal Goldbuyers, Sodom Story, Solomon Juang, Sonnee Stanley, Sonny Heston, Sonny Spagnuolo, Sonya Cashner, Sonya Schumacher Farhat, Spencer Clemson, Spencer Kiyoshi, Spencer Kuhn, Spencer Medbery, Spike McFerguson, Spike McSpike, Sta Cey, Stace Biddle, Stacee Anderson Hoebel, Stacey DeMaio Fritzinger, Stacey J Finnerty, Stacey Kaplanis Chillemi, Stacey Lange, Stacey Marsala-Caggiano, Stacey Nieto Fish, Stacey Palmer, Stacey Picolli, Stacey Pike Foster, Stacey Prussman, Staci Houchin Nash, Stacia Park, Stacy Kestler Turrel, Stacy Regan, Stahl MacIntyre, Stan Arent, Stan Rudman, Stanley Andrew Lipka III, Stasia Harris, Status

Shirts, Stefan Borzone, Stefan D Meir, Stefan Jung, Stefan Kvernmo, Stefan Skweir, Stefan Trött, Stefan Ursu, Stefanie Hahn, Stefanie Lauren, Stefanie Lewendon, Stelios Cfd, Stella marie Jurofcik, Stephanie Almasi, Stephanie Amanda, Stephanie Armstrong, Stephanie Bethea, Stephanie Carlson, Stephanie Carney, Stephanie Dessi Kiley, Stephanie Elaine McFeely, Stephanie Fenstermacher, Stephanie Gunderson, Stephanie Hart-Lesner, Stephanie Hine, Stephanie Johnson, Stephanie M Lane, Stephanie Mankin, Stephanie Marx Wallace, Stephanie Perritt, Stephanie Petersohn, Stephanie Sciochetti Donofrio, Stephanie Sherman, Stephanie Vincent, Stephen Austin, Stephen Bowman, Stephen Bumball, Stephen Coast, Stephen Cumbey, Stephen Dalton, Stephen Doyle, Stephen Elder, Stephen Gurrrola, Stephen Halpin, Stephen Hendrickson, Stephen J. Lestingi, Stephen Javakian, Stephen Kaplan, Stephen Kaufer, Stephen Kep, Stephen Langford, Stephen M. Plym, Stephen N Dempsey, Stephen Porreca, Stephen Rocamboli, Stephen Schombs, Stephen Tawil, Stephen Towery, Stephen Weber, Stephen Wokanick, Stern Fan Mutt, Stern Nation, Stern Show, Stevan Morganstein, Steve Adams, Steve Bagosy, Steve Baumley, Steve Blando, Steve Bowe Bowe, Steve Boyken, Steve Brock, Steve Burger, Steve Caffrey, Steve Ciancio, Steve Corrado, Steve Cox, Steve Crowley Antinora, Steve Curcio, Steve Denney, Steve Egan, Steve Engelson, Steve Ennis, Steve Flocco, Steve Foley, Steve Friedman, Steve Gallo, Steve Garrin, Steve Gilligan, Steve Gliner, Steve Godwin, Steve Gorman, Steve Hancock, Steve Heywood, Steve Hoffman, Steve Holt, Steve Infante, Steve Jones, Steve Juchnevicius, Steve Kabinoff, Steve Kellner, Steve Kinkler, Steve Kline, Steve Kups, Steve Lamm, Steve Lindahl, Steve Lunay, Steve Macera, Steve Mack Mackey, Steve Marshall, Steve Matasavich, Steve Mathieson, Steve Matson, Steve Moyer, Steve Olin, Steve Oudinot, Steve Perez, Steve Postiglione, Steve Quadrato, Steve Rails, Steve Rice, Steve Sabean, Steve Sajor, Steve Shirley, Steve Shuck, Steve Smith, Steve Stepleman, Steve Tepper, Steve Thompson, Steve Toplan, Steve Vaughan, Steve Viens, Steve Watz, Steve Weinraub, Steve Weiss, Steve Welch, Steve Wescott, Steve White, Steve Williams, Steve Winchester, Steve Zuckerberg, Steven Bezman, Steven Brody Stevens, Steven Burritt, Steven Darling, Steven DiLeonardo, Steven E Cavallo, Steven Geller, Steven Gibbs, Steven Girardi, Steven Gottlieb, Steven Grillo, Steven Harrison, Steven Hartline, Steven Hicks, Steven

J. Nicoletta, Steven J. Longden, Steven Leclair, Steven M. Weidler, Steven Marcato, Steven Melo, Steven Mogell, Steven Oliver, Steven R Rondina, Steven Robinson, Steven Sav, Steven Schultheis, Steven Skoblicki, Steven Smith, Steven Snakes, Steven Stetzler, Steven Williams, Sto Belongia, Stoney Weddle, Stroker Cox, Stu Baker, Stu Hellman, Stu Korn, Stuart Duncan, Stuart Glass, Stuart MacKenzie, Stuart Zweig, Sudesh Prasad, Sue Batson, Sue Caprood, Sue Chapas Fayne, Sue Hemphill, Sue NL, Sue Oppedisano, Sue Solzak Gibbs, Sugar de Jesus, Suki Hiroko, Surah Mariah Wahlberg, Susan Canyon, Susan P. Sachar, Susan Teston, Susan Tomlinson Coover, Susan Whitehead, Susana Delatorre, Susana Ruiz, Suzanne Marie, Suzanne Rocha, Suzanna Wright, Suzee Alvarado, Svetlana Balanescu, Szilva Vecserdy, T Eric Lyons, Taco Nacho, Taka Zvetc, Tal Sims, Tamara Harlan Hurst, Tamara Mary, Tamara Rizzo, Tamara Welsh, Tammy Danilovic, Tammy Phelan, Tani Golden, Tania Morales, Tanya M Tria, Tanya M Tria, Tanya Starkey, Tanya Unger, Tara Bartley Cohen, Tara Carthew, Tara Lee, Tara Melnik, Tara Napolitano Scully, Tara Sigs, Tara Smith, Tara Sutton, Tara Vassallo, Tarek El Badawy, Taris Malone, Tasha Harris, Tatiana Egas, Taunya Post, Tavahn Ghazi, Tawnya Holland, Taylor Arnold, Taylor Goodrich, Taylor Marie, Taylor Stratford, Tayyab Ashraf, Teal Bagger, Tecne Bevr, Ted Aveni Jr., Ted Gustafson, Ted King, Ted le Van, Ted Novick, Ted Panagiotis, Ted Terry, Ted Weihe, Ted Zep, Teddy Hart, Tee Reel, Terence Fitzgerald, Terence M. O'Neill, Terence Wilson, Teresa A Rivera, Terrence Castonguay, Terrence Lowis, Terry Baca, Terry Danuser, Terry Duffney, Terry Georgas, Terry Gingo, McClinton, Terry Graham, Terry Lee Smith, Terry Olivier, Terry Orel, Terry Seaholm, Terry Timmerman, Tess Stickle, Tex Watson, Thad Karbowsky, Thaddeus MacGregor, Thakoon Panichgul, Tharren Tee Poplion, Thazia Sayuri Matsuoka, Thedore Eyre Davis, Thess Chavez, TheTony Montana, Thom Baker, Thom Joseph, Thomas Abrams, Thomas Biniakewitz, Thomas Black, Thomas Brenna, Thomas Brown Jr., Thomas Burdick, Thomas Cahill, Thomas Citera, Thomas Daniels, Thomas Duffy, Thomas Duva, Thomas Gaskill, Thomas J. Goglia Jr., Thomas Laubach, Thomas M. Cooper, Thomas O'Donnell, Thomas Parmentier, Thomas Patrick, Thomas Roadkill Lewis, Thomas Rogers, Thomas Schneider, Thomas Selimoski, Thomas Sims, Thomas William

Barrett, Thomas Young, Tiffany Barbee, Tiffany Brown, Tiffany Kelene, Tiffany Mancini, Tiffany Massie, Tiffany Parks, Tiffany Rose, Tiffany Spencer Geerts, Tim Aguilar, Tim Bales, Tim Belford, Tim Belford, Tim Bell-Smith, Tim Blevins, Tim Blevins, Tim Broger, Tim Burr, Tim Buxton, Tim C Carrier, Tim Caldwell, Tim Chapanov, Tim Christiansen, Tim Comstock Sr., Tim Dominguez, Tim Dryer, Tim Ferguson, Tim Gagnier, Tim Granger, Tim Halpin, Tim Hanes, Tim Hartz, Tim Healy, Tim Huwel, Tim Kiley, Tim Krompier, Tim Laffe, Tim Lewis, Tim Liboiron, Tim Malone, Tim Mars, Tim Mattimore, Tim Mcc, Tim McDonnell, Tim Moakler, Tim Myers, Tim Needles, Tim O'Grady, Tim O'Hagan, Tim Orenbuch, Tim ORourke, Tim Osullivan, Tim Pappalardo, Tim Penska, Tim Pingel, Tim Reid, Tim Rorick, Tim Rząsa, Tim S. Brown, Tim Sabean, Tim Shales, Tim Stewart, Tim Sweet, Tim Ward, Tim Wistrom, Tim Wooters, Timmy Gill, Timmy Slawson, Timothy Andrew, Timothy Atchison, Timothy Barton, Timothy C. Johnson, Timothy Caraftis, Timothy Caughey, Timothy Harris, Timothy Hemhauser, Timothy Kuhn, Timothy L Abrigg, Timothy Leary Mitchell, Timothy Wayne Ragsdale, Tina Dickson, Tina Footes, Tina Grieco-Stanko, Tina Morgan, Tina Sanders, Tito Cruz, TJ Hazelden, Tj Hooker, TJ Roche, Tmar Switzer, Tobias Petersson, Tobie Babcock, Toby Borgens, Toby Bost, Toby Cosford, Toby Hord, Toby Jaffe, Toby Mccarron, Toby Soboleski, Toby Walker, Tod DeFazio, Todd Bechthold, Todd Bleecker, Todd Brennan, Todd Cohen, Todd Conner, Todd Corbett, Todd Dvorsky, Todd Emanuelli, Todd Frederickson, Todd Hall, Todd J Thomas, Todd J Zimmerman, Todd Kelly, Todd Lindstrom, Todd M Rehane, Todd Marcus, Todd McDonald, Todd Padavan, Todd Parish Bulge, Todd Prives, Todd Quirke Mua, Todd Ruggere, Todd TK Krbel, Todd White, Todd Youncofski, Tom Adelsbach, Tom Amerman, Tom Bailey, Tom Bosley, Tom Brennan, Tom Brown, Tom Bryant, Tom Burbine, Tom Butts, Tom Christianson, Tom Cipriano, Tom Dismore, Tom Ellis, Tom Gordon, Tom Groleau, Tom Haney, Tom Hiro, Tom Hochdorfer, Tom Holycross, Tom Hughes, Tom Jenn Mason, Tom Judd, Tom Kane, Tom Kelly, Tom Kelso, Tom Kim, Tom Kolbeck, Tom Koslowsky, Tom Kramer, Tom Lovejoy, Tom Marsula, Tom Marsula, Tom McBreen, Tom McCormack, Tom Medford, Tom Paladino, Tom Pomposello, Tom Quindley, Tom Race,

Tom Ross, Tom Sainclair, Tom Smith, Tom Somach, Tom Tagliente, Tom Taylor, Tom Teders, Tom Tommy Thomas Wylie, Tom Underwood, Tom Waddle, Tom Wagner, Tom Wandry, Tomas Welcha, Tomek Orłowski, Tommy Gonzalez, Tommy Burgess, Tommy Carrell Augustus, Tommy DiLeo, Tommy E Owen, Tommy Emolo, Tommy Festa, Tommy Kimbrough, Tommy Lane, Tommy LaRocca, Tommy Milahey, Tommy Savitt, Tommy Zito, Toni LaPlante, Tony Cannoli, Tony Ceraulo, Tony Ceresini, Tony Cerulli, Tony Chillemi, Tony Daniels, Tony DeLeon, Tony Faranda, Tony Francesconi, Tony Hacker, Tony Hubner, Tony Hughes, Tony Inzana, Tony Kost, Tony Lamesajan, Tony Landolfi, Tony Magno, Tony Marcello, Tony Mattera, Tony Mistrulli, Tony Molino Jr., Tony Mosher, Tony Nardelli, Tony Novo, Tony Pares, Tony Pierce, Tony Raffle, Tony Rodgers, Tony Romano, Tony Safoschnik, Tony Sandoval, Tony Santiago, Tony Spicchiali, Tony Wang, Tory Burk, Tory Richardson, Tracee Beebe, Tracey Gonzalez, Tracey MacDonald, Traci Arzillo, Traci Endes Johnson, Traci J. Seidman, Traci Reed, Tracie Marrow, Tracy Anacreonte-Norton, Tracy Caraftis-Lukas, Tracy Elston, Tracy L. Mooney, Tracy Lilo, Tracy Peterson, Travis Cassity, Travis Huber, Travis Moreno, Travis Rowe, Travis Schoen, Travis Thompson, Trávis Thompŝōn, Treacy Lambert, Trent Collicott, Trent Totin, Trent Willhite, Trenton Brisco, Trenton Dyer, Trevor Deery, Trevor Garner, Trevor Johnson, Trevor Wachsman, Trey Deck, Trey Olds, Tricia Lynn McKissick Watkins, Tricky Zea, Tripp McCandlish, Trish Bourgeois, Trish Buza, Trisha Marie Thompson, Trisha Tanney, Tristan, Sheazupan, Tristen Taylor, Troy Bacon, Troy Dellorto, Troy Edward Dolan, Troy Emmi, Troy Fiala, Troy McClancy, Troy Rosales, Troy St Jacques, Trudy Mangini-White, Tucker Scott, Tuomas Miettinen, Ty Koon, Ty O'Neil, Tyler Coburn, Tyler Doyle, Tyler Eveland, Tyler Sloss, Tyler True, Tyler YomTov, Uday Bhaskar, Uri Poole, Ursula Medrano, Vacious Veloria Smith, Vako Lake, Verlie Sharp, Valle Ravens Lewis Mentzer, Valorie Thomas, Vanessa Celentano, Vanessa King Stimmel, Venus Rising, Vern Morin, Veronica Stern, Vetag Kevin Jackson, Vic Cohen, Vic Doc Dougherty, Vic Freitas, Vic Montesano, Vicki Abelson, Vicki Brazzon, Vicki Lustgarten-Ahern, Vicki Ramie, Victor Benedetto, Victor Brown, Victor Cohen, Victor DiDonato, Victor Jacobs, Victor John Vulak, Victor Joseph, Victor Murphy, Victor Pashuku, Victor Sanabrais,

Victor Tangaris, Victoria Gates, Victoria Grtsn, Victoria Starr, Victoria Trance, Vidya Kumar, Viggo DeBöhriggerstein, Vince Barnett, Vince Faville, Vince Forcier, Vincent Calabrese, Vincent Farrauto, Vincent Grego, Vincent Luvera, Vincent Manganiello, Vincent Sciortino, Vincent Smith, Vincent Terranova, Vincenzo Ferraro, Vinnie Favale, Vinnie Manganiello, Vinnie Micco, Vinnie Paz, Vinny Benincasa, Vinny Bono, Vinny Conforti, Vinny Gioia, Vinny Valverde, Virginia Hall, Virginia Phillips, Visenya Fogano, Vito Faiello, Vito Laudicina, Vito Viscomi, Vivi Assam, Vivian Martinez, Vivian Palmeri, Vladimir Noskov, Von Rothinfink, Wade Barnes, Wade T Roses, Wade Watson, Wagner Randy, Walker Adrian, Walker Warren, Wally Denny, Wally Reeves, Walt Corsa, Walt Stankus, Walter Calderon, Walter Einhart, Walter Papalegis, Wanda Selimoski, Waqas Ahmed, Warren Cautious Sheprow, Warren Chalk, Warren Ruparsic, Warren Thomas, Warren Vest, Wayan Darta Nusa, Wayne Bettencourt, Wayn Brown, Wayne Dawkins, Wayne Dequina, Wayne Felber, Wayne Jershky, Wayne Johnston, Wayne Jude Muraca, Wayne Manthe, Wayne Palmer, Wayne R. Folmar, Wayne Rodriguez, Wayne Young, Wayne Ziemba, Weldy Bahls, Wells Tipley, Wenders Young, Wendi Starling, Wendy Eden Harris, Wendy Francois, Wendy Kaufman, Wendy Lee Williamson, Wendy Schneider, Wendy Smith Gumpper, Wendy Young-Hamilton, Wes Lockard, Wes Nations, Wes Pohler, Wesley Hall, Whenn Marry, Whitney Casey, Whitney Rachel, Wickie Wickie, Wil James, Wil Stebbins, Wilbur Ewbank, Wilhelm Tell, Will Bartol, Will Dodd, Will Kelly, Will Knapp, Will McAllister, Will McCandless, Will Mckay, Will Murray, Will Pearsall, Will Poteat, Will Roya, Will Shute, Will Strawn, Will Trupp, Will Umansky, Willem Knzyblocki, Willhelm Von Bailey, William Billford Staylor, William Billistik Hoerauf, William Brevaire, William Buckley, William Bundy, William Butler, William C. Carter, William Campbell, William Carboy, William Christos, William Cody Bateman, William Dunbar, William Durling, William F Holman, William Glamore, William James Handon, William Joseph, William Lemon, William Moen, William Montano, William Moore, William Morris, William Newton, William O. Williams, William Olejarz, William Rodriguez III, William Rubel Jr., William Schoemerfilms, William Seemster, William Smith, William Studer, William T

Brittingham III, William Thomas Hyer, William Willc Clifton, Willie Fistergash, Willie Taggart, Willy Cee, Willy Marciano, Winston Wacko, Wkrn Ny, Wolfie Scott, Woody Woodward, Wood Would, Wyatt Shukerow, Xanthe Matychak, Xiang Seaclear, Xiaoyan Sun, Xyane Alexander, Yakubova Swed, Yanik Pinier, Yasron Sanggacala, Yello Fury, Yevgeniy Kostenko, Yhing Ramos, Yisroel Cherns, Yona Stone Flynn, Yoshi Obayashi, Za, Zak Shaffer, Zanda Forsythe, Zaundra Witherspoon, Ze Rosario, Zeke Marchiani, Zeke Wolf, Zeki Numanoglu, Zena LeCoff, Ziggy Siegfried, Zolar Glen, Zonia Cooley, Ραυλ Τπιροδες, Анастасия Колосова, Blackhawk.

I really hope you enjoyed this book and will let me know what you think at kc@wmapradio.com.

And watch for our next release, Simply Amazing Women.

GONE!

—KC

BOOK CLUB DISCUSSION QUESTIONS

<u>Literary structure and format:</u>

What was KC Armstrong's role in the book, and was it effective in creating a unifying theme?

What was the effect of using interview transcripts rather than conventional narration to tell these stories?

<u>Judgement, assessment, application, extension</u>

Which was your favorite story, and why? In what ways were your views changed or challenged by this interview?

Is there any particular chapter in which you disagreed with a choice make by the person being interviewed? What would you have done differently?

What other questions do you wish KC had asked?

Did any of the authors remind you of anyone you know (including yourself?)

Extension:

Since this book is the beginning of a series (the new "Chicken Soup for the Soul"), and the author has announced the next book will be "Simply Amazing Women," what edition would you like to see as Volume 3?

Book Club Submission:

If you could ask a question of any of the authors, what would it be and to whom? You may submit your questions at www.wmapradio.com/author questions.) We will post selected author responses (personal responses not available at this time).

Thank you for picking up and discussing **Simply Amazing**! *If you enjoyed the book, please recommend to a friend.* Remember, inspiration and hope are great all-occasion gifts for everyone!

Tune in 24/7 to www.wmapradio.com to hear more inspiring interviews. Your favorites may wind up in an upcoming book!

Authors, business owners, survivors, amazing people . . . Book a free 10 minute interview to promote yourself your business or your project at https://www.wmapradio.com/book-online.

Leave your email for contact when our next book will be released and see readers' questions answered by the authors: www.simplyamazingbook. com

CPSIA information can be obtained
at www.ICGtesting.com
Printed in the USA
BVHW040151211118
533712BV00007B/30/P